THE
Negro
IN THE
Making of America

BENJAMIN QUARLES

With a new introduction by V. P. Franklin

A TOUCHSTONE BOOK
Published by Simon & Schuster
New York London Toronto Sydney Tokyo Singapore

TOUCHSTONE
Rockefeller Center
1230 Avenue of the Americas
New York, NY 10020

Copyright © 1964, 1969 by Macmillan Publishing Co., Inc.
Copyright © 1987 by Benjamin Quarles
Introduction copyright © 1996 by V. P. Franklin

Designed by Elina D. Nudelman

Manufactured in the United States of America

10   9   8   7

Library of Congress Cataloging-in-Publication Data
Quarles, Benjamin.
        The Negro in the making of America.
        Bibliography: p.
        Includes index.
        1. Afro-Americans—History.   I. Title.
E185.Q2   1987   973'.0496073   86-28308
ISBN 0-684-81888-4

Contents

Introduction
by V. P. Franklin

UNTIL THE RELEASE of the highly acclaimed film *Glory* in 1989, for which actor Denzel Washington received an Academy Award, it is unlikely that most Americans had any real knowledge of the significant contributions of black troops to the Union victory in the Civil War. The movie dramatized the heroic exploits of the African-American soldiers in the 54th Massachusetts Regiment, from their recruitment and triumphant send-off from Boston in the spring of 1863 to the pitched battle at Fort Wagner on the South Carolina coast in which Colonel Robert Gould Shaw, the regiment's young white commander, lost his life. Historians of the African-American experience have pointed out that more than 180,000 black soldiers served in the Union Army, and more than 25,000 in the Union Navy; and their brave actions provided substantial justification for the extension of citizenship rights to individuals previously considered some "species of property."

Benjamin Quarles in his immensely popular history *The Negro in the Making of America* not only documents the participation of black troops in the Civil War and all U.S. wars, but also presents a sweeping account of the significant cultural contributions of African Americans to the evolution of American society. Quarles, one of the most distinguished historians of the African-American experience, dedicated his professional life to revising earlier interpretations of American history that all but ignored the role of African Americans, or merely defined their presence in the United States as a "problem." In an essay published in 1946 entitled "Revisionist Negro History," which prefigured the emphasis in much of his scholarly research over the next four decades, Quarles made it clear that "when our history books do not mention the Negro, significant omissions result; when he is mentioned solely with reference to problem areas, the average reader gets a picture which is distorted because it is incomplete." What was needed was "a more balanced focus," and this is exactly what Quarles presented in his numerous scholarly and popular works.[1]

In the early decades of the twentieth century, it was no easy feat for African Americans to gain training and professional acceptance as historians of the black experience. While attending Shaw University in Raleigh, North Carolina, in the 1920s, Quarles was introduced to "black history" by Florence Walter, a white professor who discussed the enormous contributions of black Bostonians to the advancement of African Americans in the United States. Quarles was born in Boston in 1904, attended the public schools, and in a 1977 interview recalled that he "had heard the name Crispus Attucks [killed in the Boston Massacre and spoken of as the first American to die in the Revolution], but I never knew that there was such a thing as black history." The history course at Shaw "opened up a whole new world."[2]

In 1931 Quarles decided to enroll in the graduate program in history at the University of Wisconsin, but several professors discouraged him from studying the African-American experience. "There was a feeling that a black person studying black history would turn it into propaganda," he later recalled. But the white historian researching black history could be blinded by stereotypes and prejudices and was even more likely to distort or misrepresent the facts. "When [the white historian] would come across something relating to [blacks or other] minorities that didn't fit into his attitude about the role of minorities," Quarles pointed out in a 1969 interview, "he simply would ignore that. . . . [and] what he wound up presenting was a view of history that was skewed."[3]

At Wisconsin, Quarles persisted in his determination to study black history and found a professor, William B. Hesseltine, who encouraged him to write a dissertation on the great nineteenth-century black leader Frederick Douglass. In 1940 Quarles became the first African American to receive a Ph.D. in history from the University of Wisconsin. When *Frederick Douglass* was published as a book in 1948, it was acclaimed as "an excellent biography" and an important scholarly work that was "eminently readable and consistently interesting."[4]

In his efforts to revise the contemporary perspectives on African-Americans contributions to American society, Quarles next turned to the era of the Civil War. Although the war was fought primarily "to preserve the Union," in *The Negro in the Civil War,* first published in 1953, Quarles made it clear that "without slavery there would have been no resort to arms. Hence the slave was the key factor in the war." However, Quarles wanted to document the active role that African Americans assumed in the attainment of their freedom. In the film *Glory* the black soldiers took center stage; in Quarles's scholarly account, the story of the Negro's Civil War was more expansive and included the decisive actions of African Americans, slave and free, in the North and South. "The Negro's tale was not merely a passive one," Quarles announced at the outset, "he did not tarry in the wings, hands folded. He was an active member of the cast, prominent in the dramatis personae. To him freedom was a two-way street; indeed he gave prior to receiving." In assisting the Union Army as military laborers, guides, and informants; in working behind Confederate lines to sabotage and disrupt military and civilian operations; and in joining black Union regiments completely made up of former slaves from Mississippi, Tennessee, and Virginia, "the role of the three and a half million Negroes in the South reached epic proportions."[5]

Written almost as a sequel to *The Negro in the Civil War,* but clearly in keeping with his announced desire "to revise Negro history," Quarles published in 1961 *The Negro in the American Revolution.* While the documentation on black participation in the Civil War was voluminous and readily available, historical evidence about the role of African Americans in the Revolution was more fragmented and sketchy. Quarles pointed out that "the War of Independence had no all-Negro units; hence the military history of the Negro soldier in the Revolution is one with the general history of the American soldier in action." Earlier historical assessments tended to emphasize the exploits of individual "Colored Patriots"; Quarles, however, presented a complex group portrait in which the Negro's "major loyalty was not to a place nor a people, but to a principle . . . [and] whoever invoked the image of liberty, be he American or British, could count on a ready response from the blacks." Quarles described race relations in the late eighteenth century, and civilian and military attitudes about the recruitment of blacks as soldiers in the Continental Army and the British forces. He documented the activities of black troops in various military campaigns, their treatment by their fellow white soldiers and officers, and most important, what African Americans hoped to gain from the struggle for independence. Upon publication most reviewers agreed that this book filled "a long-time gap in the history of the Revolution and the Negro" and was a major contribution to "American" history.[6]

The fourth monographic work that laid the foundation for *The Negro in the Making of America* was Quarles's book *Lincoln and the Negro,* published in 1962. Abraham Lincoln, the most beloved President, was most loved by the Negro; and Quarles traced Lincoln's interactions with African Americans, slave and free, from his earliest years in Kentucky, a slave state, to his meeting with a delegation of black leaders in the White House in the thick of the Civil War. At that time, and for many years afterward, some African Americans harbored feelings of ambivalence toward President Lincoln, given his attempts (always failures) to remove the newly freed slaves from the United States and colonize them in Central America and Haiti before he issued the preliminary Emancipation Proclamation in September 1862. However, in *Lincoln and the Negro* Quarles beautifully evoked the deepest emotions that the martyred President stirred in the hearts of African Americans. Quarles made it clear that African Americans understood before and better than any others that Lincoln's greatest gift to the nation was "the new birth of freedom."[7]

These well-documented and highly acclaimed works by Benjamin Quarles were written primarily for an academic audience and were contributions to the larger African-American intellectual tradition of "race vindication." From the early nineteenth century to the present, black scholars and intellectuals devoted their energies to researching and disseminating the "truth" about Africa and people of African descent in the United States and throughout the world. Given the widespread statements and belief in the "innate inferiority of the Negro," these highly educated black scholars and spokespersons put their knowledge and training in the service of their people's quest for equal rights and "simple justice." With the publication of *The Negro in the Making of America,* Benjamin Quarles moved beyond the academic community to a broad popular audience, as had W. E. B. Du Bois, Carter G. Woodson, John Hope Franklin, and other black historians before him, to tell the truth about the African contribution to American history.[8]

With the coming of the Civil Rights–Black Power movement of the 1960s, interest in African-American history expanded greatly, and Quarles's *The Negro in the Making of America* rode that wave of increased attention, going through numerous printings and becoming a best-seller by the early 1970s. Subsequent editions included information from Quarles's later works, *The Black Abolitionists* (1969) and *Allies for Freedom: Blacks and John Brown* (1974), and he took the story of the black freedom struggle beyond the years of mass protests and demonstrations to the "quiet victories" of the 1970s and 1980s. While later historians have been less concerned with documenting African-American contributions to American life and society and more preoccupied with African Americans' efforts to help themselves, in the later editions of *The Negro in the Making of America* Quarles demonstrated a heightened appreciation for black self-determination and the distinctive nature of black culture in the United States.[9]

Introduction

Whether one is interested in knowing the historical basis for African Americans' claim for integration into the mainstream of American society, or in learning how in defining themselves African Americans came to define the American mainstream, *The Negro in the Making of America* presents that story in a manner that is as graceful and eloquent as it is accurate and convincing.

V. P. Franklin is Professor of History at Drexel University in Philadelphia and author of *Living Our Stories, Telling Our Truths: Autobiography and the Making of the African-American Intellectual Tradition* and other works on African-American history and education.

1.   Benjamin Quarles, "Revisionist Negro History," *Social Education* 10 (March 1946), 101.

2.   John Dorsey, "Benjamin Quarles: From Blacks' Roots Comes Self-Esteem," *Baltimore Sun,* 13 February 1977.

3.   Earl Arnett, "Dr. Quarles, Professor at Morgan, A Pioneer in the Study of Black History," *Baltimore Sun,* 11 November 1969.

4.   Benjamin Quarles, *Frederick Douglass* (1948; reprinted New York, 1968). Ella Lonn, "Review of Quarles, *Frederick Douglass,"* *American Historical Review* 54 (October 1948), 198. See also, August Meier, "Benjamin Quarles and the Historiography of Black America," reprinted in Benjamin Quarles, *Black Mosaic: Essays in Afro-American History and Historiography* (Amherst, Mass., 1988), pp. 3–5, 20–21.

5.   Benjamin Quarles, *The Negro in the Civil War* (1953; reprinted Boston, 1969), pp. xi–xvi.

6.   Benjamin Quarles, *The Negro in the American Revolution* (Chapel Hill, N.C., 1961), pp. x–xi. See also Richard Griffin, "Review of Quar-

les's *The Negro in the American Revolution,*" *Library Journal* 86 (15 December 1961), 4294; Meier, "Benjamin Quarles," pp. 7–12.

7.   Benjamin Quarles, *Lincoln and the Negro* (New York, 1962), p. 249.

8.   V. P. Franklin, *Living Our Stories, Telling Our Truths: Autobiography and the Making of the African-American Intellectual Tradition* (New York, 1995), pp. 11–20.

9.   Benjamin Quarles, *The Black Abolitionists* (New York, 1969); and *Allies for Freedom: Blacks and John Brown* (New York, 1974); Vincent Harding, *There Is a River: The Black Struggle for Freedom in America* (New York, 1981); Sterling Stuckey, *Slave Culture: Nationalist Theory and the Foundations of Black America* (New York, 1987); and V. P. Franklin, *Black Self-Determination: A Cultural History of African-American Resistance* (Brooklyn, N.Y., 1992).

Foreword

IF, STRICTLY SPEAKING, there is no such thing as Afro-American history, it is because this past has become so interwoven in the whole fabric of our culture. Except for the Indian, the Negro is America's oldest ethnic minority. Except for the first settlers at Jamestown, the Negro's roots in the original thirteen colonies sink deeper than any other group from across the Atlantic.

Afro-Americans helped to make America what it was and what it is. Since the founding of Virginia, they have been a factor in many of the major issues in our history, and often they themselves have spoken out on these issues. For example, if in the eyes of the world today the United States stands for man's right to be free, certainly no group in this country has sounded this viewpoint more consistently than the Negro.

Moreover, the Negro's role in the United States also throws light on some of the major trends in the history of the Western world since Columbus's time. The Commercial

Revolution of early modern times had as a basic component a plentiful supply of transplanted Africans. Three centuries later, Negroes on the plantations in the South produced the very staple—cotton—to which the Industrial Revolution owed so much of its explosive world-wide influence. And in our own times the emergence of freedom-minded nations in Africa would seem to make it advantageous for Americans to view afresh the historic role of their colored fellows.

The role of the Negro in the making of America is generally neither well known nor correctly known. Often the positive contributions of the Negro have escaped the eye of the historian, and hence do not find their way into the pages of his work. Many American histories are silent on the Negro, except for some of the problems he has presented. In describing the role of other racial groups, writers have tended to stress those traits held in common by most Americans; but in treating the Negro the approach often has been one of "deviation from the norm." It is not surprising, therefore, that many readers of history have come to feel that although the Negro has been among us, he has not been one of us.

When our history books do not mention the Negro, significant omissions result, and mentioning him solely in terms of some problem has caused an incomplete, distorted picture to emerge. In either case a more balanced focus is needed.

Such a proper perspective of Negro history would be of value to those well-meaning individuals who believe that the colored man has an unworthy past and hence no strong claim to all the rights held by other Americans. Books that seek to present an accurate picture of the Negro's past are, in effect, bridges to intergroup harmony—the Negro would be accepted more readily into the full promise of American life if his role in our history were better known. The Negro sociologist Kelly Miller once said, "We are so anxious to solve the race problem that we do not take time to study it." Those who seek an insight into human relations require the dimension of historical perspective.

Negro history not only furnishes a preface to racial understanding, it unfolds a dramatic story, if indeed not an epic one, studded with interesting and arresting personalities, colored and white alike. Moreover, the role of the Negro in this country has been rich in meaning; in 1849, Fredrika Bremer saw it as symbolic, reminding Americans that "the romance of your history is the fate of the Negro."

Afro-American history brings out the centrality of the Negro, his identification with this country's avowed goals of freedom and equality, and his role in the making of America. The black historical experience in the United States is a vital part of this country's experience from its beginnings. Would America have been America without her Negro people? This question was raised by one who already knew the answer, W. E. B. DuBois, a professionally trained historian and a figure of major importance in Afro-American life. "We have," he noted, "woven ourselves into the very warp and woof of this nation."

In essence, then, this work is a historical survey of black Americans as they engaged in the dual, simultaneous processes of assimilating and transforming the culture of their country. The Afro-American stamp is indelibly etched on the United States, both in the rich and varied contribution of the blacks, and in the depth and scope of the white response to the black presence.

Increasingly in the past two decades schools and colleges have been making room for black history in the curriculum, no longer regarding it as a fringe subject of questionable content and limited appeal. This newer assessment of the field stems in part from a realization that skin color and racial origins will remain dominant themes in our country for the discernible future. Moreover, Afro-American history is increasingly viewed as a lesson-bearing component of the current global struggle for human rights. Thus it would not be wide of the mark to say that the story of the Negro in America has had some effect in enlarging our social awareness, if not also stirring our social conscience.

Like history's other branches, Afro-American history can be viewed from different angles, from a variety of perspectives. But whatever field of history is being surveyed, to whatever extent we can restore its lost boundaries and fill in the missing pages, so too we come to a closer approximation of the true living past. If, as Abraham Lincoln advised his contemporaries, "we cannot escape history," then, as contemporary black poet Sarah Webster Fabio has admonished our own generation, "we must heal our history."

This work is designed for those seeking an up-to-date survey of the Negro's past in the United States. It is not intended for the scholars in the field; rather, it attempts to bring the fruits of their studies more fully into the public domain. It is hoped, however, that the specialist as well as the general reader will find it useful. For on all levels there would seem to be a need for a survey that seeks to get the facts straight and to reach judgments that are balanced, reflecting the point of view that history is an avenue to understanding.

The content of this edition has been updated, extending to the mid-1980s, and the bibliography has been revised. I owe many thanks to the Morgan State University Library staff for being most helpful for over three decades, and also to my wife, Ruth Brett Quarles, who read this manuscript both in its original version and its reprintings.

1

From Africa to the New World (to 1619)

"E PLURIBUS UNUM," the national motto of the United States, means "one from many." Suggested by patriots at the outbreak of the American Revolution, this motto was originally used in a political sense, to demonstrate that out of thirteen separate states one new sovereign power had come into existence. But since the time of the Revolutionary War, this Latin expression has taken on a larger meaning. It has come to suggest that America is made up of many peoples from many lands, having become, in essence, a nation of nations. One of these many groups came from the continent of Africa, a group that was numbered among the very first to arrive in the New World.

Of the varied Old World stocks that entered America, none came from as wide a geographic area as the blacks. The vast majority came from the West Coast of Africa, a 3,000-mile stretch extending from the Senegal River, downward around the huge coastal bulge, to the southern limit of present-day Portuguese Angola. A small percentage came from Mozambique and the island of Madagascar in far-away East Africa, and still fewer came from the Sudanese grasslands that bordered the Sahara.

Just as the ancestor of the American Negro came from no single region, so he was of no single tribe or physical type. The "West Coast Negro," the predominant type that came to the New World, was marked by such characteristics as tall stature, woolly hair, broad features, full lips, little growth of hair on face or body, and a skin color approaching true black. But there was no such thing as one African "race." Slave ships bound for America carried a variety of genetic stocks, from the tallish, dark-skinned Ashanti of the forest lands north of the Gold Coast to the lighter and shorter Bantu from the Congo basin. Indeed, the difficulty of generalizing about the physical characteristics of the Negroid peoples is illustrated by the Nilotics and the Pygmies, one being the tallest group in the world (averaging nearly six feet in height) and the other being the shortest (averaging less than five feet).

These varied groups had no common tongue, no "lingua Africana." Indeed, there are more than 200 distinct languages in present-day Nigeria alone. There was no such thing as "the African personality," since the varied groups differed as much in their ways of life as in the physical characteristics they exhibited and the languages they spoke.

In their political institutions, there was much diversity. "One meets in Negro Africa," wrote Maurice Delafosse, "a whole series of States, ranging from the simple isolated family to confederations of kingdoms constituting empires." In pre-European Africa innumerable village kinship groups, no larger than a clan, were completely independent in their exercise of a kind of "grass-roots" democracy. These small political systems stood in contrast to an extensive empire-state like Songhay: at the height of its power, this empire extended from Lake Chad westward to the Atlantic, covering an area as large as Europe. Its most notable ruler was Askia Mohammed I (on the throne from 1493 to 1528), whose word carried as much authority in the hinterlands as at his own palace at Gao on the central Niger.

Although there were various types of states, the fundamental unit politically, as in other ways, was the family. This was not one man's family; rather, it was a kinship group numbering in the hundreds, but called a family because it was made up of the living descendants of a common ancestor. The dominant figure in this extended family community was the patriarch, who exercised a variety of functions, acting as peacemaker, judge, administrator, and keeper of the purse. The patriarch generally sought the advice of the recognized elders.

In the immediate family the practice of plural marriage was not uncommon; one man might have more than one wife if he could afford it. As a rule, marriages were formally arranged between the families, with some form of payment—livestock generally—going to the bride's parents. This "brideprice" was not meant to indicate that the wife had been bought; rather, it was a means of recompensing the bride's parents for their loss.

In their ways of making a living, as in other aspects of their culture, there were regional variations among the Africans. Dwellers along the shores of the great rivers turned to fishing and boat-making. In the grasslands the economy was primarily pastoral, the chief livestock being goats, sheep, and cattle. Some occupations were widespread, among them the hunting of game and the gathering of beans, nuts, and fruits. Each village had its corps of artisans, often organized into craft guilds. This skilled-labor class embraced pottery makers, weavers, wood carvers, and iron workers.

Most of the people worked in the fields that surrounded their villages, the basic economy being agricultural. Crops were grown on plots of land cleared by fire or by the felling of trees. Securing adequate foodstuffs from the earth was not always easy, but the tillers of the soil had learned such secrets as transplanting. Most of the produce was intended for local consumption, but some of it might be destined for sale outside the village. So important was agriculture as a means of livelihood that private possession of a tract of earth was not permitted. The land was the possession of the collective group; the individual had only the right to its use, owning nothing but the crops he raised.

Like so much else in African life, the land system was tied in with the gods. Among the peoples of the West Coast, religious forces found full and varied outlets. There was a supreme deity and a host of lesser ones, the latter being identified with such natural objects as rivers and the wind. Each god had priests and "diviners" who interpreted his will. The gods did not exhaust the heavenly host; sharing their powers were innumerable spirits, some of them ancestral, but most of them inhabiting the everyday objects of the hut and field.

Filling a definite place in the religious life of the Africans were their art forms, particularly the statuettes and masks of bronze, wood, or ivory that were produced as adjuncts to the performance of religious and magical rites. This wedding of art to experience gave to African sculpture its enduring vitality; the modern critic Alain Locke viewed these carved works as technically so mature and sophisticated that they could be rated as "classic in the best sense of the word." Since art was functional, the urge to express it was deeply ingrained.

Music, too, found universal expression. Among its manifestations were complex compositions for voice, an ear for the subtlest rhythm, and the use of a wide variety of instruments, including the drum, harp, xylophone, violin, guitar, zither, and flute. Like music, the dance was legion, being performed for any number of observances and purposes. Any event worthy of notice was celebrated by rhythmic movement—births, marriages, or death. Each dance served its own specific purpose; the fertility dance, for example, was, in essence, a prayer that the seed might take good root in the soil and grow well.

The literature produced by the Africans was primarily oral rather than written and can be classified as professional and popular. In the former, knowledge about the history, customs, and traditions of the group was transmitted by men who made a profession of memorizing. The popular literature included tales, proverbs, and riddles passed down from one generation to another, occasionally by trained narrators, but most commonly by amateur storytellers.

In summary, the Negroes who came to the New World varied widely in physical type and ways of life, but there were many common patterns of culture. Whatever the type of state, the varied groups all operated under orderly governments, with established legal codes, and under well-organized social systems. The individual might find it necessary to submerge his will into the collective will, but he shared a deep sense of group identity, a feeling of belonging. And there was ample scope for personal expression—in crafts, in art, in worship, or in music and the dance.

African societies before the penetration of the Europeans were not backward and static, with their people living in barbarism and savagery. A more accurate view is now being unfolded by modern-day scholars in history, anthropology, archeology, and linguistics. The fruits of their researches show that the peoples of Africa from whom the American Negro is descended have made a rich contribution to the total resources of human culture.

The modern traffic in African slaves began in the mid-fifteenth century, with Portugal taking the lead. In 1441 Prince Henry the Navigator sent one of his mariners, the youthful Antonio Gonsalves, to the West Coast to obtain a cargo of skins and oils. Landing near Cape Bojador, the young captain decided that he might please his sovereign by bringing him gifts. Taking possession of some gold dust and loading ten Africans on his cockleshell, Gonsalves made his way back to Lisbon. Henry was greatly pleased by the gold and the slaves, deeming the latter of sufficient importance to send to the Pope.

In turn, the Pope conferred upon Henry the title to all lands to be discovered to the east of Cape Blanco, a point on the West Coast some 300 miles above the Senegal. Thus began a new era. With renewed vigor Portuguese seamen pressed on with their systematic exploration of the African coastline.

These pioneers found Africa to be a treasure house. It had gold, which, in addition to being valuable in itself, was indispensable as means of paying for the products they wanted from the Orient, India especially. From the West Coast, too, came pepper and elephant tusks, ivory always having a ready market in the commercial centers of the world. But the chief prize of all was the supply of slaves, which, unlike other merchandise, seemed to be inexhaustible. Within two decades after Gonsalves's voyage off Cape Bojador, the slave trade proved to be highly profitable in the European market, and within another half-century this new labor supply was finding its greatest demand in the newly discovered lands across the Atlantic. The settlements founded in America by Spain soon opened the floodgates for all the black cargoes European bottoms could carry.

With so lucrative an African trade, it was only natural that Portugal should try to shut other nations from the profits. For nearly a century she was successful; Spain, her only likely competitor during that period, was not a maritime power, preferring to stock her colonies by means of contracts *(assientos)* granted by the king to merchants of other countries.

But to keep other rivals away indefinitely was far beyond Portugal's power. By the latter part of the sixteenth century her monopoly was being successfully challenged by England and France, the latter almost displacing her in the Senegal and Gambia river regions during the 1570s. During the following century the African trade attracted the Dutch, Danes, Swedes, and Brandenburg Germans. By far the most formidable of these was the Dutch, who formed a West India Company in 1621 and sixteen years later seized Elmina on the Gold Coast, Portugal's strongest fortification in Africa. For the next fifty years the Hollanders were second to none in the slave-carrying trade, a position they slowly relinquished to England after 1700.

Whatever the nation, the actual operation of the slave trade was much the same. Usually the sovereign in Europe would grant a trade monopoly to a group of favored merchants, it being assumed that the privilege of foreign commerce resided in the Crown. The merchant company was thus protected against competition, at least from interlopers of their own nationality, and could proceed to stock its ships with the goods necessary for the exchange. Such goods consisted of textiles—woolens, linens, cottons, and silks—knives and cutlasses; firearms, powder, and shot; and iron, copper, brass, and lead in bar form for local smithies. A staple of the trade was intoxicating drink—rum, brandy, gin, or wine. Ships also made it a point to carry a supply of trinkets—baubles, bells, looking-glasses, bracelets, and glass beads—which were of negligible cost and had a fascination for native chiefs.

Upon landing for the first time, the trading company made arrangements to establish a joint fort and trading station. One of the first buildings to go up would be a barracoon, a warehouse where slaves could be kept until the voyage across the Atlantic. Thus laden with goods, and with storage space to accommodate the expected human cargo, the trader was ready to do business with the native chief. The whites did not go into the interior to procure slaves; this they left to the Africans themselves. Spurred on by the desire for European goods, one tribe raided another, seized whatever captives it could, and marched them in coffles, with leather thongs around their necks, to the coastal trading centers.

Doubtless the full enormity of what they were doing did not dawn on the African chiefs. Neither intertribal warfare nor human bondage was uncommon. Indeed, from time immemorial men in Africa had become slaves by being captured in warfare, or as a punishment for crime, or because of failure to pay debts. There was, however, no stigma of inherent inferiority attached to slave status; no hard and fast color or caste hurdles prevented a former slave from becoming free and rising to a great place. Moreover, the demand for slaves had been limited. But when the European arrived, there was a great upsurge in the market for slaves, and the native chiefs were unwilling to resist the temptations of the trade. Later, when the entire West Coast had been turned into a huge slave corral, the chiefs were unable to arrest the traffic.

With a human cargo to dispose of, the native chief was ready to negotiate with the trader. Generally the latter began by offering presents to the king—hats and bunches of beads. Then the bargaining got under way, with the Africans usually showing great shrewdness. Merchant-owner John Barbot, trading at New Calabar in 1699, gave vent to his vexation over the haggling propensities of the king's assistant Pepprell, characterizing him as being "a sharp blade, and a mighty talking black, perpetually making sly objections against something or other, and teasing us for this or that dassy, or present, as well as for drams."

Sometimes the trader might have to do business at a loss, and sometimes he had to leave empty-handed when his goods were not wanted, even though on a previous trip the identical kind of article had gone well with the same chief. But as a rule, the trader was likely to find his goods marketable. Prices varied greatly, but the average cost of a healthy male was $60 in merchandise; a woman could be bought for $15 less. Before completing the transaction, the buyer invariably took the precaution of having the slaves examined by his physician.

When enough Negroes had been procured to make a full cargo, the next step was to get them to the West Indies with the greatest possible speed. Food was stocked for crew and slaves—yams, coarse bananas, potatoes, kidney beans, and coconuts. Then, after having been branded for identification, the blacks came aboard, climbing up the swaying rope ladders, prodded on by whips. The sexes were placed in different compartments, with the men in leg irons. The ship then hoisted anchor and started toward the West Indies, a voyage fifty days in length if all went well. This was the "Middle Passage," so called because it was the second leg in the ship's triangular journey—home base to Africa, thence to the West Indies, and finally back to the point of original departure.

The Middle Passage has come to have a bad name, and

in truth the voyage was one of incredible rigor. When in 1679 the frigate *Sun of Africa* made a trip from the Gold Coast to Martinique, there were only seven deaths out of a cargo of 250 slaves, but such a light loss was exceptional. On an average, the Atlantic voyage brought death to one out of every eight black passengers. A slaver was invariably trailed by a school of man-eating sharks.

A few captains were "loose packers," but the great majority were "tight packers," believing that the greater loss in life would be more than offset by the larger cargo. On their ships the space allowed a slave was confined to the amount of deck in which he could lie down, and the decks were so narrow as to permit just enough height for the slave to crawl out to the upper deck at feeding time.

Disease took its toll, especially when the ship was struck with an epidemic of scurvy or the flux. "The Negroes are so incident to the small-pox," wrote Captain Thomas Phillips of the *Hannibal*, "that few ships that carry them escape without it." Adding greatly to the threat of a disease outbreak was the danger that the food and water would run short.

The hazards of nature were not as vexing as the behavior of the slaves. Some committed suicide by managing to jump through the netting that had been rigged around the ship to prevent that very step. Others seemed to have lost the will to live. To guard against such suicidal melancholy, a ceremony known as "dancing the slaves" was practiced: they were forced to jump up and down to the tune of the fiddle, harp, or bagpipes. A slave who tried to go on a hunger strike was forcibly fed, by means of a "mouth-opener" containing live coals.

The most serious danger by far was that of slave mutiny, and elaborate precautions were taken to prevent uprisings. Daily searches of the slave quarters were made, and sentinels were posted at the gun room day and night. But the captain and his undermanned crew were not always able to control their cargo of blacks. So numerous were slave insurrections on the high seas that few shipowners failed to take out "revolt insurance."

But, despite all risks and dangers, the slave trade flourished. The profits were great. After taking out all expenses, including insurance payments and sales commissions, a slaving voyage was expected to make a profit of thirty cents on the dollar. Such a lucrative trade was an outgrowth of the insatiable demand for "black ivory" in the New World.

The transplanted Africans found a variety of tasks awaiting them in the lands across the Atlantic. Their service dates almost from the discovery of America, cabin boy Diego el Negro coming with Columbus on his fourth voyage in 1502. Almost without exception, every subsequent discoverer and explorer sailing for the New World from the ports of Andalusia numbered Negroes among his crew, slaves having become common in Portugal and southern Spain. When Balboa first "stared at the Pacific," he carried thirty Negroes in his train. Hernando Cortez, conqueror of Mexico, made use of slaves in hauling the artillery that terrified the Aztecs. One of the Negroes with the Cortez expedition was the sower and reaper of the first wheat crop in America. Lucas Vasquez de Ayllon, exploring the Atlantic coast regions in 1526, was one of the earliest "conquistadores" to bring Negroes into the present boundaries of the United States. Panfilo de Navaez, who hoped to rival the exploits of Cortez, and his successor, Cabeza de Vaca, depended upon slave labor in their wanderings in the waters of the Gulf of Mexico.

The most renowned of the Negroes who accompanied the Spanish pioneers was the Moroccan, Estavanico—scout, guide, and ambassador for Navaez and Cabeza de Vaca. In

March 1539, with Estevanico as guide, a party of three Spaniards and a group of Pima Indians set out in search of the fabled Seven Cities of Cibola. Estavanico never found these nonexistent places, but his travels led him to the region of the present state of New Mexico, which he was the first man to behold, except for the aborigines. Negroes could also be found with the French explorers—in the Great Lakes area, along the Mississippi Valley, and in Louisiana.

A slave used as a guide, like Estavanico, was out of the ordinary. It was as a laborer, rather than anything else, that the Negro was needed in the New World. For the Spanish had decided quite early that Negro labor was more suitable than Indian labor. Catholic bishops like Bartholomé de Las Casas and Diego de Landa developed a marked sympathy for the Indians, and hence became strong exponents of Negro slavery. In support of this stand, a theory took root that the Indian was physically far inferior to the Negro, and thus less able to stand hard labor in a hot climate.

Aside from the attitude of the bishops, there seemed to be sound ground for the preference of the Negro over the Indian. The former showed a greater resistance to the white man's diseases—measles, yellow fever, and malaria. Moreover, the transplanted African was better able to adjust to the discipline of the plantation system, for he came from an economic order more complex than that of the Indian.

Although slaves were used in mining gold on the mainland, particularly in New Granada, it was to the West Indies that slavery and the slave trade owed their initial enormous growth. Indeed, at the close of the eighteenth century over half of the 800,000 Negroes in Spanish America were to be found in Cuba and Puerto Rico. The islands produced a variety of commodities—indigo, coffee, cotton, tobacco, hides, and ginger—but their mainstay was sugar. More than all other products combined, it was sugar that created the great demand for slaves in America, and it was the sugar industry that determined their geographical distribution therein. Hitherto rare in Europe, sugar now became big business, and the West Indies were commonly called the "Sugar Islands."

Sugar cane culture readily lent itself to slave labor. Its operations were not hard to learn—clearing land, hoeing, planting, weeding, and cane cutting—and they provided year-round employment. Moreover, slaves could be worked in large gangs, which were easily supervised.

Just as Portugal had been unable to prevent other European powers from coming to Africa, so Spain was unable to keep her rivals out of the Caribbean. By the middle of the seventeenth century the Spanish monopoly had been broken, and Denmark, Holland, and France were establishing themselves in the islands. Spain's weakening grasp became starkly apparent when England in 1655 wrested Jamaica from her. This possession soon became the chief slave market in the Western Hemisphere.

The European powers who now planted their flags in the islands found it expedient to permit independent merchants of their nationality to share in the slave traffic, which had grown too large to be handled by one company of licensees. The mother countries were quick to sense that West Indian possessions, in addition to supplying sugar, enabled them to build up their merchant shipping by furnishing a nursery for their seamen. Island possessions also created a market for their manufactures: "The Negro-Trade and the natural consequences resulting from it," wrote a contemporary Englishman, "may be justly esteemed an inexhaustible Fund of Wealth and Naval Power to this Nation."

Although many profited from the trade, the West India planter was its backbone; it was he who kept the wheels in motion by his constant seeking of more slaves. In making his purchases, the planter, or his agent, sometimes went to the mainland marts—Cartagena, Panama, or Vera Cruz. But, as a rule, slaves could be obtained from stocks kept in West India port barracoons. Sometimes a slave-laden ship would sail into an island port and sell its cargo to a single buyer, or to multiple buyers. Less often a slaver would sail into a planter's own waters, seeking to dispose of its blacks.

Slave purchases were made at the buyer's risk. This the planter knew. And he sensed, if he did not know, that all ship captains had orders much like that issued to Anthony Overstall, commander of the *Judith:* "You must be mindful to have your Negroes Shaved and made Clean to look well and strike a good impression on the Buyers at whatever place you touch at."

Once the slave was purchased, it became necessary to break him in—to accustom him to the routines of plantation slavery in a new and strange environment. In this season-ing process—generally running to three years—the freshly arrived blacks would be distributed among veterans, or they would be placed under special supervisors. When the slave was fully seasoned—having learned his work assignment, become accustomed to the food and climate, learned to understand a new language, and shaken off any tendency to suicide—he was worth twice as much as when he first landed.

The lot of the slave in the West Indies was no better than might be expected. In general, the owners of the plan-tations resided in Europe, leaving their properties to be handled by agents and overseers. This absentee land-lordism left the slaves in the hands of men who were inter-ested solely in profits, and to whom the slave was of little concern other than as a unit of labor.

Slave mortality was high. It was considered cheaper to

buy than to breed: the planters held that it was less expensive to get every ounce of work out of a slave and then replace him than to try to keep him in good health. One harsh master figured that he had got his money out of a slave if he lasted for four years; less severe masters might put the figure at from five to seven years. The slave population did not reproduce itself, babies not being valued highly since the cost of rearing them was reckoned as greater than that of importing a fresh supply from Africa.

The slave codes were severe; on one of the islands the list of capital offenses included "the compassing or imagining the death of any white person." The unfree black had few personal rights, because he was defined by law as part of the personal estate of the master. A Jamaican slave had a community of masters, wrote James Stephen, nine years before he drafted the British Emancipation Act of 1833, being "a slave to every white person." True, he worked for only one white, but he stood in a servile relation to all of them, being as "totally disabled from asserting any civil, or exercising any natural rights against them," as he was against his lawful owner.

The black codes reached their peak of severity in cases of slave uprisings—that haunting fear of the greatly outnumbered whites. Of five slaves found guilty of conspiracy in Antigua in 1728, "three of them were burnt alive, and one hang'd drawn and quarter'd, and the other transported to the Spanish coast," as reported by the island's governor, Lord Londonderry. Other means of keeping the Negroes from rebelling were the strengthening of the militia, the requirement that planters retain a specified percentage of white employees, and the deliberate mixing of Negroes of different tribal backgrounds. Since slavery was a means of control, there was a marked reluctance to grant a bondman his freedom. This was particularly true in the British possessions,

Barbados levying a heavy fine on a master who liberated his slave.

Despite all precautions, Negro uprisings became a commonplace in the West Indies. Slaves felt driven to revolt by the harsh treatment, and they were emboldened to take the step because of their large numbers. As early as 1522 a slave uprising in Hispaniola set the pattern for later outbreaks in other islands, including Cuba, Puerto Rico, Martinique, Antigua, Barbados, Jamaica, St. Vincent, and the Virgin Islands. The French West Indies witnessed the greatest of these outbreaks when, in the 1790s, Toussaint L'Ouverture led the slaves in Saint Dominique—later Haiti—to their freedom.

The rebellious mood of the island slaves was nurtured in part by the existence of independent colonies of runaways, the first of which dated back to 1542. These Maroons, as they were called, had established themselves in the mountains and forests, staging periodic raids for food and cattle. Often they were so strong and well organized that the colonial authorities thought it best to make treaties with them. In 1739 the governor of Jamaica signed an agreement with Captain Cudjoe guaranteeing freedom to the Maroons of Trelawney Town in return for their promise to conduct themselves peacefully. This agreement was soon extended to three other Maroon groups on the island.

With the coming of the nineteenth century, West Indian slavery ceased to bring big profits; indeed, by 1807 the typical British West Indian planter was operating at a loss. Sugar from the islands was faced with a fierce competition from sugar from other areas throughout the world, particularly from the East Indies. With the market glutted, the price of West Indian sugar fell lower and lower, and the need for slaves decreased in proportion.

But this was not the swan song for slavery in the Western Hemisphere, for the lessening need for black labor in the islands was counterbalanced by the rising demand on the mainland. As slave-produced sugar declined in the West Indies, other slave-produced staples came to the fore in continental America. The commercial revolution that ushered in modern economic development at the time of Columbus was giving ground to the oncoming industrial revolution. Slave labor was at the base of both revolutions. But there was a change of locale; the seat of slavery shifted from the islands to the mainland, and the former began to export to the latter.

Many of these island-seasoned Negroes were brought into the English colonies that bordered the Atlantic. Even in their flush times, the West Indies had always shipped some of their blacks to these mainland settlements of the British Crown, where the roots of the transplanted Africans ran as deep, if not as profusely, as in the Caribbean.

To what extent did the Negro who came to the English-speaking mainland colonies bring with him the customs and beliefs of his ancestral homelands? To what extent did he retain any cultural elements from across the Atlantic? To what extent had his rich African heritage survived the harrowing overseas voyage and the seasoning years in the West Indies? This problem of African retentions is admittedly difficult. In his authoritative work *The Myth of the Negro Past,* Melville J. Herskovits lists several factors that determined the persistence of Africanisms, one of these being the numerical ratio of blacks to whites.

But in studying the role of the Negro in the United States, it is perhaps less important to indicate what the transplanted African retained than to describe what cultural elements he lost—lost only because they had become an integral part of the total culture. For the Negro was destined to place his stamp upon the distinctive American contribution to the fields of music, the dance, literature, and art. Negro creations were destined to become national rather than racial, centering in the common core. A few illustrations of such fusions may be noted.

In the realm of song the idioms which the Negro brought from Africa were to be notably reflected in American music. Between native African music and that of the transplanted Negro there was a close rhythmic relationship and melodic similarity. H. E. Krehbiel, the nineteenth-century pioneer authority on the Afro-American folksongs, after analyzing 527 Negro spirituals, found their identical prototypes in African music, concluding that the essential "intervallic, rhythmical and structural elements" of these songs came from the ancestral homelands. Closely akin to the spirituals were the Negro burial hymns, "I Know Moonrise," and "Lay Dis Body Down," compilation songs that accompanied the common African custom of sitting up at night and singing over the dead. The product of two continents, these religious songs of the slave stand today as part of the spiritual heritage of America, and their appeal is universal.

The spirituals did not exhaust the vein of musical lore from Africa. Like his forebears, the American Negro found pleasure in singing while at work. Negroes who followed the sea improvised boat songs and rowing songs which had much the same rhythms as the spirituals. The rollicking steamboat songs and chanteys sung on the old clipper ships were the products of black-skinned roustabouts and deck hands. American Negroes, writes Joanna C. Colcord in *Songs of American Sailormen,* were "the best singers that ever lifted a shanty aboard ship." Their rhythmic tunes served as "labor-saving" devices as they stowed cotton, hoisted sail, or cast anchor, becoming part of the sailorman's repertoire ("I'm bound to Alabama,/Oh roll the cotton down").

Negro toilers on land likewise sang to ease their tasks. In such work as cleaning rice, gathering corn, or mowing at harvest, the field hands responded to the rhythms of vocal music. These plantation songs were destined to survive in the chain-gang, railroad, and hammer songs evoked in breaking stones and driving railroad spikes ("This old hammer killed John Henry, but this old hammer won't kill me").

Another musical link between the African background and the American experience was the dance. African ritual dance patterns, when brought to the New World, interacted with the secular dances from Europe, with notable results. In Latin America among the combinations springing from this fusion of African and European dance forms were the beguine, the rhumba, the conga, and the habanera. The first of these originated in Martinique; the last three are Afro-Spanish. The rhumba was first performed among Cuban Negroes as a rural dance depicting simple farm chores. The conga and the newer mambo originated among the Congo Negroes of Cuba. The music of the habanera, which takes its name from Cuba's leading city, has an African rhythmic foundation that soon came to dominate the dance melodies of Latin America, as it does today; from it came the tango (after an African word "tangana"). The national dance of Brazil, the samba, is derived directly from the wedding dance of Angola, the quizomba. The significant role of Africanisms in the dance of the Hispanic countries has been richly documented in the monumental studies of the contemporary Cuban scholar, Fernando Ortiz.

North of the Rio Grande the plantation dances of the Negro, such as the juba, were in the tradition of the circle-and-hand-clapping rounds of the Dark Continent, the feet of the encirclers beating a tattoo on the ground as a substitute for the ancestral drum. From these plantation dances emerged the Negro minstrel show. The contribution of the transplanted African to musical expression in America was summed up by Walter Damrosch in a speech at Hampton Institute in 1912: "Unique and inimitable, Negro music is the only music of this country, except that of the Indians, which can claim to be folk music."

Another African survival was the folk story. Wherever the Negro has gone, tales have gone too, and with only minor changes in plot. Negroes from the bulge of Africa brought with them legends, myths, proverbs, and the remembered outlines of animal stories that for centuries had been current at their native hearths. The best known of the adaptations of this folklore from the Dark Continent are the Uncle Remus tales, the African ancestor of Br'er Rabbit being Shulo the Hare. The very titles, such as *Br'er* Wolf and *Sis'* Nanny Goat, were carried across the Atlantic. African speech survivals are not uncommon in the United States. Lorenzo Dow Turner, after examining the vocabulary of the Gullah Negroes of coastal South Carolina and Georgia, found 4,000 West African words, "besides many survivals in syntax, inflections, sounds, and intonations."

Art too was imported. To the slave the formal fine arts—painting and sculpture—were closed, but his latent abilities were not to be suppressed. In Africa the handicrafts of the native tribes—weaving, pottery, carving in wood, ivory, and bone—were fashioned with surpassing technical finish. African Negroes had been among the first peoples to work in iron and gold, metal forging being one of their oldest arts. Bondage in the New World did not erase these ancestral skills in the handicrafts. Black artisans constructed many of the southern mansions in Charleston, Mobile, and New Orleans, embellishing them with decorative hand-wrought grills and balconies. Perhaps the best known of these antebellum colored craftsmen was Thomas Day of Milton, North Carolina, whose celebrated hand-tooled mahogany tables and divans still bring high prices on the antique market. Thus the craft work of colonial America reflected the art of Negro Africa, an art that today has won a distinctive place in modern esthetics.

The Negroes who were transported to the mainland English settlements were not brought in for their potential contribution to American music and art. The colonists had a different role in mind for them.

2

The Colonial and Revolutionary War Negro (1619–1800)

ONE DAY IN late August 1619, a Dutch frigate landed an unexpected cargo at Jamestown, Virginia—twenty Negroes, of whom at least three were women. The vessel that sailed into the Chesapeake waters was a privateer, and its coming was as casual and apparently as unexciting as its consequences were far-reaching. A new racial element had come into the first English settlement within twelve years after its founding.

The precise disposal of these first Negroes is not recorded, but it seems that they had been purchased from their Dutch captors by the colonial government itself. Acting as middleman, the government then distributed them among the private settlers. It seems, too, that these twenty Negroes were not slaves. They had been baptized, and by English law, which then governed Virginia, a slave who had been converted to Christianity became "enfranchised." This practice was based on the theory that, inasmuch as infidels were enslaved in order to make Christians of them, it fol-

lowed that when the cause of their enslavement was removed, they would become free.

These first Jamestown Negroes were not free, however.
Instead, they fell into a category that had already taken
root in the young colony—that of indentured servants who
had bound themselves to work for masters for a specified
length of time in return for paying the cost of their transportation across the Atlantic. Indentured servitude had
come early in response to a great need for labor. In Virginia,
as in the later colonies, there was an abundance of land but
a scarcity of men. In the agricultural settlements the manpower needs were pressing at the very outset, the virgin
land having to be cleared for tillage before a crop could be
raised. To this acute problem of a labor supply, indentured
servitude provided the most satisfactory answer for nearly
three-quarters of a century.

But by 1700 indentured servitude was no longer the
preferred labor base in the plantation colonies. It had been
superseded by slavery, brought about by the rising cost of
free labor, which had become scarcer, especially after England tightened up on kidnapping that had been a common
practice in her seaport towns. Moreover, by 1700 the mother
country was assuming command of the slave trade, larger
numbers of Negroes were available for import, and the agricultural colonies were in need of an increased labor supply
as plantation owners expanded their holdings, small farms
giving way to larger units of cultivation.

Bent on large-scale production of tobacco and rice, proprietors found that slavery had marked advantages over
servitude. The slave's services were for life, whereas the
indentured servant only worked for a time, generally four
years. At the end of a servant's period the master had to give
him "freedom dues"—clothing, a small sum of money, or a
plot of land—an expense never incurred with slaves. The

latter, moreover, replaced themselves by breeding, since their offspring belonged to the master. And, as a rule, it was cheaper to feed and clothe a slave than an indentured servant.

The increased need for slaves in colonial America came at a time when slavery had become synonymous with Negro. Whites were never slaves; a master might try to lengthen the term of his white servant, but he dared not try to make him a servant for life. As for the Indian, some attempts had been made to enslave him, but capturing him was not easy and keeping him captive was equally troublesome. An Indian did not make a trustworthy bondman, being unruly and dangerous. Moreover, the enslavement of Indians tended to stir up resentment among the tribes, and possibly to set them on the warpath.

The increased need for slaves also came at a time when Negro servitude had become Negro slavery. Not completed until the latter half of the seventeenth century, slavery was a gradual development, one halting step being followed by another. The legal conversion of a Negro into a chattel may be traced in Virginia, where the statutes and court decisions on slavery were more numerous than in any other colony.

For the first twenty-five years after the coming of Negroes to Jamestown in 1619, their status remained that of indentured servant. But it was not many years before it became common practice to hold a black servant after his term had expired. By 1640 Negro slavery had gained a foothold, as the John Punch case indicated. Punch, a Negro, was one of three servants caught in the act of running away. As punishment the two white servants had four years added to their periods of service, but the court ordered that Punch "serve his master or his assigns for the time of his natural Life here or elsewhere." Thus by 1640 a Negro servant who ran afoul of the law found that his period of service was likely to be extended indefinitely, taking on the hallmark of slavery—perpetual servitude.

Another instance of slavery's coming shadow was the Manuel case. A mulatto, Manuel had been purchased "as a Slave for Ever" by Thomas Bushrod. Although the Assembly declared in 1644 that Manuel was not a slave, it went on to stipulate that he must remain with Bushrod for twenty-one years, a highly exceptional length of service. Nine years later one Anthony Johnson, a Negro and a former servant who had become a large landowner in Northampton County, claimed that John Casor owed him service for life. When, in 1653, Casor contested the charge, he had already put in fifteen years with Johnson. The cases of Manuel and Casor reveal an unmistakable trend: slavery was ready to shed its cocoon. When in 1662 a Virginia law used the word "slaves" to designate an already existing class, slavery became recognized in law, as for some years it had been in practice.

But before slavery could come into its own, the colonists had to dispose of the troublesome proposition that the conversion of a Negro to the Christian faith entitled him to his freedom. This theory steadily lost ground; even religious groups opposed it, pointing out that masters would deny baptism to their slaves if such a step led to their freedom. To settle the matter, Virginia's legislature stated in 1667 that the "conferring of baptisme doth not alter the condition of the person as to his bondage or freedome." By 1706 this principle that the slave was not made free by baptism was affirmed by five other colonies: Maryland, North Carolina, South Carolina, New York, and New Jersey.

In the other planting colonies the fixing of the status of the Negro did not undergo such a long period of transition as in Virginia. In nearby Maryland slavery was recognized by law in 1664, and within a decade after the founding of the Carolinas in 1663, slavery had taken root there. Georgia permitted its settlers to import slaves in 1750, less than twenty years after the colony had come into existence.

Above the Potomac slavery likewise had an early beginning. Long before the English took the New Netherlands in 1664, the Dutch had established slavery; indeed, the colony had been founded by the slave-trading Dutch West India Company. Giving sanction to current practice, New York in 1684 officially recognized slavery as legal. When acquired by England, the New Netherlands included the territory which in 1702 became the royal province of New Jersey; the latter, too, was not unfamiliar with black bondage. When in 1681 and 1682 William Penn received the land grants that eventually became Pennsylvania and Delaware, he found that Negroes were already located in the region and that he had to recognize slavery as a matter of course.

The New England colonies had their early Negro inhabitants, dating from within ten years after the Massachusetts Bay Company made its first settlement. In 1638 the Salem-registered ship *Desire,* returning from the West Indies, landed at Boston a cargo that included a number of Negroes. Within six years Negroes had been brought into two other northern colonies—to Connecticut in 1639, and to New Haven in 1644.

Although New England's Negroes were often termed "servants," they were in most instances slaves, the former term being preferred by Puritan masters. Slaves in the farming and planting colonies likewise were sometimes referred to as servants. But, by whatever term he was designated, the Negro was to be found in every one of the thirteen mainland colonies, his presence in each dating invariably from its first years of settlement.

Chattel slavery tended to be fixed and centered on the Negro for reasons peculiar either to him or to beliefs and

attitudes concerning him. Having the mark of "high visibility"—that is, being easily identifiable by color—he could not
run away and merge into the general population as readily
as could a white servant. Moreover, it was generally
believed that Negroes could endure a hot climate and were
more resistant to malarial diseases than were whites. Negro
women could be put to tasks, particularly work in the fields,
that would not be expected of white women.

Because he differed from other newcomers in so many
ways—among others, place of origin in the Old World, cultural background, and skin color—the Negro was a natural
object of prejudice. The inhabitants of colonial America, no
less than human beings in other times and places, had psychological needs that could be resolved in some measure by
holding a derogatory view of others—superiority, security,
and social acceptance. For a man with a problem or need of
his own, a prejudiced attitude served a useful function, furnishing him with a substitute object of dislike and aggres-
sion.

For, while it is true that slavery had its root in economics, it must not be overlooked that discrimination against
the Negro antedated the need for his labor. In the early
years of Virginia, the Negro population grew slowly, in 1648
numbering only around 300 in a population of some 15,000
and in 1671 numbering 2,000 out of a population of 40,000.
It was not until the turn of the century that Virginia's Negro
population took a sharp rise. But long before that time, the
distinction between the white and the black servant had
become marked. From the beginning Negroes were thought
not to be assimilable; they were not considered fellow
parishioners in the church or even fellow roisterers at the
tavern.

In Virginia a white who mingled socially with Negroes
faced censure; as early as 1630 the court ordered one Hugh

Davis to be whipped for "defiling his body in lying with a negro." Steps were taken to prevent Negroes from issuing orders to whites, and in 1669 the court exempted a white servant from punishment because the charge had been preferred by a colored overseer. Eleven years later a law was passed prohibiting a Negro from having a white indentured servant. In fine, although racial attitudes in colonial America were basically determined by economic considerations, this was not their only root.

Economic conditions did fully determine the number of slaves in a given locality. The bulk of the black population was to be found in the colonies that were adapted to slave labor—those that produced the great colonial agricultural staples, such as tobacco, rice, and, in the eighteenth century, indigo. Leading all other colonies in the high percentage of Negroes was the greatest rice producer, South Carolina, and second to her in the ratio of Negroes to whites was the leading tobacco colony, Virginia. Because of the dual menace of the Indians and the Spanish, the founders of Georgia had tried to prohibit slavery from taking root in the colony, but they were forced to yield to the requests of the rice planters. In 1775, twenty-five years after the colony's proprietors had authorized the importation of slaves, the number reached 15,000, nearly one-half of the colony's total population of 33,000.

Of the southern colonies, only North Carolina had a relatively small Negro population. Handicapped by a lack of good ports, and prevented by Virginia from using hers, North Carolina was somewhat cut off from the mother country. Hence small farms were more typical than plantations with their goods for foreign markets. Slave labor was not in great demand; in 1754 the colony had 20,000 Negroes to 70,000 whites.

Just as the shortage of white labor in the plantation colonies led to Negro labor, so did the shortage of white artisans lead to the use of the slave. Unable to get enough white skilled labor, the plantation owners proceeded to train their slaves in the handicraft trades. For a plantation needed more than field hands. A self-sufficing economic unit, it required wood workers, such as sawyers, coopers, and carpenters; leather workers, such as tanners and shoemakers; cloth workers, such as spinners, weavers, and tailors; and building-trades workers, such as bricklayers, painters, and plasterers. It was skilled slave labor that accounted for the rise of plantation manufactures. Moreover, as Marcus W. Jernegan points out, the slave artisan had a threefold role in the commercial development of the southern colonies: in the making of containers for the exported staples, in the manufacture of staves and other forest products, and in the tanning industry—the making of leather for use at home and abroad.

Black artisans were also common above the Potomac; in colonial industry, writes Lorenzo J. Greene, there was no color line. In the North slavery did not develop on a large scale, for the thin soil and the harsh climate did not permit the plantation system of agriculture. But, although less prevalent in the northern colonies, slavery was by no means a negligible factor in their economic life; they were also plagued by a chronic shortage of labor, which led them to import Negroes.

As might be expected, many of the slaves in the North were put to doing unskilled labor, particularly of the "handyman" type. But they also did much of the skilled work, being taught the various trades. They were to be found in every skilled occupation, such as printing, goldsmithing, silversmithing, cabinetmaking, ropemaking, and carpentry. Negroes not only helped to build the New

England ships that engaged in fishing, whaling, and trading, but they were employed in manning them. Many slave women became proficient in spinning, knitting, and weaving. So numerous were slave mechanics in early America that white artisans in Boston, New York, and Philadelphia, viewing them as rivals, sought to have them barred from the skilled occupations.

Many of the slaves in the North worked in agriculture. This was especially the case in New York, its big farms along the Hudson providing employment for perhaps 8,000 of the colony's nearly 20,000 blacks on the eve of the Revolution. In the other middle colonies—New Jersey, Delaware, and Pennsylvania—slaves were also employed as agricultural laborers. In New England slaves worked on the small farms and also on the much larger holdings—averaging 300 acres—located in eastern Connecticut and the Narragansett district of southern Rhode Island, where they were employed in stock farming, sheep raising, and horse breeding.

Another typical occupation of Negroes in the colonial North was that of house servant—butler, valet, coachman, cook, maid, or laundress. It was to be expected that a well-to-do family would have its corps of domestics, but many whites of modest means managed to have a Negro in the house. Some who might have frowned on slavery from a religious or humanitarian standpoint, like certain Quaker families in Philadelphia, were nonetheless not prepared to get along without slaves for their own personal use. In fine, black labor, skilled or unskilled, agricultural or domestic, was a sought-after commodity throughout colonial America.

The treatment of the slaves was left to the colonies, the mother country permitting them to do as they chose. Hence each colony determined who was a slave and how its slaves should be treated. As a rule, a slave code was an accurate reflection of the fears and apprehensions of the colony, the extent to which the white settlers thought it necessary to go to keep the slaves from getting out of hand—staging a revolt, disturbing the peace, or running away. Hence the more numerous the blacks, the more strict the slave codes. In South Carolina the outnumbered whites adopted slave laws patterned after those of Barbados and Jamaica. In an attempt to maintain some degree of proportion between Negroes and whites, South Carolina in 1698 required a planter to acquire one white servant for every six of his Negroes, a form of control prevalent in the sugar islands.

New York's colored population was greater than that of any other colony in the North, and its slave codes were harsher than those of Pennsylvania, New Jersey, and New England. In an attempt to thwart slave conspiracies, New York would not permit more than three slaves to assemble when not working, and it decreed that a funeral could not be attended by more than twelve slaves, not including the pall-bearers and the gravedigger.

Of the New England colonies, Rhode Island had the largest proportion of Negroes—nearly 5,000 in 1755, approximately one-tenth of the population, whereas no other New England colony ever had more than 3 per cent of blacks. In Rhode Island, slaves accused of stealing, or disturbing the peace, and whites who sold hard drink to them, were punished more severely than in the neighboring colonies. But in New England as a whole, the slave codes, as might be expected, were milder than elsewhere in colonial America, particularly in permitting to the bondman certain legal rights, such as trial by jury, suing and being sued, and testifying against whites.

New England colonies had no laws against teaching slaves to read and write; indeed, some occupations to which slaves were put, such as store clerking and printing, required that they be literate. But in New England, as elsewhere, religion was the mainspring behind the movement to give book learning to blacks. A concern for the spiritual welfare of the slave led prominent Puritans, such as Cotton Mather, to establish charity schools where Bible study was the chief staple. Judge Samuel Sewall of Massachusetts, whose pamphlet *The Selling of Joseph,* which appeared in 1701, was the first direct attack on slavery in New England, urged masters to give religious instruction to their bondmen. Sometimes the members of the master's household brought to their slaves a combination of religion and letters. But the efforts of Mather and Sewall were not very fruitful, one reason being that in Puritan circles church membership carried political privileges, such as the right to vote and hold office.

The Anglicans met with more success than the Puritans in providing schools for slaves. In London in 1701 they founded the Society for the Propagation of the Gospel in Foreign Parts, one of whose purposes was missionary work among Negroes and Indians. Four years after its founding, the Society established a Negro school in New York City, followed forty years later by the Charleston Negro School, in which two former slaves, Harry and Andrew, became teachers, having been trained and freed for that purpose. The Society also cooperated with another Anglican group, the "Associates of Doctor Bray," in establishing a school in Philadelphia The Bray group set up Negro schools in Williamsburg and Newport, aided in part by support from Benjamin Franklin.

Operating mainly in the southern colonies, where their membership was most numerous, the Anglican clergymen were at some disadvantage in persuading the planters to give book learning to slaves. The church was handicapped in an environment dominated, as Frank J. Klingberg puts it, more by rice than by righteousness. Judge Sewall, writing in 1705, similarly pointed up the problem:

> Talk to a Planter of the Soul of a Negro, and He'll be apt to tell ye (or at least his Actions speak it loudly) that the Body of one of them may be worth twenty Pounds; but the Souls of an hundred of them would not yield him one Farthing. . . .

In such circumstances an Anglican clergyman could do little more than to give instruction to his own slaves—and invite secular masters to do likewise.

Like the other denominations, the Quakers made some efforts to give religious instruction to the Negro. As early as 1700 three leading Friends had publicly advocated taking steps for the mental improvement of the slaves: founder George Fox, colonial proprietor William Penn, and George Keith of Philadelphia, whose followers published in 1693 the first antislavery tract in British America. Among Quakers, alone of denominational groups, religious instruction was thought of as a step toward physical emancipation as well as a means of spiritual salvation. At a gathering held at a member's house on February 18, 1688, a Quaker group at Germantown, Pennsylvania, had spoken out sharply against slavery, invoking the Golden Rule and drafting a formal remonstrance against "the traffic of men-body." Dating from this forthright and notable Germantown Protest, the Quaker conscience could never be at ease again with slavery. During the first half of the following century the condemnation of slavery was sounded by a half-dozen Quaker reformers, the greatest of whom was John Woolman, "perhaps the most Christlike individual that Quakerism has produced," who traveled extensively in an effort

to impress upon his fellow religionists their Christian obligation toward their slaves.

Woolman made it a point to commend masters who
taught their bondmen the alphabet. But in the actual teaching of slaves, Woolman could not be mentioned in the same
breath with Anthony Benezet, his close friend and co-worker.
The leading antislavery propagandist in pre-Revolutionary
War America, Benezet was a compiler, reprinter, and distrib-
utor of abolitionist books and pamphlets. But perhaps his
dearest love was to prepare Negroes for their freedom by
teaching them how to read and write. He was the key figure
in the operation of a school for slaves founded in Philadelphia in 1770; for two years the sessions were held in his
house. The school had a handful of white students—six out
of forty-six in 1775—but its basic reason for existence
remained that of discharging a duty "to these oppressed
people"—that is, the slaves. In the light of the pioneer
efforts by men like Benezet, it is not surprising that it was a
Quaker influence that led Rhode Island in 1784, in its measure freeing its slaves, to stipulate that their children be
taught to read and write.

Outside of Quaker circles, the efforts to better the lot of the
Negro met with little success in colonial America. However,
on the eve of the Revolutionary War there were two developments that forecast a brighter day for the blacks: the growing hostility to the slave trade and the efforts of the Negroes
themselves.

Opposition to the slave trade had its roots in the fear
of slave insurrections. When Negroes became numerous
enough to endanger the peace, colonial legislatures sought
to prohibit the foreign slave trade outright or to place heavy
import duties on it. Such measures were invariably set
aside by the Crown, however, which acted on the advice of

Parliament and the British shipowners. The differing points of view held by the mother country and her colonies about the limiting of the slave trade was one of the chief reasons for the widening rift between the two.

In the years immediately preceding the war, colony after colony expressed its displeasure concerning slave importations from abroad. The Massachusetts legislature passed anti-slave-trade measures in 1771 and 1774, but the royal governor prevented them from becoming law. In the latter year, both Rhode Island and Connecticut voted to prohibit the trade, Rhode Island stipulating that any slave brought within her boundaries would immediately become free. Pennsylvania in 1773 effectively struck at the trade by levying a stiff duty of £20 on each imported slave. Three southern colonies passed restrictive measures, Virginia and North Carolina in 1774 and Georgia in 1775.

These widely adopted measures against slave importation owed their origin to more than a desire to ward off any possible uprising of a numerous black population. They also represented an attempt to strike back at Parliament for passing objectionable laws, a motive particularly influential in explaining the action of the Continental Congress in voting, on April 6, 1776, that no slave be imported into any of the thirteen united colonies. And, finally, not to be ignored in accounting for the action against the slave trade was the growing impact of a philosophy of human freedom, now gaining momentum in America as the crisis approached.

The slogans of liberty that became fashionable on the eve of the Revolution had their effect on the slaves, particularly in New England, where they made use of two techniques, freedom suits and petitions. In the former, the slave, charging that his liberty was being "restrained," took his master to court. The best known of these suits was the Jenny Slew case in 1766. Spinster Slew successfully brought charges against John Whipple of Ipswich, Massachusetts, the court awarding her as damages "the sum of four pounds lawful money of this Province." During the proceedings one of the interested onlookers was John Adams; this was the first time, he wrote in his diary, that he had ever witnessed such a case, "though I have heard there have been many."

Although freedom suits were invariably won by the complaining party, the procedure had its drawbacks. Typical of the legalistic approach, it was expensive and slow. It was also individual—far from establishing a broad principle of universal freedom, the verdict in these suits extended only to the parties immediately involved. Hence, "suits for service" gave way to formal requests addressed to the political authorities.

In Massachusetts in January 1773, a group of slaves petitioned the legislature to liberate them, calling attention to the things they lacked: "We have no property! we have no wives! we have no children! no city! no country!" In May of the following year the Bay State slaves sent to Boston another petition, stating that, in common with all other men, they had a right to their freedom. But neither the governor nor the legislature was disposed to grant relief, and the latter tabled both requests. As Negroes discovered, to have slaves freed en masse by an act of the assembly was quite another thing from the freeing of an individual Negro by a court decree.

A more direct way of obtaining liberty was by taking part in the struggle between the colonies and the mother country after the two had come to blows in 1775. To become a soldier was one way to gain one's freedom, and bearing arms was by no means a remote possibility, Negroes having set a precedent by serving in the colonial militia. In early America the general policy was to exclude Negroes from military participation and bearing arms, but manpower shortages often outweighed the reluctance to give the Negro a gun. The arming of slaves was considered particularly risky in time of war, but that was the very time when manpower needs were the greatest; hence many colonies took the calculated risk. In the French and Indian War both northern and southern colonies used Negro soldiers. Particularly was this true of New York and Connecticut, colored men serving in twenty-five of the latter's militia companies. Jeremy Belknap expressed the belief that in Massachusetts the number of slaves had declined by 1763 "because in the two preceding wars, many of them were enlisted either into the army or on board vessels of war, with a view to procure their freedom."

The use of Negroes in the colonial militia established a pattern that was followed in the first months of the war with England. Colored men took part in the first military engagement of the Revolution, the Battle of Lexington and Concord, in which the British marched to destroy the military supplies stored at Concord and then returned to Boston. Among the Negroes taking part in this skirmish was Pomp Blackman, who later served in the Continental Army, and Prince Estabrook, a casualty.

Two months later at Boston came the Battle of Bunker Hill, another British effort to prevent the provincial armies from developing a posture of strength. Bunker Hill, too, had its Negroes, among them Peter Salem of Framingham, who was seeing action for the second time, Barzillai Lew, who had fought in the French and Indian War as a Pepperell enlistee in a Massachusetts company, and, most noteworthy of all, Salem Poor. So exceptional was Poor's conduct that fourteen officers sent to the legislature a petition on his behalf. According to their statement, Poor "behaved like an experienced officer, as well as an excellent soldier." Poor later served at Valley Forge and White Plains.

Virginia had its Salem Poor in the person of William Flora of Portsmouth. Serving with the local militia in the Battle of Great Bridge in December 1775, free Negro Flora was the last sentinel to leave his post as the enemy approached. Withdrawing amidst a shower of shot, Flora returned fire eight times.

But the early use of Negro soldiers was short-lived; indeed, by the time of Flora's exploit, a pattern of exclusion had set in. The chief architect of this no-Negroes policy was the newly formed Continental Army. A military establishment that represented all of the states had to be responsive to the sentiment of all of them. Thus the federal army tended to be more selective than the local militia or the state levy. Continental commanders were aware that most Negroes were slaves, whose enlistment violated the property right of their masters. Determined that the federal army would not become a refuge for runaways, the high command, meeting at Cambridge on October 8, 1775, agreed on a policy of exclusion for both slaves and free Negroes.

This measure was not well received by Negroes already in the Army, and they carried their complaints to headquarters. Upon the recommendation of General George Washington, Congress permitted these men to re-enlist, but added that no other Negroes would be signed up. Thus both the civilian and military authorities of the central government were in agreement that the Army was no place for the Negro.

The individual states soon followed suit. By the summer of 1776, every New England state had officially barred black enlistments. In Pennsylvania nonwhites were exempted from military service, and in both Delaware and New York recruiting officers were told they must not enroll anyone who owed service to a master. In the southern states the new enlistment laws were duplicates of the colonial statutes confining military service to whites, except for Virginia, which still left a door ajar for the free Negro.

The policy of excluding Negroes was based on the supposition that the war would not last long, a supposition that proved to be a will-o'-the-wisp. As the war entered its third year—by the summer of 1777—a policy reversal was under way. The enlisting of Negroes met with decreasing opposition as the war dragged on and it became increasingly difficult to raise volunteer forces. Since recruiting officers were paid by the head—so much for each enlistee—they had little inclination to be particular. Colored recruits were also enlisted by men who were trying to get an officer's commission, which could be obtained if one brought a specified number of volunteers into camp.

Making soldiers of Negroes gained support when Congress in 1777 began to fix quotas for each state. Faced by manpower requests for Washington's army, local and state recruiting officers were inclined to send Negroes whenever available. This practice spared a like number of white men for the state or county military forces, which were usually required to put in short-term enlistments at local points.

The recruiting of Negroes was greatly advanced by the substitution system; a draftee could avoid service by producing someone to take his place. Men in search of a substitute found that a Negro was easier and less expensive to get than anyone else. Except for Massachusetts, the states above the Potomac permitted slaves to be sent as substitutes. Of the southern states only Maryland permitted slave substitutes. Virginia continued to permit free Negroes to enlist, although it confined them to the roles of drummer, fifer, or pioneer.

South Carolina and Georgia would permit no enlistment of Negroes, slave or free, even when the war was brought to their hearthstones. This unyielding attitude was of serious concern to the federal authorities, for by 1777 the Continental Congress and the Continental Army commanders had reversed their Negro exclusion policy. When the states sent Negroes to meet their troop quotas, neither Congress nor the high command voiced objection. By the fall of 1776 Washington and his generals had learned the hard facts of life and were taking whatever the states sent, and any lingering reluctance in Congress had been overcome by the dire need to reinforce the Army.

By the spring of 1779 the Congress was ready to take the giant step of recommending slave enlistment, forced into action by the British occupation of Savannah and the opening of a second enemy campaign to subjugate the South. Late in March 1779 the Congress recommended to South Carolina and Georgia that they raise 3,000 Negroes without delay, to be formed into separate battalions. Owners of the slaves were to be paid up to $1,000 for "each active able-bodied negro man of standard size, not exceeding thirty-five years of age." No bounty or pay would go to the slave, but if he served faithfully and well for the war's duration, he would receive his freedom and $50. This idea was warmly approved by Alexander Hamilton who, as a member of Washington's staff, had urged the Commander-in-Chief to support such a step.

But, despite their desperate plight, the two beleaguered states refused to sanction slave enlistments. In vain did young John Laurens, an aide-de-camp of General Washington, passionately urge his fellow South Carolinians to adopt the measure; in vain did General Benjamin Lincoln and later the able and influential commander Nathanael Greene appeal to Governor John Rutledge. But the South Carolina legislature turned thumbs down on the slave enlistment proposal, as did Georgia's lawmakers.

Outside the South, however, colored men saw action under the newly unfurled "stars and stripes." By the summer of 1778 the Continental Army was well sprinkled with them. An official return of Negroes, dated August 24, 1778, and signed by Adjutant General Alexander Scammell, totalled 755, scattered over fourteen brigades.

In this return the detachment with the highest percentage of Negroes, General Samuel Holden Parson's brigade, was made up primarily of recruits from Connecticut. This was typical: practically no town of any size in that state failed to supply one or more Negroes for the Continental Army. New England, despite its relatively small black population, probably furnished more colored soldiers than any other section. In central Massachusetts in 1777 an observer reported that he ran across no regiment without "a lot of Negroes." The Rhode Island First Regiment enrolled from 225 to 250 colored men.

Outside New England, the state that recruited the largest number of Negroes was Virginia, the total in her land and sea forces perhaps going "beyond the five hundred mark." In the fall of 1777 state recruiting agents made it a point to draft Negroes, "as it was thought that they could best be spared," explained Governor Thomas Nelson to General Washington late in 1777.

Whether he served in the North or the South, in the Continental Army, state forces, or local militia, the typical Negro soldier was a private, consigned as if by caste to the rank and file. Even more than other privates, he tended to lack identity. Often he bore no specific name, being carried on the rolls by terms such as "A Negro Man."

Only a small number of Negroes served in the artillery, and even fewer in the cavalry. The typical colored volunteer served with the infantry, where he was either assigned to functions in support of combat operations or detailed for duty as an orderly. Since white soldiers generally disliked assignment to the wagon, commissary, or forage services, it was not unusual for Negroes to find themselves enrolled in these departments. Negro drummers, too, were common. Related to the orderly and body servant duties to which he was customarily assigned, the semidomestic tasks of waiter and cook were often given to the Negro soldier.

Since Negro soldiers fought side by side with whites, rather than in separate organizations, there was no battle in which black Americans were conspicuous as a racial group. The only engagement in which Negroes were even partly distinctive as a group was the Battle of Rhode Island, which took place on the northern end of the island of Rhode Island in August 1778. A predominantly Negro regiment, the First Rhode Island, held one of the positions assaulted by the British-Hessian forces. Knowing that a large majority of the men of the First Regiment were little more than raw recruits, having been in the army only three months, the British command expected that this unit would show weakness and yield, thus exposing a soft spot in the American defense. This proved to be a costly miscalculation, for when the enemy made three spirited charges against the American right wing, the First Regiment held the ground in its sector. Meeting a resistance far more stubborn than expected, the Hessians suffered many casualties. In nearly four hours of hard fighting, the colored soldiers held as firmly as the other American troops. The upshot was a victory for the Americans. In the general chorus of praise, the predominantly Negro unit was not forgotten. The First Regiment, said commanding officer John Sullivan in orders issued shortly after the battle, was entitled to a proper share of the day's honors.

Action on land was not the only fighting contribution of the Negro. He also saw service in the Continental Navy and on other American ships of war—those of the state navies and those operated by the Army, as well as the hundreds of privateers commissioned by Congress. Faced with a chronic shortage of manpower, Navy recruiters, like those of the Army, were in no position to be carefully selective. Ship commanders gladly made use of whatever Negroes they could get.

In the Continental Navy the Negroes generally served in the lowliest ranks—officer's boy and powder boy—whereas in the state navies it was more customary to find them in the rank of seamen of various classes. The Navy of South Carolina and those of the Chesapeake Bay states—Maryland and Virginia—frequently used Negroes as pilots, a job they commonly held in peacetime.

The best-known of the pilots in the Virginia service was Caesar, the slave of Carter Tarrant of Hampton. During the course of his long service, the boats he piloted had their share of engagements with the enemy. In one of these encounters Caesar "behaved gallantly" while steering the schooner *Patriot*. On another occasion he was at the wheel when the *Patriot* captured a brig carrying stores for the British troops. Two of Virginia's slave pilots lost their lives in service: one of them, Minny, met his death trying to board an enemy supply ship that was ravaging the Rappahannock.

Some Negroes found service on the privateers, a mecca to runaway slaves, inasmuch as their officers would never ask embarrassing questions to anyone seeking to sign on. A typical New England privateer might carry two or three Negroes. In Salem, Massachusetts, slave Titus acted as a business agent for the privateers, making a good income. The best-known of the Negroes serving aboard a privateer was James Forten, who while not yet fifteen enlisted as a powder boy on the *Royal Louis,* commissioned by Pennsylvania in 1781. When the vessel was captured, young Forten was sent to the floating dungeon, the *Jersey,* where he spent seven months. After the war he became a sailmaker in Philadelphia, eventually amassing a fortune of $100,000 and joining the ranks of the abolitionists.

The morale of the Negro who served in the Revolutionary forces was likely to be good. A former slave or low-paid town laborer, he was likely to be inured to the multiple hardships of life in an army camp or aboard a cramped frigate. If he were a slave, armed service represented a step toward emancipation. If he were already a free man, he was likely to be motivated by a complex of factors, including a desire for adventure or the prospect of a bounty in land or money.

But, slave or free, the Negro, as an American, was doubtless stirred by stories about martyred patriots, such as Crispus Attucks, a runaway slave who had been in Boston on the night of March 5, 1770, when a crowd started throwing snowballs and brickbats at the British twenty-ninth regiment. In a combination of panic and self-defense, the soldiers fired into the crowd, killing three men immediately and mortally wounding two others. The first to die was Attucks, a muscular, forty-seven-year-old mulatto. His fame and that of the other four victims was fanned by the public funeral held three days after the tragic event, the impressive procession starting from Faneuil Hall, where Attucks had lain in state. The deep resentment over this affair was not allowed to subside. Colonial propagandists would see to it that this "Boston Massacre" and its victims would not be forgotten.

As Americans, Negroes were doubtless stirred, too, by the high-sounding goals of the Revolution. In breaking with the mother country, the leaders of the new nation had invoked the spirit of liberty, asserting that war was being waged to extend the boundaries of human freedom. Such ideas of liberty and the rights of man, which meant so much to slaves and others of lowly status, received their greatest expression in the Declaration of Independence.

Approved by the Continental Congress on July 4, 1776, this ringing statement held a great appeal for those who considered themselves oppressed. It stated that all men were created equal and were endowed with certain rights that could not be taken away, among them life, liberty, and the pursuit of happiness. This was revolutionary language and it was but natural that Negroes would interpret the Declaration as a freedom manifesto to mankind rather then merely an attack on a king across the water.

This fondness for freedom led many slaves to join the British, who were faced even more seriously than their opponents by a manpower shortage. From the beginning they had been receptive to the use of blacks. Moreover, to liberate the slaves of the American rebels would cost them nothing at all.

The inviting of Negroes to join the British dated from the opening months of the war. Lord Dunmore, Royal Governor of Virginia, issued a proclamation in November 1775 declaring free all slaves who would join His Majesty's troops. Dunmore's edict created great apprehension in the South, the Continental Congress recommending to Virginia that she resist Dunmore to the hilt.

But His Lordship was not able to capitalize on the

proclamation, once he was driven from the mainland a few weeks afterward, and left the Chesapeake a few months later. During that span some 700 slaves had succeeded in reaching his forces, and his proclamation had an indirect effect on thousands of others, quickening their hopes for freedom.

The most important of the slave-freeing British proclamations was issued by Commander-in-Chief Henry Clinton on June 30, 1779. It forbade any person from selling or claiming any enemy-owned slave who had taken refuge in the British lines, and it promised every Negro who deserted from an enemy master full security to follow any occupation he wished while in the British lines. This proclamation was issued after the Crown forces had shifted their military operations to the South, the heartland of the Negro population. It was issued, therefore, not only to gain a labor supply for the British, but also to reduce the military strength of the enemy. For, as was plainly evident, in the South the American authorities, civilian and military, had been putting the Negro to every war-related task except arms bearing.

The Americans had used Negroes as guides, messengers, and spies. The most celebrated of these was slave James, of New Kent County, Virginia, whose spying activities while at Benedict Arnold's base at Portsmouth in the spring of 1781 won the highest praise from General Lafayette. Other Negroes had been employed as military laborers, playing a major supporting role on the American side. It was these blacks who forged the munitions, drove the wagons, erected the fortifications, repaired the roads, and destroyed the enemy's bridges. In the South the military need for slave labor was so urgent that the authorities resorted to impressment—requiring an owner to furnish his slave for a stated period—even though such a practice aroused the bitterest condemnation of the masters. Sometimes the state governments and Continental military officers went into the market and purchased slaves or hired them.

To deprive the Americans of such a powerful black arm, British used both force and persuasion. Whenever possible, they seized and carried off enemy-owned slaves. But by far the largest number of Negroes who served under the British were those who had come of their own volition. Like a lamp unto his feet, the lure of freedom led the slave to the camps of Clinton and Cornwallis. Perhaps nearly three-quarters of the slaves who escaped to the British made their way on foot, but others took advantage of the numerous waterways that crisscrossed the low country regions. The Chesapeake Bay tributaries were particularly inviting to escape-minded slaves, as was coastal Georgia, with its nearness to British-held East Florida.

Some American masters were hard struck. Governor Benjamin Harrison of Virginia lost thirty of his best slaves, and Arthur Middleton of Charleston, like Harrison a signer of the Declaration of Independence, was deserted by some fifty of his black retainers. Another South Carolinian, William Hazzard Wigg, lost eighty-eight "prime" Negroes and eight "inferior" ones.

To keep their losses down, the Americans resorted to various techniques, the chief of which was strengthening the patrol system. In 1779 North Carolina provided special inducements for those who engaged in patrol duty, giving them a tax cut and exempting them from road work, militia duty, and jury service. A Georgia law of 1778 required that one-third of the troops in every county remain where they were as a permanent local control to check any "wicked attempts of slaves." In Virginia masters were required to remove their slaves from the vicinity of the British forces, a practice that later came to be known as "running the Negroes." In addition, Virginia's Navy Board ordered the state galleys to cruise in the rivers to prevent the flight of slaves. Meting out severe punishment was another deterrent to desertions by slaves; South Carolina in 1776 stipulated death for any bondman who joined the British land or naval forces.

Despite all precautions, tens of thousands of slaves succeeded in reaching His Majesty's lines. Like the Americans, the British put the Negroes to a variety of war-related tasks, the various services—quartermaster, commissary, and royal artillery—seeking all they could get. The striking power of the Crown forces was markedly increased by its numerous black carpenters, hostlers, axemen, miners, blacksmiths, sawyers, armorers, and turnwheelers. Unskilled Negroes were often sent out on foraging parties to run off the livestock of American patriots and strip their fields, barns, and cellars.

The British need for military laborers practically exhausted the available supply of blacks, leaving relatively few to be used as soldiers. Exclusive of the runaways who served with the Hessians, perhaps not more than a total of 1,000 Negroes bore arms for the British, the bulk of these being in the South. The British had some uneasiness about giving a gun to a former slave, sensing that such a step might pose the problem of control.

A more acceptable service for Negroes was that of spy, guide, and informer, the British not hesitating to use slaves in these capacities. The British were even more eager to use Negroes of a seafaring bent. Throughout the war slaves piloted royal vessels in the coastal waters, took part in marauding operations, and swelled the ranks of ordinary seamen. So highly did the British regard slave pilot Sampson that when they attacked Charleston in the summer of

1776, he was ordered to a safe place below deck.

When the war came to an end, the British were determined to take with them the Negroes who had come into their lines. Thousands of these had been promised their freedom; others had become the personal property of officers and soldiers. Alert to the serious danger of losing their former slaves, the Americans had formally protested to Sir Guy Carleton, the British Commander-in-Chief, the protest being voiced in person by General Washington. The interview was not satisfactory to the Americans present, Carleton insisting that his government could not ignore its obligations to Negroes who had come into the British lines under proclamations of freedom.

The upshot was that the British evacuated their Negroes with practically no American interference, 4,000 of them leaving from Savannah, 6,000 from Charleston, and 4,000 from New York. Angry Americans could only fume and sputter as their former slaves sailed away, their loss creating a diplomatic issue that would plague Anglo-American relations for a quarter of a century.

The American Revolution brought some gains to Negroes. Those who had joined the Army upon the promise of freedom usually obtained it. Moreover, since the war had been fought in the name of liberty, many Americans were led to reflect seriously upon the impropriety of holding men in bondage. The feeling that slavery was inconsistent with the ideals of the war cropped up in many quarters, becoming manifest in the formation of abolitionist societies, in the concern for Negroes displayed by religious groups, and in the antislavery activities of the state and federal governments.

In the years immediately after the war a number of

abolitionist societies emerged. The Pennsylvania Society, first formed in 1775 at Philadelphia, was revived in April 1784. Less than a year later New York organized a society, with John Jay as president. New Jersey came next, and by the end of 1790 Delaware, Maryland, Connecticut, and Rhode Island had followed suit. Supplementing these state-wide organizations were numerous local societies. These abolitionist groups held their first national convention at Philadelphia in 1794, with representatives from ten state organizations, including Maryland and Virginia. Unlike the key figures in the abolitionist movement of half a century later, the leaders in these early societies could never be regarded as hot-eyed zealots. On the contrary they were men of property and standing—orderly, law-abiding, quiet-mannered.

Meeting quarterly and working through standing and special committees, these societies engaged in a variety of activities. Although they sent petitions to the state and national legislatures, their essential technique was persuasion rather than pressure, the soft impeachment rather than the denunciatory declamation. They attempted to help the bondman by urging the abolition of the slave trade, foreign and domestic, and by the gradual abolition of slavery itself. In some instances they paid a master to free a slave; in others they guaranteed a master that if he freed his slave, they would be legally responsible if the slave failed to support himself. The Pennsylvania abolitionists tried to strike at slavery by refusing to buy the products of slave labor.

These societies attempted to make sure that the free Negro was not seized and sold back into slavery. They assisted him in finding a job, furnishing recommendations and making certain that the employer did not take advantage of him. Believing that the former slave should be educated for a life of freedom, these early abolitionists conducted night classes for adults and opened schools for children. In 1787 the New York Manumission Society founded the African Free School, beginning with some forty pupils.

The work of the abolitionist societies was seconded by church groups. Almost without exception, the religious denominations showed a quickening interest in the brother in black. The Quakers kept up their forthright attack on human bondage; their influence had been felt in making Pennsylvania the first state to abolish slavery, in 1780. Among the Baptists the most distinctive work was the licensing of preachers, slave and free. In addition to George Liele and David George, both of whom left America with the British, the Baptists also licensed Jesse Peter, who in 1783 took over the church at Silver Bluff, South Carolina, the first Negro Baptist church in the United States. Another noteworthy early Negro Baptist was South Carolina–born Joseph Willis who, prior to 1798, had become a licensed preacher and had gone into the Mississippi Territory. Willis was to have the distinction of delivering the first Protestant sermon preached west of the Mississippi River, in addition to becoming the first moderator of the first Baptist statewide organization—the Louisiana Association—west of the Mississippi.

Among Methodists antislavery sentiment was deepened by John Wesley's castigation of human bondage. In 1780, six years after he had penned his *Thoughts Upon Slavery*, the Methodist conference, meeting at Baltimore, left no doubt as to its attitude; it expressed disapproval of members who held slaves, and it required traveling preachers to free their slaves. This forthright stand was reaffirmed in 1784, but in the following year the conference suspended the rule against slaveholding. A feature of the early Methodist churches was their racially mixed congregations.

Of the fifty-one churches at the 1789 conference, thirty-six reported having colored members. "Black Harry" Hosier, a free Negro, was a traveling companion of Pranch Asbury, sometimes preaching as a substitute for the bishop.

Through such agencies as abolitionist societies and religious groups, the antislavery impulse spread. The movement was strongest in the North, where slaves were least numerous. Above the Potomac, Pennsylvania's sister states followed the lead she had set in 1780. Less than a year after the peace treaty had been signed, Connecticut and Rhode Island passed gradual abolition measures. The Connecticut Act stated that no child thereafter should be held to service after reaching twenty-five years of age, and Rhode Island declared that all children born of slave mothers after March 1, 1784, would be free.

In 1788 the New York legislature permitted masters to set free without bonded responsibility any able-bodied slave under fifty years of age. Eleven years later the assembly passed a gradual abolition measure, declaring that after July 4 of that year, 1799, a female born of a slave mother would be free after twenty-five years of service, and a male of a slave mother would be free after twenty-eight years. In New Jersey a gradual abolition bill was passed in 1804, a similar measure nine years earlier having lost by one vote. In two states, Massachusetts and New Hampshire, abolition was brought about by an antislavery interpretation of state constitutions that did not expressly prohibit human bondage. In Delaware the movement for gradual emancipation was a failure despite the work of such men as John Dickinson, who while president of the state legislature, freed six of his slaves.

In the South there were some efforts to help the slave. In 1782 Virginia empowered a master to free his bondman without first obtaining legislative consent. Three years later a law was passed declaring free a slave brought into the state and kept there for a year. But if Virginia could make it easier to free the slave, and if the Maryland legislature in 1785 could muster twenty-two votes against slavery, as against thirty-two for it, this degree of antislavery sentiment was not possible in the lower South, where Negroes were more numerous and slavery more profitable.

Until the time of the drafting of the Constitution in 1787, the central government had little to say about the Negro, for the national legislature's limited powers and its inability to enforce its enactments tended to make it avoid potentially explosive matters. The main Negro problem considered by the Continental Congress and that of the Confederation was whether slaves should be considered as part of a state's population in laying obligations—manpower and money—upon it and in giving it increased power. As stipulated in the Articles of Confederation, ratified in March 1781, Congress was empowered to fix quotas for the armed land forces from each state in proportion to the state's white inhabitants. This partial victory for the slaveholding sections was balanced by a provision stipulating that a free inhabitant of one state should enjoy the same privileges and immunities as a free inhabitant in a sister state.

The ratification of the Articles was followed by cessions of lands to the central government, necessitating a land policy for the national domain. Jefferson in 1784 asked Congress to prohibit slavery after 1800 in the region from the Great Lakes to the Gulf. This proposal was lost by a vote of seven states to six, but three years later Congress prohibited slavery in the territory above the Ohio. The Northwest Ordinance of 1787 containing this provision against the extension of slavery and involuntary servitude was the high-water mark in postwar national legislation concerning the status of the Negro. Beyond this Congress was not ready to go.

Even more conservative on matters relating to the slave were the men who that same year met in Philadelphia and drew up a constitution for the United States. These founding fathers were masters at the game of give and take; if the South wanted concessions to protect the foreign slave trade until she had time to replenish her supply, if she wanted concessions to protect masters whose slaves ran away, if she wanted concessions to count her slave population for representation in a national legislature—she could get these things if she in turn was ready to make compromises. The South did want them, and she did make the necessary concessions.

Hence, while the Constitution of the United States does not contain the word "slave" or "Negro," three of its provisions relate to persons who owed service or labor. One of the Constitution's provisions stated that Congress could not for twenty years prevent any state from importing any such persons it wished: thus the foreign slave trade was removed from congressional jurisdiction for two decades. Another provision of the Constitution stated that if a person who owed service or labor in one state were to run away to another state, the latter would have to yield him up upon claim of the party to whom such service was owed; thus masters were protected against slaves escaping into another state and claiming asylum. And, finally, in dealing with the thorny question as to whether slaves should be counted when determining the basis of representation in the House of Representatives, the Constitution stipulated that in apportioning representation and direct taxes, all free persons be counted, plus "three-fifths of all other persons."

This last-named measure, the famous three-fifths compromise, was destined to cast a long shadow. But this the founding fathers who met at Philadelphia had no way of knowing. Many of the delegates had been disposed to give slavery a minor role in their deliberations, holding that it was a local matter which should be left to the states. Others thought that it was pointless to devote too much time to a discussion of the pros and cons of an institution that was withering away: "Slavery in time will not be a speck in our country," said Oliver Ellsworth of Connecticut.

As a prophet, delegate Ellsworth was soon without honor; within half a dozen years slavery had been given a new lease on life by the coming of the cotton gin.

3

The House of Bondage (1800–1860)

THE SOUTH'S BEST-LOVED song, "Dixie," describes it as a land of cotton. So it was, but never completely so, and certainly not during the nearly two centuries after the founding of Jamestown. Cotton was the product of the industrial revolution, which first created the machines that devoured it and then created a machine that would make it accessible in abundance.

During the 1700s a series of inventions, taking place primarily in England, harnessed new sources of power and produced new machines that revolutionized the textile industry. These developments led to a sharp increase in the demand for raw materials to be fed into the new machines. For this purpose, cotton was ideal—except that the seeds had to be removed from the closely adhering fibers. Some cotton had been grown in colonial America, but in very small quantities, South Carolina's leading city exporting but seven bales in 1748. But as the century drew to a close, the great demand for a machine that would remove the seeds brought results; in 1793 a cotton gin was invented, thanks in large measure to Eli Whitney.

Quickly developed into an inexpensive and efficient tool, the new machine had an effect that was immediate. America's cotton crop of 1804 was eight times that of 1794. England's commercial restrictions, one of the causes of the War of 1812, temporarily halted the British demand, but after the war both domestic and foreign factory owners clamored for cotton. Inevitably the cotton kingdom expanded, decade by decade moving to virgin lands, primarily in the direction of the Southwest, where the growing season lasted seven months. Such expansion was made possible by territorial acquisitions such as the Louisiana Purchase in 1803 and the annexation of Texas in 1845. Florida, acquired in 1819, also had its cotton culture regions, which by 1840 were producing more than 100,000 bales a year. In the quarter of a century preceding the Civil War, the cotton fields of the South were producing three-fourths of the world's supply.

Cotton was a powerful stimulant to slavery; the two seemed to have been made for each other. In many ways, cotton lent itself to slave labor. A person working in a cotton field did not have to be highly motivated. Along with the bag to hold the picked cotton, the hoe and the plow were the basic tools, for none of the operations were sufficiently complex to require that one keep his mind on his work. Cotton provided employment for men and women, young children and graybeards, the habitually healthy and the chronically ill. Cotton was well fitted for the slave-gang system, the plant not being high enough to prevent an overseer's eyes from sweeping the field and spotting each worker, up to a total of forty. It was also a hardy crop, not easy to mutilate no matter how carelessly handled. In addition, it provided year-round employment.

In 1860 cotton accounted for three-quarters of all the Negro agricultural workers. Other staples—tobacco, sugar, rice, and hemp—had a slave-labor base and, like cotton, provided continuous employment. But, unlike cotton, they did not grow everywhere. Tobacco's stronghold was in the border states, with Virginia and Kentucky consistently in the lead; sugar was concentrated in Louisiana; rice was grown in South Carolina and Georgia; and hemp in Kentucky and Missouri.

The stepped-up demand for black agricultural laborers was supplied in part after 1807 by the internal slave trade. The foreign slave trade had been made illegal beginning on January 1, 1808, Congress having taken action on March 2, 1807, after President Jefferson had urged that the United States withdraw from "all further participation in those violations of human rights which have been so long continued on the unoffending inhabitants of Africa."

The law was one thing and its enforcement another. The importation of black cargoes from Africa and the West Indies proved hard to stamp out. The profits were high, and the risks were reduced because of the federal government's failure to vigorously search out the offenders. Slave ships, many of them fitted out in New York and Boston, carried an average of 5,000 smuggled Africans a year. Nonetheless, by the act of March 2, 1807, the foreign slave trade had been greatly cut down, forcing the cotton planters of the lower South to make their purchases in the domestic market. The states with surplus slaves—Virginia, Maryland, and Kentucky—became the sources of supply for the cotton kingdom.

Acting as middlemen between the seller in the upper South and the buyer in the lower South were licensed traders who bought and sold slaves on speculation. These traders acquired most of their slaves at auctions, held as often as not at the county courthouse. They inspected their potential wares with great care, examining a slave's teeth for signs of age and looking for whip scars that would indicate unruliness. When the slave's distinctive qualities were not observable, such as a male's labor skills or a female's ability to produce offspring, the auctioneer called attention to them. Sometimes the master who was putting the slaves up for sale made a request that families be sold together, particularly that a child not be sold separately from its mother. Most of the traders were unconcerned about preserving the unity of the slave family, however: "The selling of young children privately and publicly," writes Frederic Bancroft, "was frequent and notorious."

When he had purchased his supply of slaves, the trader's next step was to get them to the markets of the lower South. Slaves who were purchased in coastal Virginia and Maryland were put in the holds of ships sailing from the Chesapeake ports of Baltimore, Washington, and Norfolk and headed for the towns along the Gulf. Slaves who were purchased in Kentucky and in back-country Virginia made an overland trip on foot to the Mississippi, lodging at night in jails or warehouses. When the Mississippi was reached, the bondmen were put on a flatboat bound for New Orleans.

This city was mistress of the slave trade, its leading streets being studded with slave showrooms, show windows, and depots, capped by some 200 slave-auction marts, where any type of Negro could be purchased, including a pretty octoroon whom one might wish to send to Paris for her education. While in New Orleans, the traveler Frederick Law Olmsted took note of a recently purchased group of Negroes waiting for the steamboat that would take them to their new master's plantation. There were twenty-two of them, each wearing a blue suit and a black hat and holding a bundle of clothing and a pair of shoes. They stood erect and in silence, arresting the attention of the passers-by. "Louisiana or Texas, thought I, pays Virginia twenty odd thousand dollars for that lot of bone and muscle," wrote Olmsted.

The domestic slave trade averaged about 7,500 Negroes a year from 1820 to 1860. This was not the total transfer of slaves from the selling states to the buying states, since many slaves were carried by their masters rather than by slave traders. Indeed, emigrating masters probably accounted for three-fifths (445,200) of the estimated 742,000 Negroes moving from the less profitable to the more profitable sections during the four decades preceding the Civil War. Despite its volume, the domestic slave trade did not succeed in supplying masters in the lower South with all the bondmen they needed. Hence in the 1850s there was a movement to reopen the foreign slave trade, either by getting Congress to repeal African slave trade acts or by inducing the Supreme Court to declare them unconstitutional.

In making slaves available to those who needed them, the domestic slave trade was aided by the practice of slave hiring. Averaging 60,000 a year, slave hirings were common throughout the South but were most numerous in those regions that had surplus slaves. Slave-hiring brokers were ready to furnish blacks by the day, week, month, or year.

As a rule, those who hired slaves needed them only for a special task or a limited period. Leased slaves lent themselves well to such a large-scale, short-term enterprise as the construction of a railroad. In the iron and coal industries and in the hemp and tobacco factories, hired slaves were commonly used. Professional people in the towns found it convenient to use such slaves as domestics.

The hired slave was usually guaranteed wholesome

food and adequate wearing apparel, a Kentucky hirer in 1833 typically agreeing to "furnish said negro man with two summer suits of good clothes, one fall suit of jeans, and one pair of shoes." In some instances the slave received a weekly allowance of twenty-five cents. Some states permitted a slave to hire his own time, a practice generally limited to those who were skilled of hand and trustworthy of character.

Once slavery had become a dominant feature of southern life, it became necessary to defend it. Hence a proslavery argument developed, with southern opinion makers—congressmen, clergymen, newspaper editors, and college professors—contending that slavery was a positive good. One of their arguments was that the Negro was biologically inferior to the white—that race determined mental and moral traits. The Negro, as a member of an inferior race, was meant to be a slave, his normal and natural condition.

The leaders of the antebellum South did not believe in an open society, John C. Calhoun asserting that it was a dangerous error to suppose that all people are equally entitled to liberty. Another influential South Carolinian, Senator James H. Hammond, carried Calhoun's viewpoint to its logical conclusion: "In all social systems there must be a class to do the menial duties, to perform the drudgery of life." This role of "mudsill of society" fell naturally to Negroes in their proper status of "chattels personal, to all intents, constructions and purposes whatsoever," to use the language of the slave codes. The Scriptures supported slavery, ran another argument; none of the Old Testament prophets condemned it, and Paul advised a servant to return to his master. Many southern clergymen comforted themselves with the thought that if Negroes were slaves here on earth, it was but a necessary prologue to their becoming free men in the heavenly Jerusalem.

To whites in the South slavery was not only an economic way of life; it was also a system of racial adjustment. They felt that if the Negro were set free, he would run amok and lower the whole tone of society. Hence slavery was a means of keeping him under control, the best way to make sure that the South would remain "a white man's country," with all that it meant for peace, order, and stability.

Another point on which white southerners had convinced themselves was that the Negro himself was better off in slavery. By far the most able exponent of this viewpoint was attorney George Fitzhugh of Virginia, author of two widely read works, *Sociology for the South* and *Cannibals All!* In the latter, propagandist Fitzhugh wrote:

> The negro slaves of the South are the happiest, and, in some sense, the freest people in the world. The children and the aged and infirm work not at all, and yet have all the comforts and necessaries of life provided for them. They enjoy liberty, because they are oppressed neither by care nor labor.

The point of view that the Negro was happiest when he was in subjection to others was reiterated whenever the occasion permitted. In a South Carolina case in 1853 involving free Negro Reuben Roberts, the court took note that he looked to be much older than his twenty-four years, adding that "it has often been remarked that negroes wear their age better in slavery than in any other state."

It is difficult even to generalize about the actual lot of the slave, for slavery was both a labor system and a social order. Moreover, to focus properly on a slave's lot, it would be necessary to compare it with that of the laboring poor elsewhere, in the North as well as in the South. But if comparisons be confined to the slaves themselves, a bondman's lot bore a close relationship to the sort of work he did and to the kind of a master he had.

Slaves lived in varying regions, stretching from Delaware to Texas. Some of them worked in gangs on the far-flung plantations, producing cotton, rice, and sugar, each with its own sharp variations in rigor for the worker. Other agricultural slaves worked on farms producing tobacco or hemp under the direct supervision of the master. Some slaves were skilled laborers, but even here there was a difference between those of the plantation and those of the town. Some slaves were domestics; the majority of these were to be found on the plantations, but some were town dwellers.

The lot of the slave reflected something of the personality of the master—his traits and temperament. To some masters the happiness and moral welfare of their slaves meant little; to others they were matters of concern. Each state had laws governing the treatment of slaves, but these codes depended almost wholly upon the master for their observance or lack of it. Hence a kind master could ignore a law he deemed oppressive, whereas a hard master could get around a law he considered to be too lenient.

The lot of a slave might bear some relationship to the wealth of his master. Of the nearly 400,000 slaveholders in 1860, over half of them owned four slaves or less. A slave of such a small owner worked, as a rule, beside his master; he might even sit down and eat with him. Out of this close contact, some feeling of mutual regard might be engendered. On the other hand, a poorer master might not set much of a table to begin with, very likely having to resort to many penny-pinching practices that would bear hard on his black help. At any rate, slaves seemed to prefer that their masters be large owners, since they could then live in special quarters where, with no whites around, they could lead a more relaxed life. Moreover, slaves took pride in their master's wealth: "It was considered as being bad enough to be a slave," wrote a runaway, "but to be a poor man's slave was deemed a disgrace indeed!"

Possibly the slaves who were best off were those in the towns. Here the master-slave relationship was at its weakest; here were to be found slaves who were virtually free, hiring their own time. Town masters knew that if their skilled slaves were to be employed they must be permitted to go out and make their own arrangements. In many instances self-hire was a stepping-stone to self-purchase. To the normal excitements of urban life, these slaves added one of their own, mingling with free Negroes in church and at social affairs. Town slaves carried themselves with an air of assurance, their faces not marked by the "down" look often so characteristic of their rural brothers.

Sometimes the relaxed attitude of the urban blacks drew censure. Traveling in Richmond in 1852, Olmsted noted that the newspapers were carrying numerous complaints about the insolence and insubordination of the slaves. In a city of the lower South, traveler Olmsted reported that the *New Orleans Crescent* expressed great alarm about the license and indulgence permitted to the blacks, which was heightened by the forging of passes: "As things now stand, any negro can obtain a pass for four bits or a dollar."

In the agricultural regions the slaves who fared best were the plantation domestics, among them the "mammy," butler, cook, housemaid, and coachman. They dressed better than other slaves, wearing uniforms or the discarded clothes of the master and mistress. Their food was better, often differing little from the masters'. They lived in a wing of the "big house," or in a cabin close by, and they slept in beds, not pallets on the floor. The labor required of them was lighter and more congenial than that required of other slaves.

House slaves had social advantages. If the master placed trust and confidence in any slaves, it was they, particularly the "mammy," who was often a confidante to the white mistress in her loneliness and isolation. They were often taught to read and write, even in violation of the law. As maids and valets, they often got a chance to travel. House slaves tended to have more of a mulatto strain than rural slaves, some of them having a blood tie with the master.

Better cared for, often lighter in skin color, and certainly much closer to the seat of power, the house slave looked down on everyone except the "quality" whites. Human, if not all too human, the colored domestics felt that they were far superior to the other slaves. And they considered their jobs as sort of a family privilege, to be passed down from father to son and mother to daughter.

Ranking not much below the house slave in the plantation hierarchy was the skilled craftsman—shoe or harness maker, carpenter, blacksmith, chair maker, sawyer, or basket weaver. Chosen from among others because of their intelligence and manual dexterity, the slave artisans brought higher prices than their fellows. They received relatively better treatment and were likely to be less subservient: "Whenever a slave is made a mechanic," said James H. Hammond, "he is more than half freed."

Commanding a higher price in the market and a greater consideration from the master than even the slave artisan was the foreman. Hand-picked for his trustworthiness, sound judgment, and impressive physical stature, the driver, as he was popularly known, was the right-hand man of the overseer, the plantation's general superintendent. He had a variety of responsibilities. In the morning it was he who blew the horn that called the hands to work. When they reached the fields, he laid out the specific amount of work each slave was to be responsible for, and he checked at day's end to see that it had been done. If the slaves worked in gangs, rather than by the assigned-task system, it was the driver who spurred them on, either with loud exhortations or by a flick of the whip. He gave the signals for the early afternoon meal break and for putting away the tools at dusk.

When night fell, the driver was charged with maintaining peace and quiet along slave row, his authority not being limited to field labor but extending "to the general deportment of the negroes," as a contemporary puts it. If a slave proved to be unruly in the quarters, just as if he proved balky in the fields, it was the function of the driver to do the whipping. The severity of his blows reflected something of his own personality: if he were power-drunk or closely identified himself with the master, his whip would be heavy, but if he sympathized with his fellow slave he would make the whip crackle within a hair's breadth of the culprit's bare back, the latter howling in feigned anguish.

Aside from the human satisfaction of lording it over others, the driver had other rewards. Often he was exempt from field labor. He received a better ration, which might include a weekly bottle of rum. He was better clad, some masters holding that this was a way by which he could command the respect of the slaves under him.

The lot of the typical slave, regardless of locale or occupation, was influenced in large measure by the psychological and legal controls brought to bear on him. All slaves were inculcated with the idea that the whites ruled from God and that to question this divine-right-white theory was to incur the wrath of heaven, if not to call for a more immediate sign of displeasure here below. A slave was told that his condition was the fulfillment of the will of the Master on high; catechisms for the religious instruction of slaves commonly bore such passages as:

> Q. Who gave you a master and a mistress?
> A. God gave them to me.
> Q. Who says that you must obey them?
> A. God says that I must.

The exalted status of the whites was carried over into the legal realm. The testimony of a Negro, slave or free, against a white was inadmissible in any court of law. Severe punishment was decreed for harming a white person. Of the eleven offenses for which a slave could be put to death in Kentucky in 1860, six involved acts or attempted acts against whites, one of them being the administering of poison to the master or putting ground glass into his milk. Many communities had ordinances requiring Negroes to pass on the outside whenever a white person approached, stepping into the road if necessary.

But the slave's greatest legal disability was that, although he was a person, he was also a piece of property. This duality posed a problem: "Slaves are not only property," stated a Virginia judge in 1825, "but they are also rational beings, and entitled to the humanity of the Court, when it can be exercised without invading the rights of property." But this was the nub of the problem, for the human rights of the slave often ran counter to the property rights of his owner.

In the vast majority of cases involving a conflict of rights, the courts obviously tended to give priority to property. Indeed, slave marriages were not matters of legal record, because to have made them so would have been harmful to the property rights of the master. Hence, although a kind master might permit a slave to own a plot of land or make a contract, the latter might find himself in legal difficulty upon the death of his master and the settlement of his estate.

A variety of restrictive laws kept the slaves in line. There was no freedom of assembly, not more than four or five slaves being permitted to come together except at church, at a burial, or at Christmas. Firearms were forbidden. To prevent a system of signaling, slaves were not allowed to beat drums or blow horns. No intoxicants were to be sold to them. They could not leave the master's premises without a pass or letter.

To help enforce the law, each county had its mounted patrol—a sort of police system—which made unannounced visits to the slave quarters to see that everything was quiet and orderly and that no cabin contained stolen goods, concealed a runaway, or was the scene of a secret meeting. Patrol duty bore a similarity to the military draft—indeed, a patrol was made up of persons subject to militia duty—and was very unpopular, many draftees preferring to pay a fine rather than to serve. In the towns the constables were charged with seeing that the Negroes were off the streets after the curfew sounded for them, generally at nine o'clock in the winter and ten in the summer.

Slave punishments varied, the most common by far being the lash. A culprit who was muscular and bad-tempered might have to be turned over to a professional whipper—a "slave breaker." The punishment for a runaway was likely to be branding in a conspicuous place, so that everyone would give him a second look, in case he was again at large. A refractory bondman might be sold "down the river" (the Mississippi), a dreaded fate in slave circles. Some large plantations had their own jails, but since imprisonment entailed a loss of work time, it was not often used. Stoppage of food also had its drawback as a punishment—the loss of physical vigor. Similarly, the death penalty was used sparingly, for it involved a property loss that the state might have to make good.

Fearing that restrictions alone might not be enough to keep the slave in line, some masters adopted the system of rewards—in effect, using both the stick and the carrot. Slaves were given small sums or extra allowances of food, for working overtime or on Sunday or for laboring more diligently than required. Another morale-building device was the granting of holidays, which invariably included July 4 and December 25. The latter was the favorite, often running on for a week, the highlight coming on Christmas morning, when the slaves came to the big house to be greeted by the master and the mistress and to receive sundry small gifts, plus a dram of liquor. Slaves were sometimes permitted to have a dance; if no fiddler were available, they would "pat Juba." To "dance Jim Crow" was one of their favorites:

> Once upon the heel tap,
>   And then upon the toe,
> An' ev'ry time I turn around
>   I jump Jim Crow.

We have still not answered the question, What did it mean to be a slave? After stating that slaves differed in their mental make-up and in their working conditions, it must be added that on this question our sources of information are not satisfactory. It is not easy to know what a slave was thinking; unlettered, he kept no diary. Runaway slaves turned out autobiographies in sufficient number—around 100—to constitute a branch of letters, the "heroic fugitive" school of American literature. But these slave narratives tended to stress the sensational, being emotional in tone rather than analytical. Often they were ghostwritten by abolitionists and hence represented a white reformer's idea of how it felt to be a slave.

Likewise to be carefully weighed are the things slaves told the white people—the master, his guests, or travelers. A slave set a watch upon his lips whenever talking to whites. He was a "yes man" par excellence. By the intonations of his master's voice, a bondman had come to know what kind of response he wanted; to the slave the truth or falsity of what he said was unimportant compared with saying the thing the master wanted to hear.

For the slave was always playing a role, acting in the way that he believed to be to his best interests. Hence he tended to fawn servilely, to wear the mask of humility. He adopted a child posture, giving the impression of being attached to the master and utterly dependent upon him. He tended, or pretended, to be a bit stupid. This was another aspect of his technique of survival, for his apathetic gaze was self-protective; it was dangerous to know too much. So successful was the slave in acting out this role that there is a question, as Professor Stanley Elkins points out, as to whether the behavior pattern had become internalized— that the mask had become the man, that the Sambo stereotype had become a true Sambo.

There can be no question that the slave did make an adjustment to his lot. But this did not mean that he was satisfied. In many ways he struck back, from slowing up in his work to staging a full-scale revolt. The most common of his techniques of protest was what has been called his "day-to-day resistance." In going about his work, the slave might make it a point to be inefficient, pretending to be too stupid to learn, particularly if he were asked to perform a new task or use a different tool; this was a form of "outdumbing," if not outsmarting, the master.

Slaves were careless about property, abusing the livestock and damaging the farm implements. They were so hard on hoes that it became necessary to construct just for them one that was especially heavy and strong. As an additional precaution, some masters required that every tool or implement be marked with the name or initial of the slave to whom it was given. But even if a slave did not manage to break the hoe, he might use it to cut up the crop, blaming his clumsiness if called down by the driver. Obviously the slave's hostility to work had varied roots, but prominent among these was his feeling that "revenge against work" was revenge against the master.

The destruction of property by fire was a slave technique that was particularly dreaded by the master. His income for the year could go up in smoke if a barn filled with grain or tobacco were set aflame. Arson was generally punishable by death, but it had an attraction for the disgruntled slave because it required little trouble on his part and it was not easy to detect. Fire insurance companies were sometimes reluctant to write policies for slaveholders.

Another way in which the slave struck back was the feigning of illness. Whenever a slave took ill, a master grew suspicious. For, indeed, it often must have seemed that slaves were always being laid up in the plantation hospital with some kind of malady. And it always seemed that the incidence of illness went up sharply when the heaviest work was to be done, and that few slaves were ill on Sundays or holidays, when their time was their own. On a Louisiana plantation, traveler Olmsted took note of an overseer who was putting a slave to hoeing despite her groans and complaints: "We have to be sharp with them," explained the overseer; "if we were not, every negro on the estate would be a-bed."

Occasionally a slave might lame himself to avoid work, but self-mutilation was not common. Suicide bears an element of revenge, but slave suicide seems to have been rare; a scholar of Arkansas slavery, Professor Orville W. Taylor, found only one instance in the state's history, that being a runaway who had been recaptured. A Tennessee slave, Isham, took an overdose of laudanum after he had been taken to New Orleans and placed in a slave mart. In 1853 a Kentucky slave who had already been sentenced to hang died by his own hands.

One of the subtler ways of expressing dissatisfaction was through stories and songs. The Uncle Remus stories, in which B'rer Rabbit always succeeded in outwitting B'rer Fox, were popular among slaves, the rabbit becoming to them a folk symbol. Slaves found a safety valve in their songs, especially the spirituals. These songs grew out of the all-Negro church, with its slave pastor. Always attending such services, however, were some whites, to keep an eye on things. Thus, since neither the sermons nor the songs could dwell upon conditions here below, slave sermons and religious songs were "otherworldly," dealing with the kingdom to come, with Promised Lands of milk and honey. Such an approach was essentially escapist—to sing of bright mansions above would take one's mind off the drabness of slave row.

On the face of it, the words of the spirituals suggest resignation to one's lot, but many of the black singers read into the songs a double meaning. It may be straining to say that whenever the word "hell" appeared in a spiritual, the singer consciously equated it with slavery as he knew it, and that every time the word "heaven" appeared, the singer equated it with freedom up North. But it is undoubtedly true that the slave found a way of saying in his stories and songs some things he dared not say in any other way. Even the most sluggishly minded slave could hardly miss the dual meaning of these lines:

> I got a right—we all got a right,
> I got a right to the tree of life.

What slave would not instantly identify his master with Pharaoh in two of the best-known spirituals, "Go Down, Moses" and "Pharaoh's Army":

> Go down, Moses,
> Way down in Egypt's Land,
> Tell ole Pharaoh
> To let my people go.

> O Mary, don't you weep, don't you mourn,
> Pharaoh's army got drownded,
> O Mary, don't you weep.

In his autobiography a former slave states that "a keen observer might have detected in our repeated singing of:

> O Canaan, sweet Canaan,
> I am bound for the land of Canaan

something more than a hope of reaching heaven. We meant to reach the *North*, and the North was our Canaan." But whatever paradise the slave was singing about, be it in this life or the next, he was giving expression to his discontent with things as they were.

A protest technique employed by the more adventurous slaves was flight, whether to Mexico, to Canada, to the northern states, or merely to the nearest urban center (Memphis, for example, which attracted runaways from Arkansas, Tennessee, and Mississippi). The reasons for running away varied from slave to slave; some fled in order to avoid work, others because they were afraid of being put on the auction block or because they wished to search for a loved one who had been sold away. But the compelling motive in the great majority of cases was dissatisfaction with the life of a slave. Flights were of two types, individual efforts and the organized movement known as the underground railroad.

Many slaves struck out alone and unassisted. Some who, despite the laws, had become literate made use of passes and "free papers" they had forged. Some, with nothing but the North Star to guide them, took to the woods, walking by night and lying in swamps by day, covering themselves with leaves. Living off the land, their fare consisted of fruits, nuts, berries, and a stray or stolen chicken. Of the thousands who escaped by water, those who were near the Ohio River often made use of stolen skiffs or canoes. Those in southern ports used various ruses to get aboard steamships bound for the North. A typical trick was that of getting a bundle of laundry and, pretending to be a servant, boarding a ship and hiding below. Ship companies were held liable for any runaways they carried, but this did not prevent many sympathetic captains and sailors from winking at the presence of some black stowaways.

Perhaps the most dramatic of the unassisted escape was that of William and Ellen Craft of Macon, Georgia. They used a common device—disguise—but they gave it a distinctive touch. With money cabinetmaker William had saved by hiring himself out, they purchased male attire for Ellen, a light-skinned quadroon who was to assume the role of a slave owner. Posing as hard of hearing so that no one could converse with her, and wearing her arm in a poultice so that she would not be asked to sign a hotel or steamboat register (for she could not read or write), Ellen carried off well her role of an ailing planter going north for medical treatment. William, too, did well, although his role of slave to the "invalid" was far less exacting. For five days the couple traveled through the slave states, always in first-class style, as befitting a planter. Finally, as their train pulled out of Baltimore, their ordeal was at an end.

Equaling the Crafts in fame for unusual escape was Henry Brown, a slave in Richmond, Virginia. Bold and ingenious, Brown ordered a specially designed and equipped box to be built in which he would be shipped to freedom. Three feet long and two feet wide, containing food and water, and carefully marked so that Brown would be traveling with his head up, the box reached Philadelphia, via Adams Express, after twenty-six hours en route. When the box was delivered, the four men who were anxiously awaiting its arrival pried off the lid. Then, according to eyewitness William Still, "the marvelous resurrection of Brown ensued. Rising up in his box, he reached out his hand, saying, 'How do you do, gentlemen?'"

Since the dash for freedom was a perilous business, most runaways required help. Assistance was provided by a system of receiving, concealing, and forwarding fugitives known as the "underground railroad." The "railroad" was made up of a loosely knit network of stations, located at points a day's journey apart, to which a slave would be brought by a "conductor." The initial contact with the slave was made by a field agent who came among them posing as a peddler, census taker, or map maker. It required some skill to persuade a suspicious Negro of his good intent, but once this had been done, the agent soon had the runaway in the hands of another "conductor," who took him to the first station. Fed, rested, and sometimes given a disguise, the slave was ready for the remainder of the journey. The traveling was done at night; during the day the slave would be concealed in a barn, cave, sail loft, or hayrick. Sometimes a runaway would be put on board a boat or train, if the skipper or trainman were a member of the underground apparatus or a trusted sympathizer. The total number of slaves given such assistance appears to have been modest—perhaps around 2,500 a year from 1830 to 1860.

As might be expected, the "underground railroad" flourished in such states as Ohio, which were near both the slave regions and Canada. But even Connecticut, located well above the Mason-Dixon line, had a respectable system of operations. New Haven agents included the Reverend Simeon S. Jocelyn, founder of a church for colored people, the Temple Street church, and Amos G. Beman, the first Negro pastor of the church. The state's most thriving center was Farmington, the main highway to Massachusetts; any runaway who reached Farmington, writes Horatio T. Strother, was sure of food, lodging, and a lift.

That a "conductor" whose "beat" was in a slave state courted danger and tragedy is shown by the career of Calvin Fairbanks. In 1844 he came to Lexington, Kentucky, bent on helping slaves get to Ohio, where they would be put into the hands of Levi Coffin, a Quaker whose zeal on behalf of the black fugitives has earned him the title of "President of the Underground Railroad." In February 1845 Fairbanks was sentenced to fifteen years imprisonment for having successfully assisted three runaways, one of whom was Lewis Hayden, who later became a member of the Massachusetts legislature. After four years in jail, Fairbanks was pardoned on condition that he leave Kentucky. Ignoring this stipulation, Fairbanks resumed his work of "liberating slaves from hell," as he put it. Arrested again, he was sentenced in 1852 to fifteen years at hard labor in the state penitentiary. There, in a narrow cell and heavily ironed, he remained until 1864, when he was pardoned, his "underground railroad" activities having caused him to spend a total of seventeen years and four months behind bars.

The best-known of the "underground railroad" operators was Harriet Tubman, frail in body but strong in will. Born in Dorchester County, Maryland, and herself a runaway, Harriet went into the slave states nineteen times and conducted more than 300 Negroes to the North or to Canada. To join Harriet's rescue party meant to remain with it, for she threatened to put to death any one who attempted to turn back, a threat that never had to be put to the test. Unlike the unfortunate Fairbanks, Harriet led a charmed life, serving also in the Civil War—as a spy, scout, and nurse without being captured.

The operations of the "underground railroad" not only cost many a master the loss of valuable property, but also drained off the more daring Negroes, leaving behind fewer bold spirits to take part in the most desperate of all of the slave's ways of striking back, armed revolt. Such uprisings had very little chance of success—this the plotters must have sensed. But they were gripped by an inner compulsion; they simply could not accommodate themselves to a bondman's lot. Despite the very slim possibility of winning freedom by armed force, they felt impelled to take the risk, for they could not resign themselves to the outrageous fortune whose name was slavery.

Records of the existence of some 250 slave conspiracies and revolts have been found by Herbert Aptheker, some dating back to colonial times. In 1712 and again in 1741 New York City was the scene of uprisings in which a total of thirteen whites and fifty Negroes lost their lives. The largest uprising in early America took place at Stono, South Carolina, in 1739, bringing death to sixty-five altogether.

Sometimes a revolt would be fanned by the slaves'

knowledge of a revolutionary upheaval elsewhere, the greatest of these uprisings being the one led by Toussaint L'Ouverture in Santo Domingo. Here in the early 1790s the harshly treated slaves took matters in their own hands and thousands of masters fled to Cuba and to the southern seaport towns of New Orleans, Savannah, Charleston, and Baltimore. Eventually France had to give up her intention to reconquer the island, which Toussaint's successor, Dessalines, had renamed Haiti. The emergence of a new Negro-controlled nation, the child of a revolt, had an emboldening effect on the slaves in the United States.

While the blacks under Toussaint were winning their independence, slave Gabriel of Henrico County, Virginia, attempted to stage a similar uprising. In the summer of 1800, he organized some 1,000 slaves, armed them with clubs, knives, and guns, and marched toward Richmond, six miles away. They never got there. An unusually heavy rainstorm had flooded the roads and bridges, making passage impossible. Moreover, the authorities in Richmond were ready, for the plot had been divulged by two slaves. Gabriel and some thirty of his followers were hanged, and, as a further deterrent, Governor James Monroe established a standing guard for the city.

Another long-remembered conspiracy took place in Charleston, South Carolina, in 1822. Its originator was free Negro Denmark Vesey, who had brooded deeply over the plight of the slave, bringing to his reflections a knowledge of the American and French Revolutions, the uprisings in Santo Domingo, and the sharp debates in Congress over the admission of Missouri to the Union as a slave state. Organizing their plans carefully, Vesey and his followers collected a store of daggers, pike heads, and bayonets, to be supplemented by a first-step raid on the city's two arsenals. The date for the outbreak was set for a Sunday night in

July, when many of the whites would be away on vacation. But before the conspirators could strike, the plot was divulged by a slave turned informer. In the court trials that followed, thirty-five of the conspirators were sentenced to hang, Vesey among them.

No revolt equaled that of Nat Turner in its consequences. A slave preacher in Southampton County, Virginia, Turner's actions were inspired by his interpretation of the Old Testament and his belief that he was God's chosen instrument to lead the slaves out of the house of bondage. Turner's preparation consisted of prayer and looking for a sign from on high, rather than in the enlisting of a large force. Hence, on the August evening in 1831 when he set out on his crusade, his total party numbered not more than eight. They began by killing Nat's master and his family. Pushing through the countryside, they gathered additional recruits, eventually numbering seventy. Taken by surprise, with their houses open in summer weather, nearly sixty whites were seized and put to death. After forty-eight hours the rebellion came to an end, the aroused whites having mobilized volunteer companies and called out the militia. "The Prophet," as Turner was called by the slaves, was caught and sent to the gallows, along with nineteen other culprits.

The antebellum South never forgot Nat Turner. No subsequent serious outbreak of blacks ever took place, but from Turner's day on, the slave states were beset by rumors of uprisings. Sometimes this apprehension reached the proportions of mass hysteria, which could be relieved only by seizing, convicting, and condemning a number of Negroes. Southerners might claim that their bondmen were contented and docile, and hence that there was nothing to fear from them. But Nat Turner had appeared to be docile and contented; hence, the fear would not down that some other apparently satisfied slave might prove to be another unsuspected firebrand.

To prevent a recurrence of the Southampton County tragedy, the slave states strengthened their patrol and militia defenses, passed more stringent slave codes, closed ranks, and permitted no criticism at home of the institution of slavery. They tightened their controls on an element of the population which they regarded as almost as dangerous as the revolt-minded slave—the free Negro.

4

The Nonslave Negro (1800–1860)

SLAVERY IN AMERICA was a matter of race inasmuch as that status was confined to the nonwhites. But, although practically all slaves were Negroes, not all Negroes were slaves. In 1790 nonslave Negroes numbered 59,557, and in 1860 488,070. In 1790 they made up 7.9 per cent of the total black population; in 1830 this proportion reached an all-time high of 13.7 per cent, dropping in 1860 to 11 per cent. Of the nearly half a million nonslave Negroes on the eve of the Civil War, 250,787 were to be found in the South, where they were known as "free Negroes" (a term which, strictly speaking, did not apply to the North after 1800, since virtually all of its Negroes had been set at liberty by then).

Existing even before slavery, the free Negro class has a varied origin. In point of time the first Negroes to become free were those who as indentured servants had completed their terms of service. Another time-hallowed road to freedom was running away. Other slaves obtained their liberty through military or naval service in the colonial wars and, as we have seen, in the American Revolution. Following in the wake of this war, the northern states, spurred on by religious groups and abolitionist societies, passed legislation providing for the gradual abolition of slavery. A number of free Negroes were added to the population when such territories as Louisiana, Florida, and Texas were acquired.

Accounting for a large proportion of the free Negroes were private manumissions. In some instances the freed slave was the natural offspring of the master by a slave mother. Indeed, as a group, the free Negro population had a much higher percentage of mixed bloods than did the slave population. In 1850 the proportion of mulattoes was 581 to every 1,000 blacks in the free Negro group, whereas it was only 83 mulattoes to every 1,000 blacks in the slave population. Slaves who were not only given their freedom but were also bequeathed property were likely to have a blood tie to their benefactor. A number of slaves were freed because of faithful and obedient service, others because the master had an uneasy conscience about human bondage.

Some owners did not formally free their slaves by deed or will; they simply turned them loose. In such instances the master was doubtless trying to get around the legal requirement that a slave who was set free must leave the state, or he might have been trying to thwart the requirement that limited the freeing of slaves to those who were physically fit to take care of themselves. Most of the manumissions had one peril for the slave; he was not to be freed unless the master, or his estate, was unencumbered by debt. And in some cases, even years after a master had freed his slave, the latter might be seized if the former became debt-ridden or insolvent.

The free Negro class also received accessions through immigration, the census of 1860 showing that 7,011 of the colored population had been born abroad. Some small additions to the free Negro group came from the offspring of white and Indian mothers and black fathers. If this was one of the minor sources of the free Negro total, the major one was natural increase.

A final source of the free Negro class may be noted—that of self-purchase. Generally slaves who were able to buy their liberty had some special trade or skill which they put to use in hiring themselves out. The free Negro dwelt predominantly in the towns rather than in rural areas, a condition resulting in part from the town slave's better opportunity to acquire money for his freedom. Among the able slaves who purchased their own freedom and that of their families were Lunsford Lane, who raised money by curing and selling pipe tobacco in his shop in Raleigh, North Carolina, and Lott Carey, who as a slave rose to the position of foreman of a tobacco factory in Richmond, Virginia, and as a free man became a Baptist missionary to Liberia.

Some slaves obtained their purchase funds in unusual ways: self-taught George Moses Horten sold love lyrics to the students at the state university of North Carolina; Newport Gardner of Rhode Island bought his freedom in 1791 with money won in a lottery, the same source from which Denmark Vesey acquired his purchase price nine years later. Among the other notable self-purchasers was James Derham, who as a male nurse, medical assistant, and apothecary in New Orleans was able to save enough money to buy his freedom in 1783, becoming an outstanding physician within a half dozen years. After he had moved to Philadelphia, he repeated his success, winning the highest respect from his colleagues in the medical profession, especially that of the eminent Benjamin Rush.

Derham's master. Dr. Robert Love, had encouraged him in his efforts to buy himself, and this kind of sympathetic attitude was necessary if a slave was to negotiate directly for his freedom. An avaricious master might simply appropriate his bondman's earnings out of hand; a dishonest master might take the money and then repudiate the bargain, knowing that the slave had no recourse at law. Hence most slaves preferred to work through an intermediary—a kindly disposed white person or a free Negro—who, with funds supplied by the slave, would proceed to purchase him and set him free.

The total number of slaves who purchased their freedom cannot be known. To say that in 1835 Cincinnati had 476 Negroes who had bought themselves and that in 1837 Philadelphia had 250 is to do little more than furnish fragmentary statistics. But if no statement can be made as to the total number of slaves who raised money to buy their freedom and that of their families, it can safely be said that the stories represented in that unknown total—stories of great self-denial, of tenacious will, and of indomitable hope—would reveal something of the human spirit at its best.

In pre–Civil War America the nonslave Negro in the South and the Negro in the North shared a very similar experience, simply because they were Negro. But their lot differed in some significant respects, and for this reason they may be treated separately. In both sections, be it noted, the states were free to do as they pleased in the absence of any mention of race in the Constitution and the failure of Congress (until 1857) to follow a consistent policy in deciding whether the Negro was a citizen. The southern scene may be surveyed first.

Speaking of the free Negroes, U. B. Phillips says that "they complied in all things that they might live as a third element in a system planned for two." Certainly to the white South the free Negro was a totally unwanted element. He was thought to be inclined toward crime and loose in morals; he was regarded as indolent and improvident, taking no heed for the morrow and hence likely to become a public charge.

The chief objection to the free Negro was that he endangered the institution of slavery. The white South believed that the Negro lacked the capacity to take care of himself. Under freedom, he would die out; hence he needed a master. This argument was weakened by the very existence of Negroes who were not slaves. But in a more direct way, the free Negro was a threat. "Free Negroes, as everybody except the abolitionist knows, are very objectionable amongst the slave population; much of the mischief committed may be traced to them as its source," wrote a nationally known Georgian, Howell Cobb, in 1858. The free Negro was charged with a catalogue of sins against slavery, such as receiving stolen goods from slaves and selling liquor to them, harboring runaways, making the slave dissatisfied with his lot, and, like Denmark Vesey, plotting dark stratagems.

To keep the free Negro under control was a task which the South did not shirk. By law, by court ruling, and by custom, the role of the free Negro was cast. From state to state—indeed, from county to county—this role would vary, depending upon the numerical strength of the black population and the possible need of a labor supply. Moreover, the role of the free Negro in a given locale was not static, since in a period of crisis the restrictive measures against him would be enforced, whereas in a period of calm, such measures would often be relaxed, if not ignored.

But throughout the South the controls set for the free Negro had much in common. To begin with, color indicated condition: if one had a dark skin, it was up to him to prove he was not a slave. In direct contrast to the principles of

English and American law which held that a man was innocent until proved guilty, a Negro who claimed to be free bore the burden of proof. "In the case of a person visibly appearing to be a negro, the presumption is that he is a slave," ruled the Virginia Supreme Court of Appeals, adding that "the plaintiff in a suit for freedom must make out his title against all the world."

To prove that he was not a slave, a free Negro had to carry around with him a certificate of freedom. Numbered, registered, and issued by the courts, these "free papers" gave the name, stature, and complexion of the Negro and indicated how his freedom had been obtained. Free papers had to be renewed periodically, for which a fee was assessed. In Virginia a Negro who lost his free papers had recourse to law, but elsewhere it was customary to treat a noncertificated Negro as a runaway, and jail him, hire him out, or sell him. Unscrupulous slave traders were not above seizing free Negroes, charging them with being slaves. In Lexington, Kentucky, in 1860, a pair of dealers obtained by trickery the free papers of two pretty young girls who shortly afterward were placed on the auction block and sold to slave trading firms, despite the public pleas of Baptist minister William Pratt and his efforts to buy the girls before the bidding got beyond his purse.

A free Negro could be reduced to servitude for cause. If he failed to pay his debts, taxes, fines, or court fees, he might be hired out until he had earned enough to pay them. If he were picked up as a vagabond, he could be placed under a master for a specified time. He could reduce himself to servitude, like Robert Mills of North Carolina, who received $60 in 1856 for assigning to the payee "the entire control of my person and labor" for five years.

Controls on the free Negro were varied. He could not hold public office, and he could not vote, except in Tennessee until 1834 and in North Carolina until 1835. He could not testify against a white person, except in Delaware and Louisiana. The full injustice of this barring of the testimony of Negroes was illustrated in the case of William Johnson, a prosperous barber in Natchez, Mississippi. Law-abiding, conservative in his views on public issues, and careful not to excite the envy or the ill-will of the whites, with whom he had many business dealings, Johnson was shot from ambush in June 1851. His killer went free because the only witnesses against him were three Negroes, and under the law their testimony was inadmissible against a white man.

The free Negro was not permitted the use of firearms, it being illegal in most states for him to possess a shotgun, musket, rifle, powder, or shot, unless by special permit. Keeping hard drink from the free Negro was a common practice; in Kentucky he could not buy liquor without a recommendation from a reputable white person. In Georgia and Florida a free Negro had to have a white guardian to whom he must report periodically. Free Negroes, like the slaves, had to observe curfew and were denied the right of assembly, being permitted to gather only for church.

Nowhere in the South could free Negroes come and go as they pleased, because every state below the Potomac had a law forbidding their immigration. Maryland's act, passed in 1839, was typical: a free Negro entering the state was fined $20 for the first offense and up to $500 for the second; if he could not pay these fines, he would be sold as a slave to the highest bidder. This law was not ironclad, however; in 1847 the well-thought-of steward of the naval academy was granted permission to bring his wife and children to Annapolis, to live there as long as he kept his steward's job.

The opportunities for the free Negro in the South to make a living were more promising than they would have seemed, judging from the many legal restrictions laid upon him. From 1830 to 1860, the period in which such restrictions were most burdensome, he made substantial economic gains in Virginia, as Professor Luther P. Jackson points out after a careful study of the county and city tax books. In the acquisition of farm land and town lots, Virginia Negroes had made noteworthy advances. By 1860 over one-third of the rural Negro heads of families had moved out of the agricultural labor class, and had become owners or renters of land. In the towns in 1860 the number of Negroes owning real estate was 157; thirty years later the figure had gone up to 693. Almost without exception, these owners acquired their holdings by purchase, not by gift.

For the most part this relative prosperity enjoyed by the Virginia Negro was due to the economic revival the state was experiencing, particularly in manufacturing. The new mills and factories created an interest in internal improvements—railroad and canal building. In turn, these developments created a need for an increased labor supply. The free Negro was available, and by 1860 he had become a factor in the state's economy, colored men and women holding fifty-four different kinds of jobs.

If Negroes outside Virginia did not fare as well, there were some things operating in their favor. Throughout the South the free Negro could make contracts and own property. And throughout the South there was generally a shortage of labor. White immigrants did not come into southern ports; if they were landed in New Orleans, they hastened up the Mississippi, not caring to compete with slave labor. In the South, too, the Negro did not face the aggressive competition of the white artisan to nearly the extent of his black brother in the North.

In the cities most of the work in the mechanical trades was done by free Negroes. In Charleston in 1850, for example, there were 122 such carpenters, eighty-seven tailors, and thirty shoemakers. Some half a dozen Negro tavern keepers and hotel owners catered to a white clientele, one of them, Jehu Jones, owning property valued at $40,000.

A wealthy Negro anywhere was something out of the ordinary, but there were others besides Jones. Aaron Ashworth of Jefferson County, Texas, owned 4,578 acres in 1846, and 2,470 head of cattle in 1850, being the largest cattle raiser in the county. Another East Texas Negro, William Goings of Nacogdoches, grew wealthy from land speculation and employed nine slaves and several whites in his blacksmith shop. Goings had a white wife, but his fluency in Cherokee and several other Indian languages was a prize asset to the settlers, and they ignored his breaching of the color line. The richest Negro in the antebellum South was Thomy Lafon of New Orleans, who amassed $500,000 in real estate, which he was to leave to charity upon his death long after the Civil War. In 1851 a fellow Louisianian, Cyprian Ricaud, purchased for $225,000 an estate in Iberville Parish with its ninety-one slaves.

Most of the wealthy Negroes in nonurban Louisiana were slaveholders like Ricaud, and their holdings, like his, ran into substantial numbers. In 1830 seventeen Negroes in the parish plantations owned more than thirty-two slaves apiece, one master, Martin Donatto of Plaquemine Brulé, having seventy-five. Masters, white or colored, with such a goodly number of slaves were likely to view them as capital investments designed to add to income.

But the great majority of colored masters were not profit-minded. Their ownership was benevolent and temporary rather than commercial and permanent. Such owners held a relative or a friend as a slave because to have set him free would result in an automatic separation, the law, as has been noted, forbidding a manumitted slave to remain in the state. Except in Louisiana, most Negro masters were urban dwellers, and their holdings in slaves were small, both urban dwelling and small ownership being characteristic of benevolent slaveholding. Hence, free Negro ownership, as a rule, was likely to be less a system of slave bondage than it was a means of protecting and caring for a blood relative or friend.

Another way of helping each other was through clubs and organizations. Petersburg, Virginia, for example, had its "Beneficial Society of Free Men of Color," in which each member pledged himself to support the others in sickness and in death. Baltimore Negroes had thirty-five benevolent societies in 1835, as befit the city with the largest free Negro population in the country. In cities where the authorities ignored the legal restrictions, the free Negroes operated schools, the Brown Fellowship Society in Charleston being an example.

The free colored people of New Orleans were more advanced than Negroes in any other southern city. Numbering 18,000 in 1860, they owned $15,000,000 in taxable property. These free Negroes left a record of achievement in military affairs, science, and literature. In no state in the Union were Negroes permitted to join the militia, but in New Orleans two colored regiments had been in existence long before the United States purchased Louisiana. Despite their unofficial standing, these Negro regiments were summoned by Andrew Jackson as he prepared for the Battle of New Orleans in the closing stages of the War of 1812. After the battle, which was decisively won by the Americans on January 8, 1815, Jackson's headquarters issued a general order stating that "the two corps of colored volunteers had . . . not disappointed the hopes that were formed of their courage and perseverance."

In science New Orleans–born Norbert Rillieux produced in 1846 a vacuum cup that revolutionized sugar-refining methods. For this invention he is still acclaimed by the sugar corporations of the world, as evidenced by a plaque they hung in the Louisiana State Museum in 1934. In literature the most notable distinction of the New Orleans Negroes was the publication in 1845 of a 215-page anthology *Les Cenelles,* eighty-two verses written in French, the collaborative product of seventeen poets. The most talented of its contributors was Victor Séjour, who achieved his greatest fame in France, the theaters of Paris producing twenty-one of his plays.

Since both Rillieux and Séjour were the offspring of French fathers and quadroon mothers, they belonged to that class which French law designated as *"les gens de couleur libres"*—free men of color. Such a designation meant that they were not only free; they were of mixed blood and hence distinguishable from the free Negroes of pure or predominantly African descent, the "free blacks." For there were distinctions between free Negroes, and not only in New Orleans. Some of these distinctions were set up by Negroes themselves, and they included skin color, occupation, schooling, and free ancestry.

It is to be noted that these distinctions within the group were private affairs and not matters of public policy. The free Negro was basically powerless and hence, unlike the whites, could not transpose any of his prejudgments and race concepts into law, even had he been so inclined.

The lot of the Negro in the North was unlike that of his southern counterpart in three respects: the restrictions against him were markedly less severe; he could protest against them; and he had greater opportunity for self-expression through his churches, newspapers, and conventions, and by participating in reform movements, particularly the abolitionist crusade.

Because Negroes were not numerous in the North their presence did not arouse the degree of uneasiness and dread that it did in the slave states. But the North, be it repeated, was no Eden for the colored man. The doctrine of white supremacy was held almost as tenaciously above the Mason-Dixon Line as below it. Though by 1830 slavery had been virtually abolished in the North, the Negro still bore the indelible mark of a degraded inferior; he was regarded as a threat to the general welfare, if not an outright liability. Somewhat like a self-fulfilling prophecy, this attitude toward the Negro gave rise to a concerted effort to limit him to roles which fell to those of lesser breed. These roles may be noted in the fields of civil rights and employment.

In most states the Negro could not vote. During the forty years preceding the Civil War, a period when the ballot was being extended to the common man, every incoming state turned thumbs down on Negro suffrage. In 1840 in the four states in which Negroes had equal suffrage—Massachusetts, Maine, New Hampshire, and Vermont—the colored population was very small, except for the first named. In New York a Negro could vote only if he owned $250 worth of real estate.

Before the law the Negro did not always stand as an equal. In California, Illinois, Indiana, Iowa, and Ohio, he could not testify against whites in court; four of these states shared a common border with slave states and had a substantial quota of whites who had emigrated, bringing with them the belief that slavery was the natural condition of the Negro. Except in Massachusetts, the Negro was debarred from jury service. He found it hard to obtain competent legal counsel; a Negro lawyer was indeed a rarity.

Some states restricted the entry of Negroes. In 1807 Ohio passed a law requiring that a Negro could not enter into the state unless he could furnish a bond of $500 as a guarantee of good conduct. Illinois required an incoming Negro to post a bond of $1,000; Indiana's constitution of 1851 outrightly prohibited Negroes from coming in the state to reside. In Oregon's territorial elections of November 9, 1857, the vote to deny admission to Negroes was carried by a one-sided majority, 8,640 to 1,081.

In making a living, the Negro faced restrictions. He was confined to the lowest-paid jobs generally in two fields, common labor and domestic service. To get a job as a skilled worker was not easy. Many northern Negroes had, as slaves, learned a trade, but they found that as free men they were not given the opportunity to put their training to use. The colored lad who wanted to learn a skilled occupation could find no white craftsman who would take him on as an apprentice, which would cause the craftsman to lower himself in the eyes of his associates. Moreover, in the North the white worker looked upon the Negro as a job threat. Trade unions would not accept a colored applicant, thus creating a hostility on the part of the Negro toward organized labor.

Since he was almost completely excluded from the trades, the Negro's plight was not hopeless if he could obtain full employment in the unskilled fields. But after 1840 even the menial jobs—porter, waiter, cook, and maid— were being taken over by white immigrants, 4,910,690 of whom arrived from 1830 to 1860. Frequently these newcomers objected to working beside a colored person, thus hastening the process of Negro displacement. In California the Negro faced the added competition of the Chinese immigrant, who was willing to work for a very low wage.

Despite drawbacks, some Negroes managed to make a good living. In New York City in 1856, Negroes had $200,000 in bank deposits. Cincinnati Negroes in 1852 owned property valued in excess of $500,000. Most northern

cities had their well-to-do colored caterers and restaura-
teurs, food service being almost a Negro monopoly in some
places. Barbering, too, was a wide-open field to Negroes,
many of whom did very well at it. One of the steady customers of William de Fleurville of Springfield, Illinois, was
the lawyer-politician Abraham Lincoln. Prosperous Negro
farmers were not uncommon in Indiana—Rush County in
1857 having forty such heads of families who owned a total
of more than 3,000 acres.

Negroes were conspicuous in the fur trade as conducted
from St. Louis. Not only were they employed as cooks,
voyageurs, hunters, guides, and interpreters, but also as
salaried traders. One of these, James Beckwourth, who was
employed as a trader by the American Fur Company,
became in 1850 the discoverer of the lowest point across the
northern Sierra-Nevada mountains, which came to be
named Beckwourth Pass. A few Negroes became independent entrepreneurs in the fur trade, the best known being
Jean Baptiste Point Sable, whose stations were located
along the shores of Lake Michigan and who became the first
permanent settler on the present site of Chicago.

Among the self-employed Negroes were a few who gave
employment to others. Sailmaker James Forten hired white
and colored workers in his Philadelphia plant; Stephen
Smith and William Whipper were highly successful lumber
merchants in Columbia, Pennsylvania, and Henry Boyd of
Cincinnati was the owner of a bedstead factory with some
twenty employees.

In what ways did the northern Negro react to his lot? At the
outset, he made one important decision: he would remain in
America. From the time of the Revolutionary War the Negro
had been advised to return to Africa. Those giving such

advice were variously motivated. To some whites the back-to-Africa movement was a good way to get rid of the troublesome free Negro. To humanitarians the movement was a way to send to Africa a Christianized population and to discharge a moral obligation to return the Negro to his ancestral homelands. Moreover, reasoned the humanitarians, masters would more readily free their slaves if there were a place to send them outside the United States.

This sentiment to deport the Negro culminated in 1817 in the formation of the American Colonization Society. Composed of men prominent in public life, this organization sought the aid of Congress in acquiring a place to which to send the Negroes. Congress was responsive; a colony in Africa would be the answer to the vexing problem of what to do with Negroes who were captured in the illegal slave trade. Congress proceeded to appropriate $100,000 for the Society, and President Monroe appointed two agents to cooperate with it in establishing a settlement. In 1822 the colony of Liberia, on the west coast of Africa, came into existence under the auspices of the American Colonization Society, with an assist from the United States Government. Subsequently the Society received additional funds from bequests, gifts from church groups and auxiliary societies, and appropriations from state legislatures, including those of Indiana, Kentucky, Maryland, and Virginia.

But the Negro did not share this enthusiasm for colonization. By 1852 fewer than 8,000 Negroes went to Liberia, and only 2,800 of these were free Negroes, the others being some 3,600 slaves emancipated on condition they go to Liberia and some 1,000 Africans who had been liberated from slave ships. In 1855 not a single Negro from Indiana sailed for Liberia, despite increased state aid to such emigrants. Even in the South, the response was cool; in Tennessee only fifty-five Negroes had gone to Liberia by 1841, and in Virginia the colonization efforts, writes John H. Russell, "resulted in repeated failure."

The failure of Liberian colonization resulted in part from its high cost, but the key reason was the attitude of the Negro himself. Despite the Colonization Society's support by influential groups, the majority of the free Negroes disliked the proposal from its inception. They believed that deportation was a device to get rid of the free Negro in order to make slavery secure—that colonization was the twin sister of slavery. Moreover, the Negro, although not forgetful of his plight, regarded America as his home. "A few may go," said Negro leader Robert Purvis, "but the colored people as a mass will not leave the land of their birth."

It is to be noted that some Negroes—a small minority—did favor colonization. As early as January 4, 1787, a group of eighty Boston Negroes petitioned the state legislature to assist them in getting to Africa, providing them money to pay their passage and buy land. They explained that they wished to leave America because they found themselves "in very disagreeable and disadvantageous circumstances." If they were able to get to Africa, they said, they would proceed to spread the Christian religion, improve international relations, and lay the foundations for a profitable commerce between the United States and the countries of west-coast Africa. In 1795 a group of Negroes in Providence, Rhode Island, wrote to Zachary Macauley, acting governor of Sierra Leone, asking permission to settle. More tangible were the efforts of Paul Cuffe, ship captain and merchant, who in 1815 transported thirty-eight fellow Negroes to Sierra Leone at his own expense.

But acceptance of the colonization idea made little headway in Negro circles. Back-to-Africa sentiment had a little life pumped into it after the passage of the Fugitive

Slave Law of 1850, when things seemed to be worsening. In 1854 a National Emigration Convention was organized, and four years later another Negro-sponsored colonization group, the African Civilization Society, was formed. But these groups were able to do very little, having no money and not much of a following.

In developing ways to combat adversity, the Negro who had decided to remain in America, like other Americans, was a joiner. Even when patterned after those of the whites, his organizations performed a broader function—that of inspiring and uplifting a peculiarly disadvantaged group.

The earliest of these mutual-aid societies among Negroes was the Masonic order. Its founder was Prince Hall, who in 1765 had left Barbados to come to Massachusetts. Three months before the American Revolution broke out, Hall was initiated with fourteen other Negroes into the Masons by a British military lodge then garrisoned in Boston. When Hall undertook to organize a lodge of Negroes, his petitions were denied. He then proceeded to secure a charter from the Grand Lodge in England, and in 1787 "African Lodge No. 459" was formally organized with Hall as grand master. A second secret fraternal group, the Grand United Order of Odd Fellows, was established in 1843. Like its predecessor, it came into existence under a dispensation from the English lodge, after the American Odd Fellows had refused admission to colored men. After the founding of the parent lodges, affiliates were formed in cities throughout the North. These two antebellum fraternal organizations contributed much to Negro uplift.

Among Negroes a number of organizations whose goals were similar to those of the fraternal orders were not secret and not confined necessarily to males. The earliest and best-known of these was the Free African Society, founded in

Philadelphia in 1787. Its members were pledged to lead sober and orderly lives, the society not hesitating to disown one "Samuel S." for having "left his tender wife and child, and kept company with a common woman."

By far the most notable public service of the society in Philadelphia was its work during the great plague of 1793. As noted by Philip Freneau in his "Pestilence: written during the Prevalence of a yellow fever," this fearful epidemic was marked by:

> Hot, dry winds forever blowing,
> Dead men to the grave-yards going:
>> Constant hearses,
>> Funeral verses;
> Oh! what plagues—there is no knowing!

In the face of the mounting death toll in the late summer months, the Free African Society did many things to assist the stricken whites. Its leaders, Richard Allen and Absalom Jones, both former slaves of a deeply religious bent, called on Mayor Mathew Clarkson to offer assistance. Through the newspapers the grateful mayor announced that those needing help should apply to the Free African Society. The colored organization supplied nurses, and it furnished volunteers to gather the bodies, put them in the long boxes, and take them away. Jones and Allen worked around the clock; during the day they made the rounds of plague-ridden homes, purging and bleeding as recommended by Dr. Benjamin Rush; at night they made the rounds driving the dead carts. In their honor an anonymous contemporary penned an "euologium":

> Brethren of Man, and friends of fairer clay!
> Your godlike zeal in Death's triumphant day

The Nonslave Negro (1800–1860)

> Benignant Angels saw . . .

Another early and typical self-help group was the Sons of the African Society, formed in Boston in 1798 "for the mutual benefit of each other," while "behaving ourselves at the same time as true and faithful Citizens of the Commonwealth in which we live." The society's main purposes were to make certain that a member was decently buried, that his widow and children did not want, and that members watch over each other in "spiritual concerns."

Coming later than the mutual-aid organizations, but, like them, an evidence of the Negro's striving for self-improvement, were the literary societies. Founded to spread useful knowledge by providing libraries and reading rooms, these societies were widespread throughout the North, numbering at least forty-five before the Civil War. Their lengthy titles bespoke something of their earnestness of purpose: Baltimore had its Young Men's Mental Improvement Society for the Discussion of Moral and Philosophical Questions of All Kinds, and Pittsburgh had its Young Men's Literary and Moral Reform Society of Pittsburgh and Vicinity. In their 1833 appeal for contributions, books, or money, the founders of "The Philadelphia Library Company of Colored Persons" pointed out that their aim was to be of service to the "entire population" of the city.

One of the unique organizations founded by Negroes was the vigilance committee. So close was the relationship between the underground railroad and the vigilance committees that it was not always easy to distinguish between them. After the underground railroad had sped the slave on his way, the primary purpose of the vigilance committee was to help him get established in his new location—finding a home and a job—and to protect him while he was doing so. The New York Vigilance Committee's secretary was David

Ruggles, an able and dedicated reformer. In Boston Lewis Hayden was the key figure in the movement, and in Albany it was Stephen Myers, newspaper publisher and one of the very few Negro lobbyists. The corresponding secretary of the Philadelphia committee was William Still, whose father had become free by self-purchase and whose mother by flight.

Overshadowing all other organizations in influence was the Negro church—that is, the church congregations whose membership was all-Negro. In churches of any creed or color, the Negro could seek spiritual comfort, but his own church gave him two things he could not get in the white church: the opportunity for self-expression and the assurance that he would not be set apart as unwanted. For in truth the emergence of the all-Negro church resulted in part from an unwillingness by colored communicants to worship in seats reserved for them in the rear of the church or in the gallery. Most churches had a "Negro pew" to which colored parishioners were confined. In churches which distributed sacramental bread and wine, Negroes had to wait until the whites had partaken.

It was a pew incident that sparked the origin of the independent Negro church. On a winter Sunday morning in 1787, as Richard Allen and Absalom Jones, founders seven months earlier of the Free African Society, were kneeling in prayer at St. George's Methodist Episcopal Church in Philadelphia, a trustee advanced upon them, pulled Jones up, and said that the Negroes must get themselves to the rear of the gallery. When Jones's request that they be permitted to finish their prayers was denied, the two Negro leaders walked out of St. George's, never to return.

This incident strengthened the position, long held by Allen, that Negroes should have separate church facilities. Headed by Jones and Allen, the Negroes of Philadelphia launched a fund-raising campaign, and succeeded in winning the support of Benjamin Rush and several other influential whites. But before a church building had been purchased, Jones and Allen parted ways on the issue of religious affiliation, the former favoring the Anglican tradition, whereas the latter was a dyed-in-the-wool Methodist. Splitting with his friend and associate, Jones proceeded to organize the St. Thomas Protestant Episcopal Church in October 1794, becoming its first pastor.

Allen in turn gathered a congregation and purchased a building, which in 1794 was dedicated by Bishop Francis Asbury as the Bethel African Methodist Episcopal Church, whose membership was limited to Negroes. Both the newly formed churches were received into the communion of their respective denominations, for the Negroes had no differences at all with the whites on matters of doctrine or belief. What the Negroes wanted was summed up by Bishop Asbury while in Baltimore in 1795: "The Africans of this town desire a church, which, in temporals, shall be altogether under their own direction." The Negro church did not originate from a desire to be separate, but from a desire to be independent.

This desire inevitably led the colored Methodists to take a final step—that of severing their organizational tie with the whites. After Bethel came into existence, branches of the African Methodist Episcopal Church sprang up in other towns in Pennsylvania, and in Maryland and New Jersey. In 1816 these groups met in Philadelphia and organized a separate branch of Methodism, with Allen as bishop. This new church (which came to be popularly known as the A.M.E.) soon became truly national in scope; in less than ten years it had extended its operations into Ohio on the West and Charleston to the South.

The new church, however, did not make great headway

in New York City, where in 1796 the Negroes had organized a Methodist congregation, which in 1800 they named the African Methodist Episcopal Zion Church. At a meeting in 1820 this group decided against either joining the Allenites or remaining with the whites, and in 1821 they organized as an independent Methodist body (whose popular name would be A.M.E.Z.). In the following year they selected their first bishop, James Varick. Like the Allenites, they extended their field of operations, becoming more than a local offshoot of Methodism.

The Baptists, the other denomination that attracted large numbers of Negroes, also experienced the impulse toward independent organization. Prior to 1800, white and Negro Baptists had worshipped under the same roof, even in the South. But after 1800 there was a marked trend toward the all-Negro local Baptist church, especially in the northern cities. Between 1805 and 1810 Negro Baptists churches were established in Boston, Philadelphia, and New York. The key figure in this pioneer movement was the Reverend Thomas Paul, whose interest in the spread of his faith took him to Haiti in 1823, under the auspices of the Baptist Missionary Society of Massachusetts.

With other religious groups the movement toward the all-Negro congregation was less strong. Except in a few instances, there were too few Negroes to support a separate church in a given community, and Negroes joined white congregations. Even Negro Methodists and Baptists who lived in regions where the colored population was small—as in rural Indiana, for example—simply went to the white churches.

The Negro church was a many-sided institution, performing many functions besides worship. In towns which barred the colored children from the public schools, the church hall became a makeshift classroom, with deacons

and elders as teachers of the three Rs. When Henry High-
land Garnet went to Troy, New York, in 1843, his mission
was twofold: to serve as pastor of the Negro Presbyterian
Church and to conduct a school for colored boys and girls.
The Negro church was a meeting place for reformist groups,
particularly the abolitionists. More than one Negro church
was a station on the underground railroad, its alcove a sanc-
tuary for runaways. Some of the Negro clergymen, like Garnet, preached a social gospel that stressed the church
militant.

As the Negro church was the scene of many activities,
so it was a training ground for leaders. Men and women who
had practiced self-expression in their church gatherings
were ready for participation in reformist activities. Indeed,
church-trained Negroes were instrumental in launching
one of the most significant expressions of social action
among Negroes—the colored convention movement.

This movement was an expression of protest against
the status of the Negro in American life. By 1830 Negroes
had come to the conclusion that concerted action was necessary to make clear their plight and their recommendations
for bettering it. The first national convention was held at
Bethel Church in Philadelphia in mid-September, 1830. The
moving spirit behind the call was Bishop Allen, who was
elected president. For four days the forty delegates from
eight states held sessions, punctuated one afternoon by a
visit to the Lombard Street School to inspect specimens of
the penmanship and needlework of the children. The question of emigration was the main topic before the delegates,
who, before adjourning, agreed to form a permanent organization.

The convention of the following year gave its chief consideration to the founding of an industrial school for Negro
boys, a pet idea of Arthur Tappan, a New York merchant

with a humanitarian outlook. The convention endorsed Tappan's proposal and continued in session for an address by William Lloyd Garrison, then on the threshold of his career. These two conventions marked the beginning of organized activity in Negro circles.

Held annually for seven years, the conventions assembled sporadically after 1837—at Buffalo in 1843, Troy in 1847, Cleveland in 1848, and Rochester in 1853. The last named was the best attended and perhaps the most important convention: 140 delegates from eight states answered the call for "the amelioration of the condition of the colored people." Presiding over this Rochester convention was the scholarly clergyman, J. W. C. Pennington, and chairman of the committee on declaration of sentiments was the noted orator Frederick Douglass. The statement drawn up by the committee left no doubt as to what the Negro wanted: "We ask that in our native land we shall not be treated as strangers, and worse than strangers." The delegates voiced an official disapproval of colonization and supported the proposal to establish a manual labor school which would teach the skilled trades. In addition to the committee on a manual labor college, the convention established three other committees: one on safeguarding the civil liberties of the Negro, a second on business relations—a job-finding agency—and a third on publications, designed to collect data on Negroes and to refute slurs upon them.

Although the colored convention movement gave Negroes practice in the techniques of protest and petition, and apprised the country of the colored man's stand on public issues, it had serious weaknesses. After the conventions had adjourned, the delegates dispersed doing very little in their local communities to carry out plans they had made. Some Negroes refused to participate on the grounds that organizations made up exclusively of Negroes tacitly

accepted segregation—perhaps the worst kind, self-segregation. As William C. Nell of Boston put it, Negroes should
abandon separate action and become "part and parcel of
the general community."

Nell seemed to have had a telling point. However, more
often than not, the same Negroes who were active in the
convention movement and in the Negro church also supported general reform movements. A case in point was the
abolitionist crusade, which enlisted as much support from
Negroes who were prominent in the colored convention
movement as from those who shunned racially exclusive
organizations.

The Negro's significant role in the abolitionist effort has
been somewhat obscured by the attention given to the white
leaders in the movement—Elijah P. Lovejoy, William Lloyd
Garrison, Wendell Phillips, and Theodore D. Weld, to name
but a few. And truly these were notable figures. Lovejoy, a
clergyman-journalist who had become deeply committed to
the moral movement against slavery, was shot to death at
Alton, Illinois, in August 1837 when a mob seized his printing press and threw it in the river. Garrison was the editor
of *The Liberator*, organizer in 1833 of the New England
Anti-Slavery Society, and president for twenty-five years
(1840–1865) of the American Anti-Slavery Society. Fiery,
outspoken, and uncompromising, he was considered an
emotional extremist by southerners, who used him as a
yardstick to measure all abolitionists. Wendell Phillips of
Boston was a close friend and associate of Garrison. A true
patrician by birth and training, Phillips deserted the law
and turned his back on a possible outstanding career in politics. Casting his lot with the reformist groups, he brought
with him oratorical abilities unmatched in America, becoming "abolition's golden trumpet." Theodore D. Weld led, in
Whittier's words on him, "a life of brave unselfishness." A

man of deep religious convictions, his students at Lane Seminary in Cincinnati and at Oberlin fell under his spell and became ardent abolitionists. Weld trained antislavery agents for work in the field, edited reform publications, and acted as research assistant for the handful of abolitionists in Congress.

But the abolitionist movement also had its outstanding Negroes—Frederick Douglass, William Wells Brown, Frances Ellen Watkins, and Robert Purvis, to name only a quartet. Douglass, runaway from a Maryland master, developed remarkable abilities in writing and speaking. Whether one read Douglass's weekly, *The North Star,* or listened as he spoke from the public platform, one could not but think critically of slavery for what it would have done in concealing the great latent abilities of this man. William Wells Brown, also a runaway who became an antislavery lecturer, spent five years in the British Isles, arousing abolitionist sentiment wherever he went. Brown was a prolific writer, turning out, among other works, the first novel and the first play written by a Negro. Like the other Negro leaders, Brown was interested in reforms not peculiarly racial—for example, woman's rights, prison relief, temperance, and world peace. Miss Watkins (Mrs. Harper after 1860) taught school in Baltimore, her birthplace, then became an underground railroad operator in Pennsylvania As a full-time lecturer for the Maine Anti-Slavery Society, she distributed her own booklets on abolitionism. The best-known Negro poet of the reform era, her verses dealt primarily with slavery. Robert Purvis of Byberry, Pennsylvania, was one of the founders of the American Anti-Slavery Society and of the Pennsylvania Society. By pen and purse—he was the only Negro reformer with money—he supported a variety of causes for human betterment. But his first love was abolitionism and he was closely allied with Garrison and

Phillips, despite the mileage between Byberry and Boston.

With Negroes conspicuously in their ranks from the outset, the abolitionists conducted a crusade that was destined to overshadow all other reforms in antebellum America. For the abolitionists took on the role of defenders of civil liberties—freedom of speech and of the press, trial by jury, and the right to petition. By becoming fighters for freedom, they identified themselves with the highest and best in their country's traditions. And because the fundamental issues they raised could not be shunted aside, a resort to arms became inevitable.

In the pursuit of their goal, the antislavery societies adopted the standard methods of reformist groups. They held meetings—weekly, monthly, and yearly—at which reports were given, resolutions were passed, and petitions were signed. They sent out agents to give speeches and to enlist subscribers to their journals. They issued printed propaganda in prodigious quantities: sermons, speeches, essays, proceedings of meetings, poems, and a whole body of information designed for children of various ages. The abolitionists had their literary lights; John Greenleaf Whittier was their most gifted poet, and Harriet Beecher Stowe was their most successful novelist, turning out one of America's all-time best-sellers, *Uncle Tom's Cabin.* The abolitionists who believed in political action gave their support to the Liberty Party and to its successor, the Free Soil Party.

Although the abolitionists operated much the same as other groups, their reform was distinctive in two respects, as Professor Dwight L. Dumond points out. The antislavery movement was sectional; that is, it was centered in the region where slavery did not exist. The reformers were located in the North, whereas the institution to be reformed was located in the South. Such a cleavage along sectional lines was fraught with explosive danger.

Moreover, as no other reform, abolitionism was a matter of race (or, perhaps more accurately, of color). For the people to be rescued—the slaves—were all Negroes, a circumstance that had given rise to the cry in the South that the Negro had a slave mentality, and that bondage was his natural conditions. This charge the abolitionists attacked by giving Negroes a prominent role in their activities and by calling attention to outstanding colored men and women. Every abolitionist worth his salt could recite the story of Benjamin Banneker, mathematician, astronomer, and almanac publisher, whose intellectual attainments led to his appointment by President Washington to membership on the commission to survey and lay out the nation's capital. Abolitionist journals republished poems from the works of the talented Phillis Wheatley, who had been brought from Africa in 1760, when she was eight years old, and had in 1773 brought out a volume of verse that had attracted attention abroad no less than at home.

As in the other phases of the abolition movement, Negroes were active participants in newspaper work, owning and managing twenty-four periodicals during the thirty years preceding the Civil War. Generally these Negro-run newspapers were not the official organ of any of the abolitionist societies (nor was *The Liberator,* for that matter), but they gave their full support to the crusade. These journals invariably had financial problems, and some of them were issued only a few times. Their common devotion to the principles of freedom and equality is evidenced by some of their titles—*Freedom's Journal, The Rights of All, Mirror of Liberty, Impartial Citizen,* and *Herald of Freedom.*

If the abolitionists were detested in the South, they were nevertheless not honored in the North. Indeed, they were

heartily disliked by northerners of conservative temperament—those who were wedded to the status quo. It is not
surprising that men of wealth and standing would be cool to
the abolitionist agitation, but so were the white working-
men, who feared that if the slaves were set free, they would
come to the North and increase the job competition already
presented by the free Negro. The abolitionists were also
frowned upon the more by such mild-mannered reformers
as William Ellery Channing, who did not like their strong
language and fiery zeal. Channing held that theirs was "a
showy, noisy mode of action, appealing to the passions, and
driving men into exaggeration."

To resist an enthroned abuse, as the abolitionists had
come to know, was not easy. But during the ten years preceding the Civil War a number of events caused them to be
listened to as never before. First, the Fugitive Slave Law of
1850 turned out to be one of the most vulnerable measures
ever passed by Congress, and the storm of protest it aroused
was never quieted. This law denied the testimony of the
alleged runaway; it assumed that he was guilty rather than
innocent, and it was ex post facto, reaching back to fugitives
who had been living unmolested for years. This measure
became a powerful propaganda weapon for the abolitionists,
who referred to it as "the Man-Stealing Law" and "the
Bloodhound Bill."

Four years later Congress passed another measure that
rent the country. The Kansas-Nebraska Act repealed the
long-standing Missouri Compromise of 1820, which prohibited slavery in the Kansas-Nebraska Territory. As long as
the Compromise remained on the books, many people in the
North felt that slavery would eventually wear itself away,
but its repeal seemed to open the doors to the expansion of
slavery. Bitter denouncement was voiced throughout the
North and gave rise to a new Party, the Republican.

The deep resentment created by the Kansas-Nebraska Act was still at fever pitch when in 1857 the Supreme Court handed down the Dred Scott decision. By permitting slavery in the territories, this ruling gave a death blow to any belief that it would wither away. Northerners felt that it proved that slavery was on the march, with its supporters making up a "slavocracy" which was determined to rule or ruin. As if the main point of the decision were not bad enough, it had one additional feature that was obnoxious to Negroes—Chief Justice Taney ruled that they were not citizens of the United States.

The stormy fifties had one final thunderbolt—the John Brown raid late in 1859. Apparently hoping to recruit runaways to their standard, Brown and twenty-one of his followers, five of them Negroes, attempted to seize a government arsenal at Harpers Ferry in northwestern Virginia. Lacking a clear and definite plan of campaign, Brown's foray was doomed. It was staged in an area where slaves were few, and Brown had given those few no foreknowledge of his plans.

Brown was put to death, mounting the scaffold with impressive dignity. "God's angry man" was destined for a lasting fame; soon the soldiers in blue would be singing "John Brown's Body." Abolitionism had its martyr in Elijah P. Lovejoy; now the Union had its martyr in abolitionist John Brown. For he was dead less than a year when Abraham Lincoln, candidate of the Republican Party, was elected to the presidency. Feeling their security imperiled, the southern states began to leave the Union. The North-South crisis—in truth, the slavery crisis—had moved into its final phase, and the Negro was ready to move with it.

5

New Birth of Freedom (1860–1865)

IN THE CIVIL WAR the Negro was both a symbol and a participant. The nearly four million slaves who became free furnished a concrete expression of one of the great goals of the war—that of enlarging the compass of human liberty. Moreover, the Negro himself was not merely an onlooker, standing idly by and weeping in gratitude. Instead, he was active on the battlefields, behind the lines, and on the home front.

Though the causes of the Civil War were numerous, the system of slavery was unquestionably paramount. To a key figure like Abraham Lincoln, slavery was the overriding cause of the war. In his great debates with Stephen A. Douglas in the late summer of 1858, Lincoln said that this nation could not go on indefinitely half slave and half free. Four years later, on August 14, 1862, when a delegation of five Negroes visited the White House, Lincoln told them that "without the institution of slavery, and the colored race as a basis, the war could not have an existence." In his Second Inaugural Address of March 4, 1865, Lincoln pointed out that on the eve of the war, one-eighth of the population was made up of slaves. "All knew," said he, "that this interest was, somehow, the cause of the war."

If the Civil War became a crusade for freedom, it did not start out that way. The clash between the North and the South was not a week old before the Negro discovered that he had a private war on his hands—the war of his complexion. On April 15, 1861, President Lincoln issued a call for 75,000 men, upon learning that Fort Sumter in the Charleston harbor had been seized. The response was all that he could have hoped for, a wave of enthusiasm sweeping the North. The martial spirit took hold as recruits lined up at the enlistment centers.

Sharing fully in this great enthusiasm were the Negroes, who reasoned that since slavery was the root of the conflict, freedom would be the result. In city after city they offered their services. On the day after Lincoln's call, a group of Boston Negroes, meeting in the Twelfth Baptist Church, pledged to the President their lives and their fortunes. In Providence a Negro company offered to march with the First Rhode Island Regiment as it left for the front. New York's governor was tendered the services of three regiments of colored men, their arms, equipment, and pay to be furnished by the Negroes of the state. Philadelphia Negroes formed two regiments, which drilled at Masonic Hall, and in Pittsburgh the Hannibal Guards offered their services, pointing out that as American citizens they were anxious "to assist in any honorable way or manner to sustain the present administration."

Negroes in Cleveland, meeting at National Hall, declared their allegiance to Lincoln's government and offered to supply money, prayers, and manpower to help with the war. At Detroit Captain O. C. Wood and the thirty-five members of his Detroit Military Guard sought to enlist; Dr. G. P.

Miller of Battle Creek asked War Department permission to raise "from 5,000 to 10,000 freemen." Among the last of the volunteering letters was one to Lincoln from clergyman J. Sella Martin, who had just returned to Boston after a lecturing tour in England: "If I can be of any manner of service here, should your excellency ever think it best to employ my people, I am ready to work or preach or fight to put down this rebellion," wrote Martin, enclosing a personal photograph and a batch of London newspaper clippings about himself.

Nothing came of any of these proposals. Every city to which Negroes offered their services adopted a thumbs-down attitude. Negroes met a similar response at Washington. When Jacob Dodson, a Senate attendant who had seen service with John C. Frémont in crossing the Rockies, offered the services of 300 Negroes for the defense of the nation's capital, he was officially informed that the War Department had no intention of using colored soldiers.

These refusals to accept Negroes for military service were grounded in traditional practices and beliefs. Since the close of the Revolutionary War, it had been the custom to bar Negroes from the armies of America. The national militia act of 1792 restricted the enrollment to whites, and state militia laws, North as well as South, followed suit. Opposition to the Negro as soldier was rooted in fears that he lacked the qualities of a fighting man, that arming him would be an admission that white soldiers had not been valiant enough to do the job, that putting a gun his hands might lead to slave insurrections—and in the deep, although unspoken, fear that to make the Negro a soldier would bring about a change in his position in American life.

This desire to keep the Negro in status quo had its weight in Washington, where both Lincoln and Congress sought to avoid questions relating to the Negro, slave or free. The Administration had no intention of making the war an abolitionist crusade. In Lincoln's thinking, the war was being launched to preserve the Union and not to interfere with slavery.

But this intention to bypass the Negro had to be abandoned. The war was not turning out to be a parade at arms; it had not ended in ninety days, as some had expected. And as both North and South girded for a contest of indefinite duration, the government at Washington had to take a second look at its "hands-off-the-Negro" policy.

Congress preceded Lincoln in making a reversal, declaring on August 6, 1861, that any property that was put to use in aid of the rebel cause would be confiscated; if such property consisted of slaves, they were to be set free. This measure was an attempt to make the Confederacy discontinue its use of slaves as military laborers. Most congressmen would have been startled had they known that this was only the first of a series of enactments that would set the stage for slavery's downfall.

Two important measures were passed in the spring of 1862. By an act of March 13, military commanders were forbidden to return fugitive slaves to their masters. A month later slavery was abolished in the District of Columbia, giving freedom to some 3,000 Negroes.

As if appetite had come with the eating, Congress outdid itself in the summer of 1862. Early in June it passed a measure authorizing the exchange of diplomatic representatives with Haiti and Liberia, the latter having been granted its independence in 1847 by the American Colonization Society. Later that month Congress abolished slavery in the territories, and on July 17 two measures were passed. The first provided that all rebel-owned slaves coming under United States control should be considered captives of war and made free, a measure which differed from the first confiscation act in that it was now not necessary for the rebel-owned slave to have been put to use by the enemy. The second enactment authorized the President to receive Negroes into the service of the United States to perform "any labor of any war service" within their competence, the volunteer's mother, wife, and children to be given their freedom if he were a slave.

Like Congress, the chief executive found it necessary to address himself to the Negro. His slowness on this score was rooted in a natural conservatism, an inclination to bide his time. Moreover, when he took office he was of the opinion that the President had no right to interfere with slavery. Too, he was always thinking of the border states—Maryland, Kentucky, and Missouri—which held slaves but had remained in the Union. Kentucky-born himself, he knew that the prevailing sentiment in these states was against any change in the status of the colored man.

If Lincoln could not be rushed into anything, neither was he the last to lay the old aside. In waging the war, he invoked the spirit and used the phrases of the Declaration of Independence—revolutionary language for revolutionary times. Lincoln had been in the White House less than a year before sensing that he faced both a war and a revolution and that, although one was military and the other social, they were interrelated.

Lincoln's response to the social revolution was to project two plans, one for the slaves and one for the free Negroes. His plan for the former was gradual compensation—freeing them gradually over a period extending to some thirty years and paying their masters out of the national treasury. To carry out his proposal, it was necessary to enlist the cooperation of Congress and the particular states that were involved. With the former, Lincoln was successful: upon his recommendation Congress, on April 10,

1862, passed a joint resolution stating that federal financial aid should be given to any state which adopted a plan for the gradual abolition of slavery. But the response from the border states was negative: their spokesmen on Capitol Hill said that the cost of the program would run to the prohibitive sum of $478,000,000, and that even if that amount were appropriated beforehand, their constituents would vote the proposal down.

This setback to compensated emancipation had a discouraging effect on the second of Lincoln's plans for the Negro—free as well as slave—that of shipping him out of the country. Deportation would get rid of both slavery and the Negro. Again, Congress lent a helping hand. In April 1862 the lawmakers voted to set aside $100,000 to aid in colonizing Negroes of the District of Columbia, and two months later an additional $500,000 was appropriated for the colonization of the slaves of disloyal masters.

With this $600,000, of which he was sole trustee, Lincoln took up the related tasks of getting the Negro to agree to be colonized and of finding somewhere for him to go. To get his views before the colored people, Lincoln arranged to have an interview on August 14, 1862, with a five-man Negro delegation. The interview was widely published, as Lincoln had intended, and was widely read by Negroes, as he had hoped.

Their response, however, was something less than he had hoped for. A number of colored leaders wrote open letters condemning his proposal, and Negroes in various cities held protest meetings. The general sentiment of these gatherings was expressed in an "Appeal" sent to Lincoln by the Negroes of Philadelphia:

> Many of us have our own house and other property, amounting, in the aggregate, to millions of dollars.

> Shall we sacrifice this, leave our homes, forsake our
> birth-place, and flee to a strange land, to appease the
> anger and prejudice of the traitors now in arms
> against the Government?

At the same time he was trying to stir up colonization
sentiment among Negroes, Lincoln was seeking a site for
the potential emigrants. Representatives from the government of Liberia had assured him that American Negroes
would be welcome to their country, but Lincoln wanted a
place nearer to the United States. He decided upon
Chiriqui, a province in Panama, then a part of the republic
of Colombia. But the project fell through when its promoters, the Chiriqui Improvement Company, were revealed as
speculators whose land titles were faulty. Moreover, Colombia's neighbors in Central America had vigorously protested
against the proposal. Abandoning Chiriqui, Lincoln proceeded to sound out the European powers who owned territories in Latin America. But these powers, not wishing to
incur the condemnation of the proud and sensitive Hispanic
nations, were guarded in their replies.

By October 1862 Lincoln had but one remaining colonization possibility in the Western Hemisphere, Haiti. Here
again, however, he made the mistake of dealing with land
speculators of questionable honesty. After he had, late in
December, signed a contract with Bernard Kock for the settlement of 5,000 Negroes on Cow Island in Haiti, Secretary
of State Seward, rightly suspicious of Kock's integrity,
refused to certify the contract and thus saved a grateful Lincoln from embarrassment.

One of Lincoln's chief reasons for advocating Negro migration was his momentous decision to issue a proclamation
freeing the slaves. It would, reasoned Lincoln, be easier to

defend such a step if there were a place to ship the freed slaves. But he was prepared to issue a proclamation, emigration or no. He had been urged to take such a step by newspaper editors, groups of clergymen, and a number of influential congressmen. Moreover, military operations were moving slowly, and a morale booster was necessary.

Impelled to take action, Lincoln issued a preliminary emancipation proclamation on September 22, 1862. In it he stated that as of January 1, 1863, all slaves would be free in those states which were then still in rebellion. As was to be expected, the South did not look upon Lincoln's edict as an extension of the olive branch, and they condemned it roundly. But when January 1 came, Lincoln carried through his ultimatum and signed the final Emancipation Proclamation. A lengthy document, its chief provision was a declaration freeing all persons held as slaves in those states, or parts of states, which had not laid down their arms.

In reform circles, and especially among Negroes, the Proclamation was received with great joy and thanksgiving. Celebration meetings were held in the cities of the North and in the Union-held regions in the South. It was, in the words of a Negro leader, "a day for poetry and song." The Negro's attitude toward the edict was voiced by Frances Ellen Watkins Harper:

> It shall flash through all the ages;
>   It shall light the distant years;
> And eyes now dim with sorrow
>   Shall be brighter through their tears.

Like Mrs. Harper, most Negroes focused their thoughts on the Proclamation's antislavery articles. They ignored its other aspects—that it was only a declaration, that it applied only to those areas in rebellion, that it was matter-of-fact in style and legalistic in tone. To Negroes it was enough that the Proclamation contained the words "henceforward shall be free." To them, the whole was more than the sum of its parts.

The esteem that Negroes had for the Emancipation Proclamation was an important factor in making it one of the most far-reaching pronouncements ever issued in the United States. Negroes were instrumental in creating the image of the Proclamation that was to become the enduring image. For in its own day Lincoln's edict was destined to reflect the luster and take on the evocative power reserved only for the half-dozen great charter expressions of human liberty in the entire Western tradition. The Proclamation soon assumed the role that Negroes had given to it at the outset, becoming to millions a fresh expression of one of man's loftiest aspirations—the quest for freedom.

Lincoln issued the Emancipation Proclamation "upon military necessity," to use his own words. He had come to realize that by undermining slavery he could reduce the striking power of the Confederacy. For by January 1, 1863, it had become crystal clear that the slave was contributing greatly to the southern war effort. Industry in the eleven states of the Confederacy depended upon black workers. As the armories and munitions plants tried to increase their output, they sent out appeals for more and more skilled Negro laborers. The Tredegar Iron Works of Richmond had a standing "help wanted" advertisement for 1,000 such factory workers. Equally great was the war-spurred demand for slave blacksmiths, harness makers, shoemakers, carpenters, wheelwrights, and miners.

So great was the need for slaves in constructing fortifications and embattlements that the Confederacy resorted to impressment. The army was authorized to impress slaves, and six states gave a similar power to their governors. As in the Revolutionary War, the owners of the slaves bitterly opposed impressment, but the need for black military laborers left the military and civilian authorities with no other choice.

On the plantations the slave was "the stomach of the Confederacy," producing its crops—potatoes, corn, peanuts, oats, barley, and wheat. "Much of our success was due to the much-abused institution of African servitude," wrote Jefferson Davis, President of the Confederacy. White men were enabled to bear arms, explained Davis, by leaving to slaves the cultivation of the fields, the care of the livestock, and the protection of the women and children. Sharing this opinion of the role of the slaves was General Ulysses S. Grant, who described the entire South as a military camp. Because slaves were required to work in the fields without regard to age or sex, said Grant, "the 4,000,000 of colored non-combatants were equal to more than three times their number in the North, age for age, sex for sex." As suggested by both Davis and Grant, the support received from its Negro population was one of the key factors enabling the Confederacy to hold out for four years, despite the North's great superiority in manpower supply and material resources.

Designed in part to weaken the South's hold on its slaves, the Emancipation Proclamation did lead to a slight increase in the number of runaways. But when Lincoln signed the document on January 1, 1863, he was actually doing little more than giving sanction to a movement that had already reached flood proportions. In terms of striking the shackles from the slave, the Proclamation was merely an accessory after the fact, for Lincoln did not initiate the movement to free the blacks; rather, he caught up with it.

As soon as the war broke out, Negroes began to make themselves free. The military operations of the war were conducted mainly on southern soil, and whenever the Yankee troops drew near, the black population poured into their lines. Officially this mass flight may be dated from May 23, 1861, when three Virginia slaves ran away and sought asylum at Fortress Monroe. Commanding officer Benjamin Butler refused to return them to their master. Quickly the news was whispered along slave row, and many a bondman became obsessed by one idea: if he succeeded in reaching the "stars and stripes," his freedom would be assured.

A freedom-minded slave no longer needed assistance from the underground railroad. With the camps of the Union armies within reach, opportunity beckoned as it had not done since the British invaded the South. And so began a series of migrations, by individuals, by families, and by groups. All manner of slaves took flight—the old and the young, the sick and the well, the trusted house servant and the lowly field hand.

The Emancipation Proclamation struck another blow at the Confederacy by authorizing the enrollment of freed slaves in the Union Army and Navy. The sanction of Negro levies by Lincoln marked the beginning of the large-scale tapping of this great reservoir of manpower. Northern state governors, desperately anxious to fill their quotas, now saw their way out, as did white men who had been drafted and who were looking for substitutes.

The recruiting of Negroes in the North ran into one serious handicap—the relatively sparse population. Since many potential Negro soldiers were available in those portions of the South which had come under the Union flag, however, into those regions came recruiting agents from the states and from private parties. These agents soon found a formidable rival in the national government. On March 25, 1863, Secretary of War Stanton dispatched

Lorenzo Thomas, Adjutant General of the Army, to the Mississippi Valley, to organize brigades of colored troops. Thomas proved to be a zealous recruiter, raising twenty regiments in less than three months.

The Negro's response to invitations to become a soldier was good. By the end of the war, some 180,000 colored men had volunteered, comprising between 9 and 10 per cent of the total Union enlistments. These Negroes in blue took part in 499 military engagements, thirty-nine of which were major battles. Their death toll was high, amounting to nearly 37,000, which comprised more than one-fifth of their total.

On the whole, the Negro volunteer acquitted himself acceptably. He knew that he faced a number of discriminations: his period of enlistment was longer than that of others, he had little chance of rising to the rank of commissioned officer, his pay was lower than that of whites, he did not receive the same hospital or medical care, he was furnished with inferior firearms, and if he were captured by the enemy, he ran the risk of being treated not as a prisoner of war but as a rebellious slave taken in arms. Despite such disadvantages, however, his morale was likely to be above par. Black regiments did have their deserters, nearly 15,000 Negroes taking informal leave of the service. But the typical colored volunteer made a dependable and resolute soldier. He knew why he had donned the federal uniform. He was fighting for a new dignity and self-respect, for an America in which his children would have greater opportunities. He felt that the army had something to offer him—it gave him the opportunity to make something of himself.

Proof of the high spirits of the Negro soldier was furnished by his conduct on the battlefield. Secretary of War Stanton, in a letter of February 8, 1864, to Lincoln, attested to the valor of Negro troops: "At Milliken's Bend, at Port

Hudson, Morris Island and other battlefields, they have
proved themselves among the bravest of the brave, performing deeds of daring and shedding their blood with a heroism
unsurpassed by soldiers of any other race." The three battles mentioned in Stanton's letter took place within the
space of three months in 1863: Port Hudson on May 27, Milliken's Bend on June 27, and Fort Wagner on July 18. Each
deserves a descriptive word.

In the spring of 1863, Port Hudson was the last remaining Confederate fortification on the Lower Mississippi, its
twenty siege guns and thirty pieces of field artillery posing a
serious threat to Union warships. To reduce Port Hudson
would be of great assistance to General Grant in his operations against Vicksburg. Numbered among the troops
selected to assault the Port were five Louisiana colored regiments. Charging up to the Confederate bastion, the Negro
soldiers were met by a hail of fire. Repulsed, they wheeled to
the rear and dressed into line. Again they charged, only to
be cut down again. A third and a fourth time the colored soldiers advanced, met each time by a tempest of bullets and
shells, but the strongly entrenched enemy was not to be dis-
lodged. The losses in Negro troops were severe, one regiment losing six successive flag bearers. As a military
operation the assault was a failure, but the Negro soldiers
had borne themselves well. "No body of troops—Western,
Eastern or rebel—have fought better in the war," editorial-
ized the *New York Times* of June 13, 1863.

On the last Sunday in June, 1863, the little garrison at
Milliken's Bend, a small town twenty miles from Vicksburg,
was manned by 1,410 Union soldiers, of whom only 160
were white. The rest were former slaves from Louisiana and
Mississippi who had joined the army exactly sixteen days
earlier. The Confederate command had decided that the
Milliken's Bend camp must be wiped out. Striking suddenly,

the soldiers in gray drove the Negro pickets back and then rushed upon and over the fort's entrenchments. A fierce hand-to-hand bayonet fight took place, the longest engagement of its kind in the entire war. The tide finally turned with the arrival of the Union warship *Choctaw,* rushed to the scene by Admiral Porter. The weary Confederates beat a retreat, leaving behind 130 of their dead for whom there was no room in the ambulances. The Union casualties were also heavy, totaling 652 killed, wounded, or missing. Milliken's Bend would be remembered because its defenders had not flinched under ordeal. "It is impossible for men to show greater gallantry than the Negro troops in this fight," reported General Elias S. Dennis to the assistant secretary of war. Another high-ranking officer was to express a similar opinion: "These men were very raw," wrote Ulysses S. Grant in his *Memoirs,* "but they behaved well."

Fort Wagner, a strong Confederate fortress situated on Morris Island, South Carolina, was a prize which the Union forces wanted to gain, for it controlled the sea approaches to the key city of Charleston. Heading the assaulting column was the Massachusetts Fifty-Fourth, the first Negro regiment recruited in the North. Led by a gallant young white colonel, Robert Gould Shaw, the Fifty-Fourth pressed forward to the attack, unaware that in their path lay a defile—a narrow passage between the sand hillocks and the sea—and unaware, too, that the enemy was in full readiness for them. As the colored soldiers approached the defile, the Confederate batteries suddenly became alive, showering them with fire. Shaw and a few dozen of his soldiers managed to reach the top of the parapet, but the assault was doomed; the outnumbered Union soldiers were forced to fall back, with heavy casualties, among them Colonel Shaw. Although the Fifty-Fourth had been repulsed, its bravery under fire won praise throughout the North, for the storming of a formidable bastion furnished the severest test of valor. In the dread twilight on that barren stretch of Carolina shore, the Fifty-Fourth had forged forever the Negro's right to the title of citizen-soldier.

Matching the Negro's services with the land forces was his role in the Union Navy. Throughout its history, the Navy had never barred free Negroes from enlisting, and in September 1861 it adopted the policy of signing up former slaves. Suffering during the entire course of the war from a shortage of men, the Navy was anxious to attract colored recruits and to have them re-enlist when their terms expired. The Negroes responded in goodly numbers to the naval recruiters, eventually comprising one-quarter of the men sailing the Union fleet. The Navy treated its 29,000 Negroes fairly well, quartering and messing them with whites and offering them some opportunity for promotion.

Four of these Negro sailors won the Navy Medal of Honor. Perhaps the best known of these was Joachim Pease, loader of the number one gun on the *Kearsarge*. One of the fifteen Negroes on board this warship when she met the most famous of the Confederate raiders, the *Alabama,* in a historic sea duel off the coast of France, Pease was cited by his superior officer as having shown the utmost in courage and fortitude.

Negro civilians, too, made some noteworthy contributions to the war effort. Some Negro women worked in hospitals or camps. Others formed groups designed to raise money for the families of the men at the front, to purchase flags and banners for the regiments, or to buy delicacies for the sick and convalescent soldiers. A number of Negro women's organizations had as their primary goal the assistance of the newly arrived slaves, distributing food and clothing to them. Typical of these charitable groups was the Contraband Relief Society, made up of forty women of the District of Columbia who were devoted to helping fugitives who had found their way to the nation's capital. Some women's organizations sent money to assist former slaves still in the South, the Colored Ladies Sanitary Commission of Boston on one occasion sending $500 for the suffering freedmen of Savannah.

Under the auspices of freedmen's aid societies, some Negro women volunteered to teach the three Rs in those regions which had come under the Union flag. The best known of these was young Charlotte Forten, who had been educated in Massachusetts and was personally acquainted with many of its notable reformers, including John Greenleaf Whittier, Charles Sumner, and William Lloyd Garrison. In the fall of 1862 Miss Forten arrived at St. Helena's in the Sea Islands of South Carolina. Here she entered enthusiastically upon her duties as a schoolmistress, sustained by the golden opportunity to carry out her life goal of doing all she could for "my oppressed and suffering fellow creatures."

If Negro women took the lead in sewing for the soldiers and in assisting the former slaves, Negro men on the home front were active in trying to influence public opinion in support of the war effort. Negroes sensed that the war would bring about an improvement in their lot. They started to read the newspapers more closely and to take a keener interest in public affairs. Negro spokesmen prodded mayors, governors, and congressmen to stand firmly behind the war effort, and they acted as a whip and spur to Lincoln, successively urging him to permit Negroes to join the Army, to declare the slaves free, and to support equal suffrage.

The last named—the right to vote—was the issue that particularly gripped the attention of the Negro during the last year of the war. Colored leaders held the opinion that freedom without suffrage was somewhat of a sham, political equality being the basis upon which other equalities were built. Negroes had repeatedly informed high-ranking government officials of their desire for the ballot. In one instance, a suffrage petition sent by a group of New Orleans Negroes was addressed jointly to the President and Congress, dated March 13, 1864, and bore 1,000 signatures, of which twenty-seven were those of men who had borne arms under Andrew Jackson at the Battle of New Orleans in the War of 1812.

The greatest wartime expression of this desire for the ballot was a national Negro convention held in Syracuse, New York, in early October 1864 and attended by 144 delegates from eighteen states. After four days of deliberation, the delegates drew up an "Address to the People of the United States," which claimed that Negro Americans had fully earned the right to vote and raised some questions: "Are we citizens when the nation is in peril, and aliens when the nation is in safety? May we shed our blood under the star-spangled banner on the battlefield, and yet be barred from marching under it at the ballot-box?" Negroes wanted the franchise, stated the "Address," because they were men and wanted to be as free in their native country as were other Americans.

One of the factors contributing to the Negro's morale, on the battlefield as well as on the home front, was his attitude toward Lincoln. Negro leaders might be disappointed in Lincoln because of his lukewarm attitude toward equal suffrage. They might also be puzzled by the persistence with which he held to the fetish of colonization. In mid-April 1863 nearly 500 Negroes had been sent to Cow Island, Haiti, but the venture proved a complete fiasco, and Lincoln had to send a transport to bring the emigrants back to Virginia. But Negro leaders did not press any criticisms against the President, realizing that the Negro rank and file would not listen, particularly after the Emancipation Proclamation.

With few dissenters, Negroes viewed Lincoln as a man who was personally well disposed toward them. They had heard of his graciousness to Negroes who had put in an appearance at the White House, whether on public occasions, such as a New Year's Day reception, or on personal visits, such as that of the delegation of Baltimoreans who presented him with a huge, ornamented Bible. Negroes saw in Lincoln a humanitarian whose love for his fellows embraced all sorts and conditions of men. They sensed that he was a growing man—ever learning, particularly in his concepts of liberty.

Lincoln's growth was nowhere better illustrated than in his Gettysburg Address of November 19, 1863. In a short speech at the dedication of the battlefield as a national cemetery for the soldiers who fell there, he pointed out that the living should highly resolve that America should have "a new birth of freedom." Thus did Lincoln reveal that he had fully grasped the great truth that the war had become not a war to restore the Union as it was, but a war to reconstitute the Union on a broadened base of human liberty.

Within a month after the Gettysburg Address, Congress began debating a constitutional amendment prohibiting slavery throughout the United States and its territories. Few men were more concerned about the adoption of this measure than Lincoln; he needed no one to tell him of the limitations of the Emancipation Proclamation. In the campaign of 1864 Lincoln placed his party on record as supporting the proposed Thirteenth Amendment. Upon his request, the Republicans, at their convention in Baltimore in June 1864, wrote such a plank into their party platform.

At this convention the Republicans also renominated

Lincoln for the presidency, a very popular choice with Negroes. Lincoln won re-election by a comfortable majority, a victory which he regarded as a mandate by the people that Congress pass the amendment abolishing slavery. This viewpoint gained support on Capitol Hill, and on January 31, 1865, the House, following the lead of the Senate, gave the necessary two-thirds majority vote to send to the states a constitutional amendment doing away with slavery. Lincoln and the Negroes would have concurred with the editorial appraisal appearing in a New York newspaper the following morning: "The adoption of this amendment is the most important step ever taken by Congress."

During the month of April, 1865, the two most important events to the Negro, as to the country, were the collapse of the Confederacy and the assassination of Lincoln. The former took place on April 9 when, at Appomattox, Lee surrendered his army to Grant. The latter took place five days later when, at Ford's Theatre, John Wilkes Booth fired a fatal shot at Lincoln's head. As Negroes had been elated over Lee's surrender, so they were stricken by Lincoln's death.

But as that fateful April drew to a close, the Negroes felt that they stood on the threshold of a new era. Slavery was dead, and they had played a part in bringing this to pass. Taking inventory of the war's four years, the Negroes felt that now they had a stake in America, that their future was here and not in Liberia, Haiti, or elsewhere. The Civil War had deepened the Negro's sense of identity with the land of his birth, giving him the feeling that he mattered, that he belonged.

It was good for the Negro that his faith in America had been strengthened. For there were trying times just ahead.

6

The Decades of Disappointment
(1865–1900)

WITH THE CIVIL WAR ended and with slavery gone, the
Negroes throughout the country were optimistic, linking
their freedom to a deepening sense of patriotism. "We are
part and parcel of the great American body politic," declared
a convention of colored men in Kentucky; "we love our country and her institutions and we are proud of her greatness."

Among many of the former slaves one of the fruits of
this new pride in their country was a new sense of personal
responsibility. In June 1865 a group of Petersburg, Virginia,
Negroes pointed out that they understood freedom to mean
industry, not idleness and indolence. The Negroes in the
Sea Islands had given ample proof that they would work
without the threat of the lash: as early as the summer of
1862 they had been working for wages, and their diligence
had surprised their northern supervisors. Like farm workers elsewhere, the former slaves wanted to have land of
their own, to work in their own sweet potato patches. Gen-

eral Rufus Saxton, who had been charged by the War Department to ascertain the readiness for freedom of the former slaves, sent a glowing report to Secretary Stanton: the Sea Islands, said he, "have shown that they can appreciate freedom as the highest boon; that they will be industrious and provident with the same incitement which stimulates the industry of other men in free societies." General Saxton's superintendent of plantations, William C. Gannett, added a revealing comment: "the freeman works to accomplish his ends; the slave, to end what he is obliged to accomplish."

Another eyewitness, John T. Trowbridge, who toured the South immediately after the war, was similarly impressed by the former slaves' willingness to work. He noted that they felt great pride in supporting their families. In Louisiana he found no shirking among the colored gangs producing sugar: "and so the business went on with black engineers, black crushers, black filterers, black sugar makers—all black throughout—but the sugar came out splendid in quantity and quality." Visiting Memphis, Trowbridge noted that out of more than 16,000 freedmen in June 1865, only 220 were indigent and these unfortunates were maintained by the Negroes themselves through their benevolent societies. General Edward Hatch, stationed in Mississippi and Alabama at the close of the war, testified that in his experience with the freedmen he had "seen no instance where they were not willing to work when they have been assured of their rights."

Not all former slaves sought work during their first months without a master. Many folded their hands, waiting to receive forty acres and a mule which never came. Others left their home plantations to go in search of lost relatives. Taking no thought of the morrow, many former slaves felt that the only way to test whether they were actually their own masters was to take to the open road, going wherever it led them.

Fortunately for the southern Negro, whether a wanderer or not, there were nearly 100 privately financed freedmen's aid societies ready to lend a helping hand. The work of these benevolent groups was much the same as that of the Bureau of Refugees, Freedmen and Abandoned Lands—popularly known as the Freedmen's Bureau—which Congress had established in March 1865 in the War Department. Unlike most of the other aid societies, the Freedmen's Bureau extended considerable assistance to impoverished whites.

Headed by an able commissioner, General O. O. Howard, the Freedmen's Bureau offered a variety of services. It had a health program, distributing a total of some twenty-one million rations, establishing forty hospitals, and treating nearly half a million cases of illness over its seven-year existence. The Bureau acted as legal guardian to the freedmen, adjudicating many cases in its own semimilitary courts, where technicalities might be brushed aside. Though the Bureau was placed in control of confiscated and abandoned lands, most of the acreage at its disposal was inferior and undesirable. President Johnson's pardon of many planters had enabled them to reclaim their estates, and to protect the former slaves in their negotiations with landowners, the Bureau drafted labor contracts calling for a fair wage. The Bureau was empowered to enforce such contracts, becoming in effect the first mediating agency between capital and labor in America.

The Bureau also established over 4,000 schools, from the elementary grades through college, charging no fees and often furnishing free textbooks. Nearly a quarter of a million former slaves received varying amounts of education through such efforts.

Despite its many accomplishments, the Freedman's Bureau met with one signal failure: the promotion of mutual confidence between Negroes and whites. Aside from those who were aided by the Bureau, the great majority of whites were strongly opposed to it. Basically the southerner was a conservative, and hence some of the hostility to the Bureau was a predictable resistance to change. Moreover, the very presence of the Bureau was a reminder of a lost war.

The white planters, preferring to deal without interference with their Negro field laborers, objected to the go-between role of the Bureau agents. Moreover, white southerners were opposed to the school-founding activities of the Bureau, for they believed that the Negro could not absorb book learning. Even worse about the schools, in the eyes of the southerners, was the feeling that the Yankee teachers were fostering social equality by eating with Negroes and addressing them as "Miss" or "Mr."

The Bureau's efforts on behalf of the Negro ran counter to the white South's image of him. Whatever the southerner had surrendered at Appomattox, he had not surrendered his belief that colored people were inferior to white. Deeply imbedded in the regional culture, this view outlasted slavery. Much more than he feared the Negro, the southerner feared losing his grip on the world, almost a loss of his identity.

Any effort by the newly freed slave to extended the olive branch was doomed. In June 1865 a group of Petersburg Negroes stated that they had no feeling of resentment toward their former masters, but were "willing to let the past be buried with the past." But to expect such magnanimity on the part of people who had been crushingly defeated on the battlefield, who had lost $2 billion in slave property, and whose world was in disarray, was to expect too much.

The role that the white South had for the former slave was unfolded in the so-called Black Codes, laws for the control of the Negro. These were the work of state legislatures which had come into existence under the Reconstruction policies of Lincoln and Johnson, who had assumed that the seceded states had not left the Union, that their restoration should be speedy, and that the executive arm should take the lead in bringing it to pass. By the end of 1865 the eleven former states of the Confederacy were functioning again as states within the Union, although Congress, in recess until December, had not recognized them.

The Black Codes, passed in the fall and winter of 1865–66, were designed to take the place of the defunct slave codes, and the two had some features in common. The South Carolina code stipulated that in the making of contracts, "persons of color shall be known as *servants* and those with whom they contract shall be known as *masters.*" In South Carolina, too, the Negro farm worker could not leave the premises without permission. Vagrancy laws were common. Mississippi's vagrancy laws applied only to Negroes, who were fined if they had no lawful employment; upon failure to pay the fine, they were to be hired out by the sheriff.

A local ordinance in Louisiana required that every Negro be in the service of some white or former owner who was to be held responsible for his conduct. In some instances the Negro's job opportunities were restricted, South Carolina forbidding him to engage in any vocation other than farming or domestic service.

As a rule, the codes forbade Negroes to join the militia or to possess firearms. A special license to preach might be required. In some states and communities a former slave might be fined or imprisoned for committing any insulting act or making an insulting gesture. "Jim Crow" regulations were a part of the picture. Mississippi, for example, forbade Negroes to ride in first-class passenger cars, and in Florida a Negro could be given thirty-nine lashes for "intruding himself into any religious or other assembly of white persons." The codes placed the Negro at a legal disadvantage, in some instances not permitting him to testify against whites. The former slave could not seek redress at the polls, for the ballot was denied him.

The Black Codes, however, did differ from the slave codes on some points. They granted Negroes the right to own property, to make contracts, to sue and be sued, to testify in court in cases involving other Negroes, and to have legal marriages. But they left the Negro, in one sense, even more at the mercy of the whites than the slave codes, which had given him at least the powerful voice of his owner, bent on protecting a valuable piece of property.

In enacting the Black Codes, the southern legislatures made one fatal miscalculation: they had no idea of the storm of opposition such measures would arouse in the North. To southerners the codes seemed natural and necessary, but to northerners they seemed like an effort to establish a modified form of slavery. Even northerners who had been sympathetic to the prostrate and defeated South began to raise questions about the good faith and loyalty of the former Confederate states. Dying but not yet extinct in the North were the embers of the abolitionist crusade and the moral fervor it had aroused.

As nothing else, the Black Codes played into the hands of the Republicans, who were looking for reasons to postpone the readmission of the southern states. For these states, if readmitted, would elect enough Democrats to insure that party's control of the government. Hence the Republicans were determined to keep the South in political limbo until the ascendancy of their party was assured. To achieve such ascendancy it would be necessary to enfranchise the southern Negro.

The Republican-controlled Thirty-Ninth Congress, which opened on December 4, 1865, refused to seat the recently elected representatives from the South. Instead, it denied the legal existence of the southern state governments and proceeded to appoint a Joint Committee on Reconstruction. Charged with inquiring into conditions in the former Confederate states, the Joint Committee of Fifteen, as it was popularly known, was dominated by Radical Republicans, among them Charles Sumner and the powerful House figure, Thaddeus Stevens. Of stern visage, and with a club foot, Stevens was regarded by southern whites as a diabolical fanatic, and he returned their hatred, matching epithet with epithet.

For four months the Joint Committee held hearings and took testimony; subcommittees were sent to investigate the southern states. Giving full publicity to its findings, which inevitably tended to support its own point of view, the Joint Committee slowly but surely began to influence northern opinion. Reflecting something of its own temper, Congress in early April 1866 passed a Civil Rights Act, which extended citizenship to the former slaves and stipulated that discriminations against them were to be tried in federal courts.

On April 30, 1866, the Joint Committee made its report to Congress, recommending a proposed amendment to the Constitution, the Fourteenth. The first section of this far-reaching measure declared that all persons born in the

United States were citizens and that no state could abridge the rights of such citizens or deprive any person within its jurisdiction the equal protection of the laws. Another section stated that if a state withheld the ballot from its adult male population, its representation in the House would suffer a proportionate reduction.

Congress duly passed the Fourteenth Amendment and on June 13, 1866, sent it to the country for ratification. To the South this measure was a blow at two of its most sacred canons; states' rights and Negro inferiority. With the exception of Tennessee, the former seceded states turned it down by large majorities. But this very rejection was turned by the Republicans to their advantage, enabling them to claim that the South had been offered a reasonable proposal and had spurned it.

Another factor that aided the Republicans was the incidence of rioting in the South. In Memphis during the spring of 1866 there was an outbreak of violence in which over forty Negroes were killed, nearly seventy were severely wounded, and over a dozen colored schools and churches were burned. A similar race riot took place in New Orleans in late July, costing the lives of nearly forty Negroes. The Republicans proclaimed that these bloody disturbances were fresh evidence that the South was unrepentant and that the Negro was being oppressed and thus needed the protection that the ballot would bring.

By election day in November 1866, when a new Congress would be chosen, the Republicans had succeeded in winning a majority of northern voters to their way of thinking. The counting of ballots revealed that the Democrats had been decisively defeated. The Republicans, now completely dominated by the Radical wing, obtained more than a two-thirds majority in both houses, thus immunizing the veto power of President Johnson.

With what they construed as a mandate from the people, and with sufficient strength to carry out their program, the Radical Republicans were ready to go to work. As a starter, the Congress, on January 8, 1867, passed a bill conferring the suffrage on the Negroes of the District of Columbia. This was followed three weeks later by a measure forbidding territorial legislatures from denying the ballot to Negroes.

It was in the Reconstruction Act of March 2, 1867, that Congress unfolded its design for establishing loyal governments in the South. Calling the existing regimes illegal, Congress stipulated that the former Confederate states (except Tennessee) should be divided into five military districts, each of which was to be under a major general who was directed to prepare his province for readmission to the Union. This process entailed a series of steps, beginning with the registration of loyal voters who would elect delegates to a state constitutional convention. When the constitution had been approved by the voters and by Congress, the state then had to ratify the Fourteenth Amendment, which, in turn, required the vote of three-quarters of the states for final ratification.

A distinguishing feature of the Reconstruction Act of March 2 was its requirement that the Negro be given the vote. For example, the delegates elected to the state constitutional conventions had to be chosen by an electorate which included Negroes. Moreover, the constitutions that were drawn up by the states were required to embody the same rule of suffrage for the colored man. Thus the former slave was assured of the right to take part in the reconstructed governments of the southern states.

Thus, too, the Republicans were able to procure the support they needed in the South. Among Negroes the party could represent itself as having freed the slave and as now

adding to its benefactions by giving him the vote. Losing no
time in imploring the Negro with a sense of both his obligation and his opportunity, the Republicans organized and
financed political clubs, headed by whites. The best-known
of these agencies, the Union League, had worked during the
Civil War to keep up morale on the home front. With the war
over, it moved South early in 1867 and acquired both a new
name—the Loyal League—and a new purpose—Negro suffrage.

Through its many branches, the League operated as a
secret society, with grips, ritual, and a password—*Lincoln,
Liberty, Loyal, League,* the four Ls. Meeting in church or
school buildings, the local leagues held joint social and political gatherings, with banquets and barbecues alternating
with business sessions devoted to prayer, oratory, and taking an oath to support the Republican ticket. On election
day the typical Loyal League member was eager to do his bit
at the polls.

In its efforts, the League had the willing cooperation of
the Negroes. Many of the former slaves sensed that if they
wished to become fully free, they must do something on
their own behalf. Thus even before the League had moved
South, Negroes in such cities as Norfolk, Nashville, Raleigh,
and Charleston had held conventions expressing their
wishes to vote. "Give us the ballot," stated a convention of
Alexandria Negroes in August 1865, "and we will protect
ourselves." And as the prospect for equal suffrage had
become brighter, many Negroes in the North decided to
move to the South. Some were northern-born (like Philadelphia's Mifflin Wister Gibbs, who settled in Arkansas, where
he became a city judge and a register in the United States
Land Office), while others had been born in the South (like
P. B. S. Pinchback, who became lieutenant governor of
Louisiana).

From the North, too, came many whites who were interested in politics. Along with other northern whites who had seen service in the Freedmen's Bureau or some other government agency, the newcomers were soon numbered among the leaders of the enfranchised Negro. Many of these Republican migrants were men of unquestioned honesty and ability, while others were plunderers (like General Milton S. Littlefield who operated in North Carolina and Florida, his assets a suave manner and a confident air, and his sole goal the quick dollar). Northern whites shared their leadership with native-born whites, who likewise varied in honesty and ability.

Urged on by the Loyal League and led by the whites, the newly enfranchised Negro shared in the work of bringing the southern states back into the Union and then in electing men to office in the new state governments. But, although he was an active participant in politics, he did not exercise political control. The total membership in nine of the constitutional conventions was 713 whites as compared with 260 Negroes. In no state legislature were Negroes ever in control. In South Carolina, where Negro political strength was greater than elsewhere, the state senate, as well as the governorship, was always white.

If Negroes in the state legislatures never played a dominant role as a group, many of them were prominent and influential as individuals. In South Carolina Jonathan J. Wright served for nearly six years as associate justice of the state supreme court. In Louisiana William G. Brown discharged the duties of superintendent of education with marked ability. Jonathan C. Gibbs was Florida's secretary of state for four years and its superintendent of instruction for two years. A score of additional Negroes held high posts, including such offices as prosecuting attorney, superintendent of the poor, sheriff, and mayor. However, the vast majority of Negro officeholders were local officials, such as justices of the peace.

By far the most notable group of Negroes to hold office were those who went to Congress. From eight southern states came twenty-two colored congressmen. Two of these sat in the Senate—Hiram R. Revels and Blanche K. Bruce, both from Mississippi. Of the twenty Negroes who sat in the House, South Carolina accounted for eight, North Carolina for four, Alabama for three, and Florida, Georgia, Louisiana, Mississippi, and Virginia for one apiece. Thirteen of the total had been born in slavery. Ten of them had college training, including five with college degrees. The best educated was Robert B. Elliott, who had graduated from Eton in 1859 and who read French, German, Spanish, and Latin. Perhaps the most respected of the Negro congressmen was John R. Lynch, who at the age of twenty-four had become speaker of the Mississippi House and who in Washington made many influential friendships, including that of President Grant.

The Negro congressmen were not destined to leave any mark on national legislation. Their numbers were small, and their tenure in office was short, the two Senators serving a total of seven years and the twenty House members serving a total of sixty-four years. But as legislators they won praise, including that of fellow congressman James G. Blaine, who characterized them as studious and earnest. A present-day scholar, Vernon L. Wharton, says of the Negroes from Mississippi: "The three who represented the state in the national Congress were above reproach."

Far more lasting than the work of the colored congressmen was that of the Republican-Negro regimes in the southern states. To begin with, the new constitutions adopted by these states as a condition of their readmission were a distinct improvement over the documents they supplanted.

They provided for expanded suffrage by removing all property qualifications for voting and holding office (North Carolina's abandoning the religious test for those seeking election to public position). Equally important, every one of the new constitutions provided for a statewide system of free public education. Without redistributing the land, the new constitutions exempted small property-holders from taxation. Imprisonment for debt was abolished in many states, and such punishments as branding, whipping, and the stocks were declared illegal. In the South Carolina constitution the number of capital crimes was reduced from twenty to two.

The state governments under the Republican-Negro regimes likewise had much to their credit. During their period in office, "there were efforts to increase the efficiency of government through a reorganization of the judicial system, the redistribution of powers in towns and counties, and the modification of registration and election laws," writes John Hope Franklin. As a rule the Negroes who sat in the state legislatures showed no inclination to press for special advantages for the former slave. Generally, they were not revenge-minded or vindictive, Mississippi's colored lawmakers petitioning Congress to remove all political disabilities from the whites.

The constructive work of the Republican-Negro regimes was marred by evidences of fraud and corruption in such states as South Carolina, Florida, Alabama, and Louisiana. In the first named, the legislature reimbursed a Speaker of the House the sum of $1,000, which he had lost on a horse race, and such items as wines, cigars, and groceries were listed under legislative expenses. It should be carefully noted, however, that fraud and corruption in public life were new neither in the South nor in the nation. Moreover, during a postwar period, public morality among officeholders often reaches a new low throughout the country. Certainly extravagance and mismanagement in governmental affairs were widely prevalent in the years immediately following the Civil War, a period which has been ruefully labeled as an "Era of Good Stealing."

Without doubt, then, there were among Negro office-holders those with itching palms and a limited sense of their public responsibility. But an even larger number were just the reverse. "In retrospect," writes a present-day authority, Professor C. Vann Woodward, "one is more impressed with the success that a people of such meager resources and limited experience enjoyed in producing the number of sober, honest, and capable leaders and public servants they did."

Perhaps the most distinctive type of legislation passed by the newly organized southern states were the militia laws, which provided for an active-duty state guard and a reserve force. Open to men from eighteen to forty, the militia was under the state governor, who selected its officers. As was to be expected, the militia forces contained a goodly number of Negroes. They were quick to fill the muster lists, attracted by the pay and by the appeal of a uniform. Moreover, to many of the former slaves, service in the militia seemed like both a defense and a guarantee of their freedom. In the seven southern states which had militia forces, there were "heavy concentrations" of Negro troops in four, and there was "a noticeable mixture" of Negro and white troops in the other three, says Otis A. Singletary. The militia was avowedly created and organized to protect the public peace, but it also bolstered the fortunes of the Republican party.

For, however well or ill they served the South, the new governments certainly aided the Republicans. In the presidential elections of 1868 the Republican party received the expected and necessary support from the South. Indeed, the elections revealed fully the crucial importance of the Negro vote, which overwhelmingly favored Ulysses S. Grant, the Republican candidate. Without the 450,000 votes cast for him by Negroes, Grant would have been perilously close to defeat, for his popular majority was not large. The Democratic nominee, Horatio Seymour, polled a heavy vote, although some 300,000 less than that of Grant.

The lesson was not lost on the Republicans. Fearing that when the conservative whites in the South came into control, they would strike the equal suffrage provisions from the state constitutions, the Republicans bestirred themselves. Launching a movement to protect the Negro vote, they proposed a constitutional amendment that a citizen's right to vote should not be denied by a state or by the national government because of race or color. Sent to the states in February 1869, the measure was ratified on March 30, 1870, as the Fifteenth Amendment.

Negroes and reformers were overjoyed. "We have washed color out of the Constitution," exulted Wendell Phillips, and Negroes throughout the country held ratification ceremonies. The greatest was in Baltimore, where, on a beautiful day in mid-May, a parade of some 20,000 Negroes marched through the downtown streets. The public meeting which followed was addressed by such notables as the postmaster general, but appropriately enough the featured speaker was the slave-born son of Maryland, Frederick Douglass. "We have a future," said he, "everything is possible to us."

But as concerned the Negro, the ratification of the Fifteenth Amendment was high tide, if indeed the tide had not already begun to recede markedly.

White southerners bitterly resented the Republican-Negro regimes. The new state governments were scorned and hated by the masses no less than the planter-business class. In part this hostility was based upon fear of "Negro domination." To see former slaves holding high public office and parading in the militia, this was the wormwood and the gall. Striking at the Negro would put him in his place and at the same time constitute a mortal blow to the hated Yankee from the North. Taking the name Conservative, the aroused and angered whites vowed to bring about some changes.

Believing that they were faced with political and social self-preservation, Conservatives launched a counterrevolution. Ready to go to any lengths, some of them joined secret societies like the White League of Louisiana, which passed an official resolution declaring "that it was the intention of the founders of this government, that this should be a white man's government, as far as our efforts go, it shall be."

By far the best known of these undercover agencies was the Ku Klux Klan. This organization had a modest beginning in 1865 at Pulaski, Tennessee, as a group of merrymakers bent on a good time. But by the spring of 1867 the Klan had become a highly organized movement cutting across state lines, and unswervingly bent on combatting the influence of the Loyal League.

To keep the Negro in the place to which it had assigned him, the Klan used a variety of techniques. In some cases, simple fright was enough, many rural Negroes regarding with awe and dread the queer costumes of the Klansmen— black robes with red crosses on the breast and white circles around the eyes. If fright did not prove effective, the Klan would resort to threats. The next step would be the burning down of one's home. If these failed, the Klan was quite ready to fall back on force, the tradition of violence being deeply rooted in the South. The Klan would waylay a Negro who persisted in disobeying its orders, and then administer some form of corporal punishment—whipping, tar-and-feathering, or lynching. A similar fate might overtake white Republicans or whites who fraternized with Negroes.

In essence a popular movement, the Klan was singularly successful. Inevitably it attracted lawless elements, those who liked violence for its own sake. In 1869 the head of the Klan, Nathan B. Forrest, alarmed at the recklessness of some of the local dens, ordered the organization dissolved, but his edict was ignored.

Hardly more effective in curbing the Klan were the laws passed against it in Congress and in the state capitals. Congress did not furnish adequate money or machinery to protect the Negro from intimidation and violence. Moreover, charges against Klansmen were difficult to prove, for witnesses were afraid to give testimony and juries might be made up of Klansmen or their sympathizers. Every federal judge was studied with a view to any weakness he might have: "If he is convivial, they wine and dine him; if he is more avaricious or impecunious than honest, they bribe him; if he is timid, they frighten and bully him."

In Klan cases involving the laws of a state, the Negro was at an even greater disadvantage. Sheriffs, probate judges, and clerks of courts were white, and they saw to it that Negroes did not serve on juries. "In controversies between our race and white men, and in criminal trials where the accused or injured is a black man, it is almost if not quite impossible for a black man to obtain justice," ran the words of memorial sent to Congress in December 1874 by a group of Negroes in Alabama. If the offense against a colored plaintiff were too flagrant to be ignored, a sympathetic judge would levy a token fine and make no effort to see that it was collected.

The Klan was most successful from 1868 through 1871. By the latter year, the Loyal League was in a state of rout. The Conservatives were capturing political control of the state governments, beginning in 1870 with Virginia and North Carolina. Many white Republicans took note of the changing order, renounced their party affiliation, and became Democrats.

Once in control of the machinery of government, the Conservatives hastened to minimize the Negro vote. They used such devices as holding elections at sites whose whereabouts were kept secret from the Negro voter and falsely arresting the Negro the day before election and releasing the day after, with apologies for the error. Other techniques to nullify the Negro vote included stuffing the ballot box, "repeater" voting, and the doctoring of the election returns. Even more important, once in charge of the state governments, Conservatives proceeded to revise the constitutions, striking from them all guarantees of equal rights.

By the spring of 1877 the Conservatives were in charge of state governments throughout the South. The Republican-Negro regimes had been liquidated, having lasted for a period of from three to ten years.

A contributing factor to the victory of the southern Conservatives was the North's loss of interest in the Negro. The industrially booming America that emerged from the Civil War was notable for its absence of a crusading spirit, its retreat from idealism. The postwar North was engrossed in the problems of a rapidly evolving urban society, with its disputes between labor and capital, the growth of manufactures, and the expansion of commerce. Moreover, by the mid-seventies, the Negro had lost his two greatest champions in Congress, death taking Thaddeus Stevens in 1868 and Charles Sumner six years later. As of no other figure from Abraham Lincoln to Franklin D. Roosevelt, Sumner's passing saddened the Negro population: "Dark is the way without thy beacon light," mourned Charlotte Forten Grimké.

Unfortunately for the Negro, he was no longer needed by the Republican party after 1876, for the vital industrial-capitalist legislation of the Civil War was no longer in danger of being repealed. With big business firmly in the saddle, eastern industrialists had begun to think seriously about southern markets and trade. Wanting a peaceful climate in those states, they decided that it was best to adopt a "hands-off" policy on the Negro question and leave to the South its own handling of this sectionally divisive issue.

The wishes of the business community were reflected in the behavior of the Republican party. The event that signalized the party's new laissez-faire policy was the "Hayes Bargain." The presidential election of 1876 between Rutherford B. Hayes and his Democratic opponent was extremely close. Three southern states sent in two sets of election returns, one Republican and the other Democratic. A specially created Electoral Commission decided in favor of Hayes. Anxious to placate the white South—which, naturally enough, had not supported the Hayes ticket—the campaign managers of the President-elect promised that once he had taken office the remaining federal troops would be withdrawn from the South.

Hayes lived up to the bargain made by his managers, and the withdrawal of the federal troops removed the last prop of the tottering Republican-Negro regimes and furnished a final proof that the party of Lincoln had all but abandoned the former slave. Indeed, many prominent Republicans, including President Hayes and later Presidents Arthur and Harrison, were ready to play down the Negro question in an effort to attract southern whites.

To stifle any twinges of conscience about forsaking the Negro, the Republican party saw to it that Hayes and his successor, James A. Garfield, appointed a handful of Negroes to public office. Frederick Douglass was made Marshal of the District of Columbia, John Mercer Langston became Minister to Haiti, and former Congressmen Blanche K. Bruce and Robert B. Elliott received lucrative posts in the Treasury Department. Thus did the Republican party seek to still any criticism by the more prominent Negroes and at the same time preserve the fiction of being the colored man's friend.

Despite its loss of interest in the Negro, the Republican party continued to enjoy such political support, North and South, as the colored voter was able to give. The Negro knew only too well that the Republicans took him for granted. But, although he could, and did, express his bitterness, he felt that he had no place else to go. For better or worse, he was wedded to the Republican party, even though it had become evident that what had taken place was less of a mating of kindred spirits than a marriage of convenience, with the reciprocal advantages no longer equally shared.

If the Conservatives in the South were aided by the do-nothing policy of the Republican party, they were abetted in a more positive way by the Supreme Court. This high tribunal consistently interpreted the Fourteenth and Fifteenth Amendments in such a way as to weaken their protection of the Negro.

A variety of considerations moved the Court in its handling of the war amendments and the acts of Congress relating to the Negro. Rightly concerned with maintaining a proper balance between the powers of the national government and those of the states, the Court tended to restrict federal powers which it felt were excessive. Moreover, the Courts of the nineteenth century did not regard the purely human factor as crucial as the assumed first principles of the law: the letter of the law took precedence over its spirit. And, finally, the men of the Supreme Court could not escape the influence of public opinion on matters of race and color; for all their apparent Olympian aloofness, the justices were subject to the all-pervasive temper of the times.

In a series of cases, the Court set up four basic principles that worked in the interests of the southern whites. To begin with, it decreed that the war amendments applied only to actions taken by states of their agents, and not to private parties. Hence if a private individual or group kept a Negro from voting, the latter had no recourse in the federal courts. Another principle related to the emphasis on appearance rather than reality: if a state law were not plainly discriminatory, the Court would not attempt to ascertain whether it was being applied alike to black and white. A third principle was that of holding the state's police power paramount and therefore more important than the rights given to the individual under the Fourteenth Amendment. The state's police power—its inherent right to protect the public health, safety, or morals—of necessity had to be broad. At any rate, the Court obligingly found that state "Jim Crow" laws were a valid exercise of this power. Finally, the Court favored the white southerner in its ruling that there was a substantial difference between "race discrimination" and "race distinction," the latter not being contrary to the Constitution.

The two most publicized of the Court's decisions affecting Negroes were the Civil Rights Cases of 1883 and *Plessy v Ferguson,* thirteen years later. The former related to the Civil Rights Act of 1875, a measure which sought to secure equal rights for all citizens at hotels, theaters, and other places of public amusement. It also stipulated that no person should be disqualified to sit on juries because of race. This bill had been strongly supported by Negroes, James T. Rapier of Alabama, in a speech in Congress, having called attention to the fact that there was "not an inn between

Washington and Montgomery, a distance of more than a thousand miles, that will accommodate me to a bed or meal."

The Civil Rights Act remained on the books for only eight years before the Court struck it down. Negroes were up in arms, holding a series of indignation meetings, heaping ridicule and invective on the Court, and offering it lessons in constitutional law. Anxious to soften the blow to its colored population, many nonsouthern states, numbering eighteen by 1900, passed state civil rights bills. But the national legislature was not destined to pass another such measure until seventy-five years after the Court's adverse ruling in 1883.

After the Court's action in the Civil Rights Cases, no one should have been unprepared for the Plessy decision. The high-water mark of the constitutional sanction of state "Jim Crow" laws, this decision in 1896 upheld a Louisiana law calling for separate railroad accommodations for white and colored passengers. Revealing something of the popular belief in white superiority, the Court ruled that laws were "powerless to eradicate racial instincts or to abolish distinctions based upon physical differences." In his dissenting opinion, Justice John Marshall Harlan pointed out that the "Constitution is color-blind, and neither knows nor tolerates classes among citizens." He ventured the opinion that "the judgment this day rendered will, in time, prove to be quite as pernicious as the decision made by this tribunal in the *Dred Scott Case.*" Prophetic words, but in 1896, Justice Harlan's was a lone voice. "*Plessy* was bad law: it was not supported by precedent," writes Barton J. Bernstein. But it remained the law of the land for over half a century.

The Court's rulings encouraged the white South to launch a final bloodless offensive to relegate the Negro to his proper political and social sphere. Regarding voting, the white South felt that the time was ripe to exclude the Negro legally, that it could adopt better and more permanent techniques of disfranchisement than those of intimidation and violence.

Mississippi was the first state to employ the new devices. In 1890 her constitution established three conditions for voting: a residence requirement, the payment of a poll tax, and the ability to read or to interpret a section of the state constitution. Five years later South Carolina adopted these same requirements, adding to them a list of crimes—such as larceny, which had a high incidence among Negroes—which disfranchised the offender. Another requirement southern states found useful was the good-character test: an applicant seeking to become a voter had to produce a responsible witness to vouch for his worth and standing. In many states, tricky registration procedures were legalized, giving local registers broad powers to thwart the Negro applicant. "White primary" laws were passed, asserting that the Democratic party was a voluntary association of citizens and could therefore limit voting as it pleased in party elections.

So sweeping and effective were these measures to disfranchise the Negro that they caught in their dragnet a number of whites, particularly the poor and illiterate. Hence some southern states hastened to pass "grandfather clauses," bestowing the franchise upon those whose grandfathers had voted. This measure added to the total number of voters, but all the persons on whom it bestowed the vote were white, since no Negro's grandfather had voted or been eligible to vote. (Such measures were declared unconstitutional in 1915.)

The white South's grim determination to keep the Negro voteless was strengthened by a halfhearted, unsuccessful attempt by Congress in 1890 to pass a "Force Bill," which would enforce the section of the Fourteenth Amendment stipulating that if a state denied the suffrage to its adult population, its representation in the House would be proportionately reduced. The South was more angered than alarmed by the "Force Bill," but it aroused her spirit of defiance and thus fanned her zeal for Negro disfranchisement.

More than any other factor, the white South's determination to totally separate the Negro from the ballot stemmed from the Populist revolt. Populism was the outgrowth of an effort by the American farmer to improve his lot. Believing that both major political parties were the creatures of business interests in the North, the aroused farmers formed a People's Party.

In the South the leaders of the agrarian crusade—Tom Watson, for example—sought Negro support, holding that the poor white man and the poor colored man were in the same economic strait jacket. Seeking cooperation across the color line, many southern Populists appealed to the remaining Negroes who could vote and tried to obtain the vote for those Negroes from whom it had been wrested. Taking alarm, many of the businessmen and planters decided to fight fire with fire. They, too, sought the Negro vote, opening their pursestrings for barbecues and entertainment, and for the services of Negro spellbinders. Where Populism was successful at the polls, as in North Carolina, Negroes were placed in such offices as alderman, magistrate, deputy sheriff, and collector of the port. But this re-emergence of the Negro voter and officeholder as a power to be reckoned with during the mid-nineties was short-lived.

Reviving the cry of "Negro domination," defeated or ambitious politicians charged that the Populists were taking the South back to the days of the carpetbagger. The Populists were stigmatized as the lineal descendants of the

173

Loyal Leaguers. Such charges spelled doom, for in the South no political accusation was more fatal than that of being the party of the Negro. Although the reform measures championed by the Populists were directly aimed to benefit the poor white farmer, he tended to forget everything else whenever someone shouted Negro, and the white South closed ranks, determined to eliminate the agrarians Populism's failure in the South stemmed in large measure from its attempt to bridge the color line.

To Negroes the aftermath of the Populist revolt was particularly galling. Seeking a scapegoat, many of the party's former leaders turned on the Negro, blaming him for its downfall. Moreover, the growing political influence of the poor whites and their pronounced anti-Negro bias led to the widespread adoption of "Jim Crow" legislation. To bolster their own self-esteem, the lower-class whites insisted on their social superiority to the Negro, and even such titles as "Hon." or "Mr." for the exceptional Negro were abandoned. In most southern states this sentiment received more formal expression in the laws requiring that Negroes be segregated at inns, hotels, restaurants, theaters, and on public carriers. And, as was to be expected, those who advocated "Jim Crow" measures had no trouble in convincing themselves that segregation was in the Negro's own best interests—indeed, that it upheld a status that he himself wanted.

The experiences of Reconstruction had a lasting influence in the South and still mark that region in many ways. One of these legacies was the legend of the Old South. Turning backward to the antebellum period, southern writers metamorphosed the planters into aristocrats whose lineages could be traced back to kings in Scotland and Ireland. To these literary glorifiers, the Civil War became a "lost cause" which deserved a better fate, and Reconstruction became a wailing wall.

As a result of the Reconstruction period, the South came to regard as intermeddling any undue interest by outsiders in its affairs. The long-held "leave us alone" psychology became greatly intensified. In the South the fetish of states' rights and the cry for "local self-government" struck a deep and responsive chord. Hostility to outside devils became a phobia.

Reconstruction profoundly affected political life in the South. Since the Republican party was associated with the humiliation of the South, no self-respecting white could vote other than Democratic. Hence the South became politically "solid," a one-party section. Political life in the South might come to lack vitality, but this price its citizens were prepared to pay.

Equally as tenacious as hostility to the Republicans was a hatred of Negro suffrage. Vividly kept alive as the menace of menaces was the memory of the colored man voting and holding office. Southern politicians found no surer way of appealing to the white voter than posing as guardians of white suffrage. A candidate for public office would vow to outdo his opponent in keeping the Negro in his place.

Leaders of the white masses found that it was not hard to make the Negro a whipping boy, a scapegoat. The strong prejudice against the Negro participating in politics was rooted in a fear of which "no amount of power or privilege ever relieves them," wrote George Washington Cable of his fellow southerners. Another turn-of-the-century observer, Ray Stannard Baker, held a similar point of view: "Traveling in the South, one hears much of the 'threat of Negro domination,' by which is generally meant political control by Negro voters of the election of Negro officeholders. But there exists a far more real and sinister form of Negro domination. For the Negro still dominates the *thought* of the South."

Finally, Reconstruction tended to leave the South with a casual attitude toward the law and legal procedures. During the days of the Republican-sponsored regimes, the white southerners felt that they had no recourse except violence and force, and they soon became habituated to such methods, especially in matters relating to the Negro. The practice of taking the law in one's own hands was to last long after the heyday of the carpetbagger.

By 1900 the South's white-supremacy doctrine met with little disapproval in other quarters. Increasingly there had been a merging of the southern and the national image of the Negro. At the turn of the century the idea that certain races were naturally inferior became more tenaciously held than ever. The belief that the Anglo-Saxons were superior to other races waxed in the 1890s.

By 1898, when the Spanish-American War brought Cuba and the Philippines into United States orbit, the people of the conquering country had no difficulty in believing that they were peculiarly fitted to rule the darker-skinned, non-Anglo-Saxon populations formerly under Spain. The shibboleths of white supremacy were eagerly seized upon in the North. It followed then that if the stronger and superior Americans were justified in imposing their will upon lesser breeds across the oceans, there could be no objection to white southerners doing the same on the domestic scene. Thus did the North and South effect a reconciliation on matters of race and color.

Colored Americans might protest that this road to reunion was paved at their expense. An eminent northern Negro might sorrowfully ask of his white fellows in Massachusetts: "Are we of this generation worthy descendants of tea spillers and abolitionists? Are we living up to the principles of the fathers in relation to the treatment of citizens of color?" But attorney William H. Lewis was speaking to Bay Staters who, like their fellows throughout the North, did not see the Negro steadily or whole; theirs was a southside view.

If Reconstruction left its mark on white America, it also affected black America's political life and means of earning a living. Reconstruction made the Negro a Republican, as has been noted. In the words of Frederick Douglass, the Republican party was the deck, and all else was the sea. A goodly number of Negroes became Democrats, but they had to bear the reproaches of their fellow Negroes and sometimes even the contempt of whites of their own party.

Politically, too, the experiences of Reconstruction led the Negro to look to the national government rather than to the states for protection. To the Negro in the South "local self-government" meant a denial of his right to take part in politics. Inevitably, then, the southern Negro looked to the federal government to insure his rights; he became, as he remains today, an ardent supporter of federal control and the extension of federal power.

In getting a job and making a living, the period after Reconstruction was particularly galling to the Negro. A laboring class shorn of political power is largely at the mercy of fate. This was the lot of the Negro, on the farm or in the factory, during the quarter of a century following Reconstruction, a period which Professor Rayford W. Logan has incisively characterized as "the nadir."

In the rural regions of the South the typical Negro was propertyless. Some Negroes who had acquired homesteads during the last months of the war lost them when President Johnson restored to the white planters their confiscated lands. Southern whites were reluctant to sell land to

Negroes, sensing that a propertied Negro might feel himself entitled to full citizenship rights. But even in instances in which the large plantations had been broken up and land was available to Negro purchasers, few had the money to buy. With no way to secure a loan, and with no Freedmen's Bureau to guide him, the landless Negro became a share tenant or a sharecropper.

Share tenants provided their own stock and farming utensils and received a portion of the crop they produced, while sharecroppers were able to furnish nothing but their own labor. Since they needed credit for everything—work animals, tools, fertilizer, feed for stock, cabins, and rations of hogback, cornmeal, and molasses—sharecroppers received smaller portions of the crop than tenants. Most share tenants were white, whereas most sharecroppers were colored.

Sharecropping would work well in instances in which the landlord was honest, the worker was industrious, the strip of land was productive, and the cotton crop brought a good price. But such a combination was rare indeed, for sharecropping had a built-in system of evils. Landlords, who in many cases lived in town and doubled as merchants, tended to charge high prices for the things they sold to the sharecropper, and to add on exorbitant interest charges. The landlord also kept the books, for his tenants were often illiterate. Sharecroppers had a tendency to overbuy, thus compounding the likelihood that they would remain hopelessly in debt. On "settling-day" the dismayed and angered cropper not only found himself with no income but owing money. He had no other choice than to pledge his labor to the landlord for another year. If he were no longer a chattel bound to a master, he was not unlike a serf or peon bound to the soil.

Landlords themselves were the victims of the declining price of cotton. When one was asked by a tenant for some overalls, he replied that he needed a pair himself. Share-cropping was "a lazy descent to hell," the worker having little incentive to increase his output or to try to repair or brighten his unpainted shack. In sharecropping, as in slavery, the laborer consciously withheld efficiency.

The relatively small percentage of Negroes who worked as salaried agricultural workers were hardly better off, receiving an average annual wage of $60. With that sum they had to clothe themselves and "purchase necessary articles for subsistence," other than one peck of corn or meal per week.

Like his rural brother, the town Negro had his problems in the postwar South. White laborers brought strong pressure to drive the colored worker out of the skilled jobs. In instances in which the Negroes were able to retain their skilled occupations, they were forced to accept lower wages: colored carpenters in 1890 averaged $.75 to $1.25 an hour, whereas white carpenters received $1.50 an hour and up.

In jobs traditionally held by Negroes, the picture was somewhat brighter. In Georgia, for example, Negro janitors outnumbered whites by eight to one in 1900, Negro draymen and teamsters outnumbered whites by three to one, and Negro stonemasons outnumbered whites by more than two to one. Barbering was among the better jobs held predominantly by Negroes; Alonzo Herndon, who opened his shop at the Markham House in Atlanta, became well-to-do, owning and renting fifty houses in 1908.

Lesser occupations, notably those in domestic service, were likewise monopolized by Negroes. But the pay was low (cooks averaging $5 a month in 1902), and, as in other jobs traditionally held by Negroes, competition was rearing its head (in this instance from German and Swedish domestics who were often more reliable and efficient than Negroes fresh from the farm areas). Negroes also faced competition from prison inmates who were hired out cheaply under the notorious convict-lease system.

The plight of the city Negro in search of a job was intensified by the deepening color line. The doctrine of white supremacy and black separation permeated the job market as it did other aspects of southern life. Increasingly the Negro found himself driven out of the "clean" and better-paid occupations. At the close of the Civil War five out of every six artisans in the South were Negroes, but by the turn of the century the skilled Negro workers probably numbered not more than 5 per cent of the total. Though hot and heavy work might still be available, this only underscored the fact that in the southern mill towns, as on the farms, the relationship between the races had become one of "boss and black."

In the North the Negro workingman found his major problem not so much in the reluctance of the industrialist-employer as in the attitude of the white laborer. Indeed, the latter had opposed freeing the slaves lest they come to the North and become competitors. After the war this hostility of the white laborer was reflected in the attitude of the national labor unions, which ideally may have wanted to unite all workers, regardless of color, but were in fact bent on excluding Negroes.

Caught between the theory of working-class solidarity and the Negro-exclusion attitude of the white laborer, the national unions tended to adopt a "hands-off" policy. Upon organizing at Baltimore in 1866, the National Labor Union, the first important coast-to-coast federation, sought the cooperation of the Negroes, inviting them to form locals. But at its second annual session, held at Chicago in August 1867, the delegates passed a resolution stating that the question of Negro membership was so involved and had aroused "so wide a diversity of opinion amongst our members" that it was not expedient to take action one way or the other. The annual meeting held the following year made no mention of the Negro. The 1869 convention had nine Negroes among the 142 delegates, and the 1870 convention went on record as denouncing discrimination on the basis of race or color. But by this time the National Labor Union was in a state of rapid decline, and the Negroes had formed two national unions of their own.

Both the National Negro Labor Union and the National Labor Convention of Colored Men were established in Washington in 1869. Although the latter established a Bureau of Labor to encourage and support the formation of Negro locals, both organizations were dominated by public figures who were civil rights advocates rather than labor union officers, such as Frederick Douglass and John Mercer Langston.

The fact that the national Negro labor union movement became political in its leadership was one of the reasons for its short life of less than five years. Leaders like Douglass tended to equate the Republican party with the workingman's party and to subordinate the latter to the former. But there was another reason for the failure of the movement: the white workers were not to be won over. In an address issued in January 1870, the National Negro Labor Union urged whites to "join us in our movement, and thus aid in the protection and conservation of their and our interests." But this invitation brought no response.

The national Negro unions thus remained fatally outside the mainstream of organized labor, and by 1874 the separate national Negro union movement was dead. The Negro weekly *The New National Era,* in its May 17 issue of that year, carried a lead editorial entitled, "The Folly, Tyranny and Wickedness of Labor Unions," portraying the disillusionment of the black bourgeoisie and, to some extent, the black worker.

The despair of the Negro laboring man yielded to hope with the emergence of the Knights of Labor, an industrial organization welcoming both the skilled and the unskilled. Founded in secrecy in 1869, the Knights came out into the open in the seventies. Emphasizing that there was to be no color prejudice in their union, the Knights made a determined, and highly successful, effort to organize Negroes on a large scale. By 1887, after seven years of working among Negroes, the Knights had enrolled some 90,000 of them, approximately one-eighth of the total membership.

But if the rise of the Knights was meteoric, their decline was even more rapid. In 1886 the Knights became embroiled in a series of violent strikes and was blamed unjustly for a bloody riot in Haymarket Square, Chicago. From these blows the Knights never recovered, the public coming to believe that the union was controlled by socialists and anarchists.

The successor to the Knights in the national labor union movement was the American Federation of Labor, launched in 1881. Like the Knights, the Federation proclaimed that workers should unite irrespective of creed or color, and in 1890 one of the conditions of affiliation was an oath not to discriminate on account of race.

But by 1900 the Federation had begun to retreat from its policy of Negro inclusion. The Federation was made up of craft unions of skilled workers. The army of unskilled or semiskilled was outside its purview, and this was the very class of workers that made up the bulk of Negro labor. Moreover, the Federation believed that each local should have a high degree of autonomy; the principle of craft sovereignty was paramount. Anxious to increase union membership, the leaders of the Federation, particularly president Samuel

Gompers, believed that it was necessary to permit local affiliates to do as they pleased about the Negro.

For these reasons the Federation abandoned its original policy of no discrimination on the basis of color. By 1900 it was admitting locals whose constitutions barred Negroes, the Boilermakers and Iron Shipbuilder's Union having been granted a charter in 1896, although its constitution restricted membership to whites. Realizing that this practice left the Negro defenseless, the Federation authorized its executive committee to issue charters to local unions of colored workers. And to keep such membership small, the Federation shunned the use of Negro organizers.

Though the Negro might rail against the Federation for the failure to exert moral leadership, the leaders of organized labor bore no special malice toward him. They had not created color prejudice. Moreover, since they believed that to insist on job equality for the Negro would have been to disrupt and weaken the labor movement, they fell back on evasion or compromise.

However, organized labor's lack of forthrightness on the color issue inevitably turned the Negro into a strikebreaker. Since he was unable to get jobs through the union, the Negro got them directly from the employer. When white laborers struck for better living conditions, Negroes were offered their jobs. Ironically in many steel plants in the North the only way the Negro could get employment was by scabbing, which—it hardly need be added—widened the rift between the black worker and his white counterpart.

As the nineteenth century drew to a close, the general outlook for the Negro was not bright. A realist, the Negro was not given to blinking the hard facts of life. But as an American, he was of an optimistic turn of mind. A new century was dawning, and with it perhaps a better day. For even the most lonesome of roads must have its turning.

7

Turn-of-the-Century Upswing (1900–1920)

To HIS LOT in the America that took shape in the post-Reconstruction years, the Negro brought a variety of responses. He might rail at the fates, but he did not permit himself to become immobilized by them. An American, he must bestir himself—take steps, do something. The most popular solution hit upon by the Negro sharecropper was migration. Much of this movement by colored families was from one part of the South to another—from country to town, from poorer to richer lands, and from the older states to the newer ones.

As part of the general westward expansion, many land-seeking Negroes went into Indian territory. Here they were often welcomed by the tribes, becoming known as "linksters" because they could speak English. Hundreds of Negroes moved into the Southwest, where opportunity beckoned especially to those who had been in the saddle from childhood. In the early 1870s a Negro cowboy on the Texas plains was no novelty; indeed, the Negroes as a group had a reputation for night riding and the identification of brands.

Ever in search for more freedom, many of the Negro cowboys shifted to the northern ranges during the mid-seventies. The best known of these was Nat Love who, on July 4, 1876, at Deadwood in the Dakota Territory, won the title, "Deadwood Dick" for his surpassing skill in riding and marksmanship. To the Rockies and beyond went Negroes; "they were found on every mining frontier from California in 1849 to the end of the gold rush in the Black Hills of Dakota," writes Professor W. Sherman Savage.

Although the spirit of equality was characteristic of the frontier settlements of the West, some of the Negroes who left the South to escape discrimination found it waiting for them elsewhere. Believing that prejudice was inevitable in a biracial society, some Negroes thought that a separate state might be the answer. Such a quasi-independent all-Negro state was proposed in 1890 by the Texas Farmers' Colored Association. A similar impulse was behind the visit to the White House made by a delegation of twenty Negroes who urged President Harrison to appoint a Negro as secretary of the Oklahoma Territory.

To suggest making Oklahoma a Negro state was bound to arouse great resistance by whites and Indians. But since land was cheap and plentiful, the whites were not averse to the formation of small, all-Negro towns. Beginning with Langston in 1891, a number of such Oklahoma towns came into existence. The largest of these was Boley, founded in 1904, whose inhabitants for five years voted in the Okfuskee County elections; when it was found that these Negroes held the balance of power between the Republicans and the Democrats, however, the alarmed whites disfranchised them.

Oklahoma's all-Negro towns were destined to live on,

but they were also destined to fall short of the hopes of their founders. Indeed, in 1914 when an adventurer, "Chief" Alfred Charles Sam of the Gold Coast, proposed to transport Negroes to Africa, his greatest response came from the all-Negro towns of Oklahoma, especially Boley.

The largest movement of Negroes from the South in the post-Reconstruction years was the "exodus" to the Middle West in 1879. After the crop failures of 1878 the Negroes were more restless than ever. Colored conventions were held in New Orleans in April 1879 and in Vicksburg and Nashville three weeks later. The Nashville group recommended that a request be made to the national government that $500,000 be appropriated "to aid in the removal of our people from the South."

The moving figure behind the 1879 migration was Benjamin "Pap" Singleton, an unlettered, Tennessee-born ex-slave. Singleton issued circulars describing the opportunities in "Sunny Kansas" and distributed them to train porters and steamboat hands who would scatter them in the outlying regions. In person as well as in print, Singleton exhorted Negroes to follow his advice.

Singleton's colloquial persuasiveness spurred hundreds of "exodusters" to head north and northwest, their possessions tied in bags, bundles, and red bandannas. Their hopes were high, many having deluded themselves into believing that land and mules without price awaited them in Kansas and that one might do little other than bask in the sunshine between meals. By August 1, 1879, over 7,000 needy Negroes had arrived in Kansas, and lesser numbers were making their way to Missouri, Iowa, and Nebraska.

Negro leaders were sharply divided as to the wisdom of migration. In its support, Richard T. Greener, dean of the Howard Law School, argued that the Negroes who left would be better off and so would those who remained, since the excess labor supply would be reduced. On the other hand, Frederick Douglass criticized the movement; it was promoted, said he, by railroad companies to drum up passenger trade. Moreover, argued Douglass, emigration was a solution by flight rather than by right, and the Negro would be unwise to leave a section of the country where he had a virtual monopoly on the labor supply.

The debate over migration waned as the movement suddenly lost momentum. For word was seeping back that the migrants were faring badly. Those who went to Kansas found that the weather was cold and that jobs were few. White workers voiced their fears that the black migrants would bring about a lowering of wages. The mayor of St. Louis issued a proclamation advising Negroes without money to avoid the city.

The severe winter of 1879–80 turned out to be a nightmare for the penniless newcomers. Most of them were destitute, lacking food, clothing, and shelter. Many died of exposure, their plight arousing national concern. Relief societies raised funds; their efforts were augmented by Negro church groups and by Negro leaders who made public appeals on behalf of the migrants. Some of the migrants were thus able to weather the storm, eventually finding jobs or obtaining public lands. But others returned to the South or struck out in new directions.

The exodus ceased partly because some efforts were made to remove one of its major causes, the exploitation of the workers. A Senate committee appointed to investigate Negro migration placed the problem and its solution squarely in the hands of the southern landlords and industrialists, stating that Negroes pulled up their roots only because their job outlook was so bleak. Influenced by this criticism, some employers took such steps as finding off-season jobs for their workers. But, on the whole, such ameliorating measures were of short duration. For as soon as the migration ceased, the concessions also ceased, most businessmen and planters reverting to their previous practices in dealing with their Negro hired hands.

Cut off from political life and not faring well in the world of work, the postwar Negro turned increasingly to his traditional center of hope—the church. The fading of the great expectations of Reconstruction days led the Negro to look anew to the church as an agency of uplift and inspiration. And, as it happened, the Negro church in the South was able to assume an even larger role than in antebellum days, for the Civil War had freed the Negro church from the controls established during slavery times. The white preacher and the white observer were no longer on the scene.

Equally as important, the war brought about a separation of white and Negro churches in the South. The theories of race held by most white southerners, which had led them to establish "Jim Crow" practices in secular life, made it next to impossible for them to welcome Negroes into their church congregations. And the relatively small percentage of whites who were not averse to retaining their Negro membership were willing to do so only on condition that such members would continue to sit in the galleries formerly reserved for slaves and would not expect to take part in the church's social or business affairs. Negroes were unwilling to accept such stipulations.

As a consequence, southern Protestantism divided into all-white and all-Negro denominations. In 1866 Negro Baptist congregations in the South Atlantic states of South Carolina, Georgia, and Florida organized an association of their own; this was followed fourteen years later by a South-wide convention of Negro Baptist churches held in Montgomery,

Alabama. By 1880 white and Negro Baptists in the South were going their separate ways.

Other denominations were experiencing a similar separation. Late in 1870 the Colored Methodist Church in America was organized, an offshoot of the Methodist Episcopal Church, South. Negro Methodism in the South was further strengthened after the Civil War by the coming of the African Methodist Episcopal Church and the African Methodist Episcopal Zion Church, which up to the Civil War had confined their work largely to the North. Like the Methodists, Negro Presbyterians in the South began to form their own churches, over two-thirds of them taking this step by 1870. It was not until 1898, however, that the General Assembly of the Presbyterian Church in the United States actually transferred its Negro units to a newly organized Afro-American Presbyterian Church.

The problem of church separation touched even the Episcopalians, whose Negro membership was small. After the Civil War, this denomination continued to hold special services known as "colored Sunday school," for its Negro communicants. This practice did not win Negro converts. Indeed, in Baltimore, where the Episcopalians were relatively strong among Negroes, the "colored Sunday school" had disappeared by 1900, its former members having either joined the two local Negro Episcopalian congregations or become Methodists or Baptists. The only major denomination to escape the challenge of the color line was the Catholics, largely because of their late start in Negro work; their first organized effort did not begin until 1871, with the arrival of five Josephite Fathers in Baltimore, and their first Negro priest was ordained in 1893.

By 1900 Christianity had divided along the color line even more markedly than ever before. For, although some churches in the North still kept their doors open—there were, for example, from 10,000 to 12,000 Negro Presbyterians in white churches in 1900—the southern churches were almost completely segregated. "There may be in the South a black man belonging to a white church today," wrote W. E. B. DuBois in 1907. "But if so, he must be very old and very feeble."

White and colored, the denominations which attracted large memberships in the South were desperately lacking in funds. This meant, particularly among Negroes, that the church congregations were too poor to pay the salaries of college-trained men. But, unfortunately, an applicant's lack of formal schooling was not often a barrier to a call to a pastorate. Indeed among some congregations an educated clergyman was suspect.

"Oh, for a studying ministry," lamented H. Edward Bryant in 1894. Presiding Elder of the Selma, Alabama, District of the A.M.E. Church, Bryant spoke from experience: "I have visited many preachers, and have seldom found one with a single work on systematic theology, a dictionary, commentary or work on ethics," he wrote. Without formal training in theology or the arts and sciences, many Negro ministers were, in the words of another contemporary churchman, "all sound and no sense, depending upon stentorian lungs, and a long-drawn mourn, for their success." Under such pastors, church services tended to become intensely emotional, with trances and weird singing.

Of necessity, the role of the Negro clergyman was not confined to pulpit preaching and spiritual leadership. He was, writes Carter G. Woodson, a "walking encyclopedia, the counselor of the unwise, the friend of the unfortunate, the social welfare organizer, and the interpreter of the signs of the times." The Negro clergyman was a natural leader because his support came from the mass of people; he was therefore in a position to speak more frankly on their behalf than a Negro leader whose job required that he have the good will of the white community.

The role of the Negro church, like that of its pastor, did not stop with Sunday service. The Negro's church was a highly socialized one, performing many functions. The church served as a community center, where one could find relaxation and recreation. It was a welfare agency, dispensing help to the sicker and poorer members. It was a training school in self-government, in the handling of money, and in the management of business. The church was the Negro's very own, giving him the opportunity to make decisions for himself, which was seldom available elsewhere.

As a patron of schools, the organized Negro church performed one of its greatest services. Bent upon giving its young people a "Christian Education" and upon the better training of its future clergymen, Negro church groups markedly expanded their school-founding efforts. Every major Negro denomination was represented in the movement. Negro Baptists were supporting eighty elementary and high schools by 1900. In existence, too, at that date were eighteen Baptist institutions of college or semicollege rank designed for Negroes, all located in the South. But the major financial support of these schools, along with their control, rested in the hands of white Baptists in the North, who worked through the American Baptist Home Mission Society.

The Negro denominations of the Methodist Church were likewise busy; the A.M.E.s established six colleges between 1870 and 1886, the C.M.E.s established four colleges between 1878 and 1902, and the Zion Methodists founded Livingston College in 1879. These denominations received support from white friends, but the major support from the white Methodists went to the schools founded by the Freedmen's Aid Society of the Methodist Church, an auxiliary of the Methodist Episcopal Church, North. By 1878 this society had founded five colleges, two theological seminaries, and two medical schools. Here again the control was vested in those who had put up the money.

Other northern denominations were not idle. The Presbyterians, having founded Ashman Institute (afterward Lincoln University) in Pennsylvania in 1854, expanded their efforts after the war, founding Biddle Memorial Institute (afterward Johnson C. Smith University) in 1867, Scotia Seminary in 1870, and Knoxville College two years later. Although numbering relatively few Negro members, the Congregationalists were particularly active. Operating through their agency, the American Missionary Association, the Congregationalists founded seven colleges for Negroes in the four-year period from 1866 through 1869, and by 1876 the Association was also running fourteen normal and high schools. Not to be left out, the Episcopalians founded St. Augustine at Raleigh, North Carolina, in 1867.

The typical church-related school or college was notable for the eagerness of its students, many of whom were adults responding to opportunity no matter how belated it had come. Having to meet the student where he was, most of these schools, even those designated as colleges or universities, spent most of their time on basic elements of knowledge. As a rule, these schools were open to all students without regard to color, the Congregationalists particularly believing in mixed schools as a matter of principle. But in practice almost no white student was likely to be found in attendance. But if the student body was not mixed, the faculty was. As a group, the teachers were likely to be conscientious and dedicated. The great majority of teachers were female, and a goodly proportion of them were Negroes.

Some of these were graduates of Spelman College, founded in Atlanta in 1882, while others had taken degrees "from Oberlin, Wellesley and Vassar, from Cornell and Ann Arbor," to quote Mary Church Terrell in 1898, who herself had graduated from the first named.

All the church-related schools shared in common a desperate need for money, and many of them led a hand-to-mouth existence. Fortunately, in the closing decades of the century two additional sources of support for Negro schools—state governments in the South and educational foundations established by philanthropists in the North—became available.

Just as the impetus for publicly supported schools in the South was a result of the state constitutions drafted by the Republican-Negro regimes, so the strengthening of these schools resulted from the example set by the Negro and church groups. The poorer whites began to acquire some of the Negro's faith in education, and to gradually overcome the opposition of economy-minded legislators and the planter-banker groups they represented. The new South had become school-minded.

In building schools with public monies, it was not possible to ignore the Negro. But less could be spent on him than on the whites, on the grounds that he paid few taxes and that there was little point in giving him any training beyond the basic elements of reading and writing. Guided by this point of view, white school boards and superintendents established separate schools which were never equal. The length of the school year differed for white and colored, as did the salaries for teachers. A school building for Negroes often turned out to be a hired hall, church basement, or vacant store.

The southern states offered little support to college-level work of Negroes. The Morrill Act of 1862, which provided for the founding and maintenance of agricultural and mechanical colleges across the nation, was silent about dividing federal funds on a racial basis. Three southern states did, however, make available to Negroes a portion of the funds received from the national treasury. The second Morrill Act, passed in 1890, specifically authorized the use of land-grant funds for Negro colleges; it stated that such funds should be "equitably divided" between the white and Negro colleges. But such an equal division was slow in coming. As late as 1916 none of the sixteen existing Negro land-grant institutions was offering college-level work.

Negro parents supplemented the school monies which the state provided. Some went into their own pockets, giving what they could. Others raised money by holding rummage sales, giving suppers, and selling raffle tickets.

Such sacrificial giving, although meager compared to the total need, had its influence in enlisting substantial contributions from the great educational foundations then being established. Some of these philanthropic agencies showed either an exclusive or special interest in the Negro. Among the former was the John F. Slater Fund, established in 1882 for the "uplifting of the lately emancipated population of the Southern states, and their posterity, by conferring upon them the blessings of Christian education," in the donor's words. With no less a personage than Rutherford B. Hayes as its first president, the Slater Fund contributed not so much to the founding of new schools as to the support of already existing ones, particularly those devoted to the training of teachers. Slater's original gift of $1,000,000 was supplemented by some $350,000 when the George Peabody Fund came to its final liquidation in 1918.

Another bequest exclusively for Negroes was the Rural School Fund, founded in 1907 by Quaker Anna T. Jeanes. "Others have given to the large schools," said she; "I should like to help the little country schools." Miss Jeanes's gift had points of similarity with that of Slater, both being in the amount of $1,000,000 and both being subsequently increased from other sources. The Jeanes Fund, as it came to be popularly called, distributed over $2,225,000 over a thirty-five-year period. Fittingly enough the two funds—Jeanes and Slater—were consolidated in 1937 to form a new corporation, the Southern Educational Foundation.

Negro rural education attracted the interest of Julius Rosenwald. Beginning in 1911, Rosenwald offered to furnish a portion of the cost of constructing school buildings in the rural South. The remainder of the cost was to come from the local communities, through public tax monies and private donations. By the time of his death in 1932 the Chicago humanitarian had contributed over $4,000,000 to the building of more than 5,000 "Rosenwald" schools. In 1928 a fund bearing his name was established exclusively for Negro education.

Some philanthropic foundations had a special rather than an exclusive interest in the Negro. The Phelps-Stokes Fund, founded in 1911 by a gift of $900,000, expressed its intention of helping existing schools "of proven experience and of assured stability." Giving much attention to the making of surveys, the Fund spent over half a million on its Negro activities during its first twenty-five years. Another agency that embraced the Negro in its interests was the General Education Board. Established by John D. Rockefeller in 1903, its stated purpose was the promotion of education "without distinction of race, sex or creed." In the first ten years of its existence this corporation gave nearly $700,000 to Negro education, showing a particular interest in programs to provide better teachers.

In addition to gifts from foundations, Negro schools received support from individual philanthropists. One of the earliest and most generous of such benefactions was Andrew Carnegie's grant of $600,000 to Tuskegee Institute. Carnegie took this step out of his admiration for Booker T. Washington, founder and principal of Tuskegee. "To me he seems one of the foremost of living men because his work is unique," wrote Carnegie in making the gift in 1903. Like other men with large sums of money to give to Negro schools, Carnegie liked Washington's ideas as to the best kind of training for colored youth.

Washington believed in vocational education, the mastering of trades with the aim of becoming a skilled wage earner. At Hampton Institute, where he had been a student, and at Tuskegee, the young women became proficient at cooking, sewing, and nursing, and the young men learned how to become better farmers or were taught the trades of carpenters, blacksmiths, plumbers, and painters. "I have never seen a commencement like Tuskegee's before," wrote Mary Church Terrell. "On the stage before our very eyes students actually performed the work they had learned to do in school. They showed us how to build houses, how to paint them, how to estimate the cost of the necessary material and so on down the line."

Washington was aware that many Negroes resented industrial education, connecting it with slavery. But the type of education he advocated developed character as well as mechanical skills. In 1907 Washington stated that he had made careful investigation and had not found a single Tuskegee graduate "within the walls of any penitentiary in the United States."

Though by no means the originator of vocational education, in his day Washington was its greatest exponent in America. Moreover, his influence outstripped that of anyone else. Before making gifts to Negro colleges, prospective white donors sought Washington's assurance that their

monies would be earmarked for his kind of education.
Struggling Negro colleges were only too anxious to add
trades to the curriculum in order to get badly needed funds.

Washington's influence on education extended beyond
the Negro world. An appreciation of schooling became
increasingly evident among whites, and they proceeded to
follow the pattern molded by Hampton and Tuskegee.
Booker T. Washington was not boasting when, in 1908, he
pointed out that "it was the Negro schools in large measure
that pointed the way to the value of this kind of education."

The turn-of-the century Negro took many paths in seeking
to improve his lot. But, as in education, all roads seemed to
lead to Booker T. Washington. As he put his stamp on Negro
schools, so he put it on other aspects of Negro life, including
economic activity, political preferment—appointment to
offices—and the persuasive presentation of a philosophy of
getting along with the white man.

Washington's emergence as a Negro leader of broad and
unparalleled influence may be dated from an address he gave
at Atlanta on a hot September afternoon in 1895. Invited to
make one of the opening speeches at the Atlanta Cotton
States and International Exposition, and introduced by the
governor of Georgia, Washington's homespun eloquence left
few hearts untouched. A practiced public speaker, Washington's moving words were essentially a plea for better understanding and good will between the races. He urged Negroes
to stay where they were—"Cast down your bucket where you
are"—and he urged the whites to lend them a helping hand.
Playing down the Negro's grievances, Washington spoke
instead of his possibilities. But nothing so pleased the whites
in the audience as Washington's assertion that sensible
Negroes understood "that the agitation of questions of social
equality is the extremest folly."

The Atlanta Exposition speech was acclaimed in the North almost as fervently as in the South, and Washington was flooded with offers to write articles and to take to the lecture platform. One bureau offered him $50,000 to deliver a series of addresses. Some Negroes may have felt slightly unhappy about the speech, feeling that Washington had been too anxious to avoid giving offense to anyone. But unquestionably the Atlanta speech was a resounding personal success.

Washington's prestige was increased five years later with the publication of his autobiography, *Up From Slavery*. This simple narrative was presented in the quiet style that bespoke the man. It was clearly written, and its pull on the heartstrings is unmistakable even today. Above all, it was an affirmation of faith in the future. It quickly became a best-seller, winning high praise even from literary critics such as Barrett Wendell and William Dean Howells. It added to Washington's reputation, reinforcing the picture of him as an exponent of good will and a living example of the triumph of the human spirit over adversity. It further endeared Washington to whites, giving him an influence that the years did little to dim. "You have the attention of the white world," wrote Kelly Miller in 1911; "you hold the pass-key to the heart of the great white race."

One of the areas in which Booker T. Washington wielded influence was business enterprise. As might be expected from one who preached self-reliance and self-help, Washington shared the belief that the Negro's entry into the business world would furnish a road to racial advancement on all fronts. It would make for a well-to-do merchant class which would create jobs for ambitious youngsters whose color kept them out of the white-collar occupations.

Believing that one way to stimulate Negro business was to bring its practitioners together, Washington founded the National Negro Business League in 1900. This organization became the colored man's Chamber of Commerce, whose members might receive encouragement and inspiration from one another. One of the League's objectives was the formation of state and local branches, of which some 600 were in existence by 1915.

Like anything else he was connected with, the League took on the personality of Washington. Its perennial president, he dominated the annual meetings, always ready to give advice and admonition. At the last meeting he attended, in Boston in 1915, he warned the delegates that the newly arrived Greeks were taking over a former Negro monopoly, the shoeshining business: "Just think of it—the black boy is studying Greek and the Greek boy is blacking shoes!"

Washington's efforts to make the Negro a force in the business world could hardly be called a success, for the Negro's achievements in the field of trade and commerce were relatively meager. There were numerous individual success stories, however, and there were even instances of Negro businesses hiring whites. A Negro newspaper in Baltimore employed white compositors, for example, and the Negro-owned Chesapeake Marine Railroad and Dry Dock Company, located in the same city, employed white carpenters.

But, on the whole, the Negro was a failure as an entrepreneur. In general the only large-scale Negro businesses that managed to survive were those in fields in which there was no white competition. Negroes had met with some success in the insurance business, most companies not preferring to "write up" Negroes, whom they considered bad risks. Similarly, in the field of banking Negroes were able to make a good start because white banks tended to discourage the deposit business of Negroes, feeling that it would cost too much to handle accounts which were likely to be both small and subject to frequent withdrawals. By 1914 Negroes had established some fifty banks, the initial capital coming from the deposits made by burial societies and fraternal organizations.

Negroes were likely to do well in the service fields which catered to a colored clientele. Negroes who operated undertaking establishments were likely to survive and hardly less likely to prosper. Even more profitable was the beauty culture business. From the manufacture of products to improve the hair and skin, "Madame" C. J. Walker and Mrs. A. E. Malone each amassed over $1 million.

But, outside the personal service and those fields which specialized in "race products," Negro businesses were generally small-scale, lacking in capital and in trained and experienced managers. Like Booker T. Washington, many Negro businessmen were motivated by a sense of race pride. But the fate of Negro business was more likely to be determined by the economics of buying and selling, of credit and debit, than by the exhortations of Mr. Washington and others.

During the age of Booker T. Washington the Negro, as has been noted, wielded little political power. But some Negroes did receive small-sized appointive plums from the Republican party. And more likely than otherwise a Negro who landed a federal appointment had very probably first been handpicked for it by "Booker T." A Negro who got an important letter from Washington, D.C., invariably owed his good fortune to something that had been done by the Washington from Tuskegee. No Negro ever equaled Washington in influencing the political patronage involved in naming Negroes to federal posts.

Washington had strong contacts at the White House,

three successive Republican occupants holding him in high regard. At his request, President William McKinley journeyed from Atlanta to Tuskegee in December 1899, and in his address in the chapel spoke glowingly of his host's "genius and perseverance." President William H. Taft, speaking on behalf of Hampton Institute at Carnegie Hall in February 1910, stated that a race that produced a Booker T. Washington should feel that it could "do miracles." And President Theodore Roosevelt, in a letter to Owen Wister in April 1916, said that he did not "know a white man of the South who is as good a man as Booker Washington today." Washington had dined at the White House in October 1901, but the invitation had been extended on a sudden impulse while he was making a visit to discuss race problems. Roosevelt never repeated the invitation, for he was somewhat dismayed at the widespread criticism by white southerners, who felt that a Negro dining at the White House, even a Booker T. Washington, was a studied insult to them and their traditions.

The dinner episode did not affect Washington's popularity with the President. "I enclose you a list of the principal Negro appointments, and you might ask Booker T. Washington as to their character," wrote Roosevelt to henchman Lawrence Fraser Abbott. But most Negro appointments originated with Washington rather than with the White House. Federal appointments over which Washington exercised control included the recorder of deeds for the District of Columbia, register of the Treasury, auditor for the Navy, and several port collectorships. Two of Washington's more prominent recommendations were Robert H. Terrell to a municipal judgeship in the District, and William H. Lewis to the assistant attorney-generalship. In matters relating to the Negro in general, Roosevelt sought Washington's counsel.

Washington also worked in an unpublicized way to

201

undermine such practices as segregation in railroad accommodations and discrimination against Negroes as jurors in court cases. But anything Washington did in protest against "Jim Crow" was almost completely overshadowed by his statements and actions that seemed to please, if not appease, the white people.

For it cannot be denied that Washington outwardly seemed to be the soul of conciliation, of apparent acquiescence to the subordinate place of the Negro. He seemed to view things from the point of view of the whites, especially when he delivered himself of such placatory remarks as: "The old soil of Virginia draws no color line. The sun draws no color line. The rain draws no color line." Because he wore so ingratiating a mask, Washington was considered by many Negroes as a "white man's Negro," an "Uncle Tom." By 1904 these critics had found a leader who dared to challenge the formidable Booker T.

William Edward Burghardt DuBois was cast in a different mold from Washington and, indeed, from almost every other Negro. Both his ethnic and educational backgrounds were rich. His ancestry was a mixture of Negro, French, Dutch, and Indian ("Thank God, no Anglo-Saxon," he added). Unlike others who wielded influence in Negro circles, he was a bookish man, destined to make his mark almost wholly in the realm of ideas. He studied at Fisk University and the University of Berlin. He received three degrees from Harvard, becoming in 1895 the first Negro ever to receive a Ph.D. His doctoral dissertation, *The Suppression of the African Slave Trade,* became the first published work in the Harvard Historical Studies.

Possessed with intellectual interests broader than the field of history, DuBois was a pioneer in the sociological study of the Negro. His thrusting mind ranged beyond the social sciences, however; on his twenty-fifth birthday, in 1893, he had announced his plans "to make a name in science, to make a name in literature, and thus to raise my race."

Impressed by the scholarly attainments of DuBois, Washington had at first sought to enlist him as a lieutenant, but DuBois's ambition and abilities, plus his haughtiness, made him unsuitable as a subordinate. Possibly it was this effort to assume leadership among Negroes that led DuBois to attack Washington's policies. But conviction also played a role, for by 1903 he had come to the conclusion that Washington was "leading the way backward."

DuBois sounded his challenge in *The Souls of Black Folk,* a collection of essays. In one, titled "Of Mr. Booker T. Washington and Others" and written in a prose style more ornamental than Washington's but no less moving, DuBois charged that the Washington program was a tacit acceptance of the alleged inferiority of the Negro. As he saw it, Washington was asking the Negroes to give up political action and civil rights agitation and instead to "concentrate all their energies on industrial education, the accumulation of wealth, and the conciliation of the South."

DuBois also charged Washington with being hostile to Negro liberal arts colleges and their graduates. DuBois had a high regard for degree-bearing Negroes like himself, designating them as "The Talented Tenth" who would furnish the leaven for the rise of the race. College-trained men and women, almost as if in response to DuBois's expectations, began to form Greek-letter societies, a total of six coming into existence in the ten years after 1904. College-trained Negroes had a more direct response to DuBois's esteem for them: many of them joined him in the anti-Washington movement. This was particularly true of those who had been graduated from northern colleges—men like the

uncompromising editor of the *Boston Guardian,* William
Monroe Trotter, a college mate of DuBois at Harvard.

In the summer of 1905 DuBois officially launched his
own movement at a meeting held at Niagara Falls, Canada,
which was attended by twenty-nine members of the Talented Tenth from thirteen states and the District of Columbia. Avoiding any open criticism of Booker T. Washington,
the conferees drew up a manifesto which called for freedom
of speech and of the press, the abolition of discrimination
based on race or color, and a recognition of the principles of
human brotherhood. The delegates proclaimed that until
they got the rights belonging to freeborn Americans, they
would never cease to protest "and to assail the ears of America with the story of its shameful deeds toward us."

Basically the men at Niagara were asking for nothing
new. The combating of injustice and "Jim Crow" had been
the goals of the Afro-American National League, an all-
Negro movement organized in Chicago in 1890, the brainchild of T. Thomas Fortune, the ablest Negro editor of his
day. But at its meeting in Knoxville the following year,
attendance was sparse, and by the summer of 1893 the
League was defunct, its plans too grandiose for its meager
resources.

The men who met at Niagara hoped for a better fate.
With DuBois as chief executive officer, they held annual
meetings, choosing such historic freedom spots as Harpers
Ferry and Boston's Faneuil Hall. The parent group managed to form some thirty branches, whose activities varied.
The branch in Baltimore reported that it had worked effectively to prevent the city's Negroes from losing the ballot,
the Illinois chapter protested the opening of *The Clansman*
at a Chicago theater, and the Massachusetts chapter urged
the state legislature to withhold any appropriation to the

Jamestown Exposition unless its sponsors guaranteed that all comers would be treated alike.

Aside from these few scattered victories on the local level, however, the Niagara Movement fell far short of its early hopes. Its numbers remained very small; a white member was a rarity, and the movement received almost no support from the Negro masses. Indeed, its leaders, particularly DuBois himself, seemed to be uncomfortable in the presence of the rank and file. The Niagara Movement was desperately poor, whites with money taking their cues from Booker T. Washington, who was bent on scuttling the organization. In 1910, after five fitful years, the Movement quietly passed off the scene.

But it had not been without some success in bringing to the forefront the grievances of the Negro. And it served as a forerunner of the National Association for the Advancement of Colored People, whose foundations it helped to lay. The two kindred groups—the Niagara Movement and the N.A.A.C.P.—had a binding tie, W. E. B. DuBois, who was to be almost as dominant a figure in one as he had been in the other.

On the centennial of the birth of Abraham Lincoln, February 12, 1909, the grandson of William Lloyd Garrison, Oswald Garrison Villard, wrote a call urging all believers in democracy to join in a national conference for "the renewal of the struggle for civil and political liberty." Among the fifty-three signers were social worker Jane Addams, president of Mt. Holyoke College Mary E. Woolley, Rabbi Stephen S. Wise, and the Reverend John Haynes Holmes. Negro signers, in addition to DuBois, were Ida Wells Barnett, the Reverend Francis J. Grimké, and Bishop Alexander Walters. In response to the call, two meetings were held in New York. Out of them emerged the National Association for the Advancement of Colored People.

The basic aim of the new organization was to wipe out discrimination in American public life, or, in its own words, "to make 11,000,000 Americans physically free from peonage, mentally free from ignorance, politically free from disfranchisement, and socially free from insult." Control of the organization was vested in an interracial board of directors, which appointed the paid, administrative staff. Like other reform agencies, the N.A.A.C.P. was designed to operate through state and local branches.

With one exception, the first national officers of the organization were well-known whites, and to them much of the early success of the movement can be credited. The president was Moorfield Storey of Massachusetts, who gave generously of his great legal talents in Supreme Court cases involving Negroes. Another national officer of equal zeal was the disbursing treasurer, Oswald Garrison Villard, biographer of John Brown and the crusading editor of the *New York Evening Post*.

DuBois was the only Negro on the first roster of national officers. He was named director of publications and research, but he was a host in himself. Hoping to edit a magazine of news and opinion, he launched the publication of the *Crisis* in 1910. Although this monthly was the official organ of the Association, DuBois ran it almost as a personal journal. Fortunately for his editorship, the *Crisis* proved to be a success almost from the first issue, and by 1914 it had a monthly paid circulation of 31,450.

During their first years the *Crisis* and the parent organization had to devote much attention to an unexpected adversary—the Woodrow Wilson Administration. As the candidate of the Democratic party in 1912, Wilson had run for the presidency as an advocate of what he termed the

"New Freedom." In an America that was approaching the climax of ten years of reform agitation, Wilson's eloquent appeals to justice and his pledge to curb monopolies and destroy privilege gave hope to many, including thousands of Negroes. In his campaign he had told Bishop Walters, president of the recently formed National Colored Democratic League, that Negroes could count on him for "absolute fair dealing." Many Negroes wanted to believe in Wilson, especially since the party of Lincoln appeared to be more indifferent to them than ever before. (Some influential Republicans, the "lily-whites," had espoused a policy of purging the party of its southern Negro officeholders and stalwarts in order to win white support in the South.) With such considerations in mind, many colored voters cast their votes for Wilson.

A tragic disappointment awaited them. Within a few months after his inauguration, it had become evident that members of Wilson's cabinet were quietly but effectively establishing the color line in their departments. Particularly in the Post Office and the Treasury, in both of which Negroes were numerous, office spaces in these departments began to be segregated or screened off, as were lunchrooms and restrooms. Soon the few good jobs traditionally held by Negroes, such as Register of the Treasury and representatives to Haiti and Liberia, were assigned to whites. Moreover, in May 1914 the Civil Service began to require photographs of persons taking examinations (the stated purpose being to prevent impersonation)—a practice which, added to the customary one of permitting an appointing officer to make his own choice among the three top applicants, tended to increase the incidence of racial discrimination. And in the South, officials of the Post Office and Treasury showed little hesitancy in dismissing or downgrading colored employees.

Wilson was quite aware of the actions taken by his subordinates. Indeed, he approved of segregation, holding the typical white Virginian's viewpoint that it was beneficial to both races. Other considerations also guided his behavior; he was preoccupied with pushing through a series of domestic reforms for which he needed the support of congressmen from the South. In Wilson's scheme of things the Negro problem presented no special urgency. Unlike the money trust, it could wait.

But it could not be ignored, even by as busy a man as the President. The N.A.A.C.P. saw to that. In May 1913, on behalf of the Association, Villard asked Wilson to appoint a National Race Commission to inquire into the status of the Negro. Wilson considered the idea but decided in the negative, though he did invite Villard, a hitherto stanch political supporter, to the White House for a heart-to-heart talk. Somewhat sorrowfully, according to Villard, the President said that he saw no solution to the Negro problem: "It will take a very big man to solve this thing."

In protest against federal "Jim Crow," the N.A.A.C.P. sponsored a series of mass meetings in northern cities, with addresses by Villard and John Haynes Holmes, among others. The Association also voiced its protest through petitions, collecting signatures of whites and Negroes to be sent to the White House. The largest of the petitions was one bearing 20,000 names which was delivered to Wilson in person on November 6, 1913, by a delegation of six Negroes headed by William Monroe Trotter. The *Crisis* vigorously joined in the hue and cry, although at first DuBois was a bit red-faced, having supported Wilson for the presidency.

In opposing federal discrimination, the N.A.A.C.P. reflected a widespread sentiment among Negroes. With rare unanimity they condemned the Wilson Administration. At its convention in 1913 the National Negro Press Association, representing 126 newspapers, sent a strong protest to the President. No occupant of the White House ever received so many private letters of protest from Negroes. White groups were not silent, many church organizations passing resolutions protesting federal "Jim Crow" policies and the efforts of some southern congressmen to push legislation in support of such policies.

The full-scale attack on segregation in government jobs was not without its effect. Early in 1914 the Treasury Department began to abandon its discriminatory policies, almost as quietly as it had initiated them. Other federal departments were slower to root out prejudices, but the advocates of segregationalist practices no longer dominated the thinking of the Wilson Administration.

To Negroes the fight against "Jim Crow" in the federal government brought with it an increased sense of racial solidarity and a keener interest in national affairs, sentiments that would be deepened by America's entry into World War I in April 1917.

During the fifty years following the Civil War, America's attention had been riveted on domestic problems. Foreign affairs had been a major concern only during the brief interlude of less than four months in 1898 when the United States went to war with Spain. Although this conflict stirred America less deeply than any other foreign war, it spelled a farewell to her traditional policy of isolation and brought new peoples, many of them nonwhites, under her flag.

When the war broke out, there were four Negro units in the regular army—the Twenty-Fourth and Twenty-Fifth Infantry and the Ninth and Tenth Cavalry. Retained after the Civil War, when other Negro regiments had been disbanded, these four units had seen action against the Indian tribes in the West. These "black regulars" formed a portion of the expeditionary force of 15,000 that landed in Cuba late in June 1898.

The Spanish-American War was a popular one in the United States, and the Army had no problem in securing volunteers. But Negro civilians who wished to enlist had a problem: since they were not members of the National Guard, they were not eligible for summons to the Army. To satisfy the clamor of the Negroes, Congress passed an act authorizing the formation of ten colored regiments. Only four such units were organized, however, for Negroes resented the War Department stipulation that officers above the grade of second lieutenant be white. Rather than join these national regiments, many Negroes enlisted in the troops recruited by the states, in which there was no ban on Negro officers (except in Alabama). Each of eight states recruited a regiment that was wholly or partly Negro.

Only the Negro regiments in the regular army saw battle service. These four units took part in much of the heavy fighting of the short war, particularly at the outposts to Santiago. They behaved well in the celebrated charge up San Juan Hill. In the confusion and disorder of the charge, white Frank Knox had become separated from his regiment, but, as he wrote, "I joined a troop of the Tenth Cavalry, colored, and for a time fought with them shoulder to shoulder, and in justice to the colored race I must say I never saw braver men anywhere. Some of those who rushed up the hill will live in my memory forever." The first lieutenant of the Tenth Cavalry, John J. Pershing, felt that the storming of San Juan Hill had forged a deeper bond of unity between the victors, white and Negro regiments showing that they were "unmindful of race or color" in the dedication to their common duty as Americans.

The naval service had its Negro component. When the battleship *Maine* was sunk in the Havana harbor—an event which helped to bring on the war—twenty-two Negro sailors lost their lives in the explosion. Some 2,000 Negroes, nearly 10 per cent of the total forces, were enlisted in the wartime Navy. As a rule, they served in menial capacities, with few opportunities to win individual notice. Elijah B. Tunnell was an exception: a Baltimore clergyman who enlisted as a cabin cook on the torpedo boat *Winslow,* he left the galley and came on deck to take a more direct part in the action and was killed some minutes later by a bursting shell.

If the Negro did not expect that the war would improve his lot, he certainly did not think it would be to his disadvantage. But in one sense it was, for it brought under American control hundreds of thousands of nonwhites, notably those in the Philippines. The United States found it necessary, at the outset at least, to govern these peoples without their consent. As a justification for this denial of the democratic principle, some influential Americans—congressmen, newspaper editors, and high-ranking military officers—put the theories of racial inferiority to a new use, applying them to the overseas peoples who had recently come under the "stars and stripes." The United States had entered the war in order to free Spain's colonies, and this had been accomplished. But another of the war's fruits was America's increased devotion to the fetish of racialism—that men are inherently separated into greater and lesser breeds.

When the United States declared war on Germany in April 1917, some 20,000 Negro fighting men were available. Half of these were members of the regular army; the other half were the Negro regiments of the national guards of the several states. These two groups were quickly brought to combat strength, and then the War Department faced a problem: What should be done with the young Negroes who were coming to the recruitment centers?

As might be expected, the Negro had shared fully in the general burst of patriotism brought on by the declaration of war. Negroes took great pride in the fact that the District of Columbia National Guard, under the command of colored officer Major James E. Walker, had been mustered in to protect the nation's capital city, taking over the assignment on March 25, twelve days before the war. This unit was not inexperienced, having been sent to the Mexican border when trouble threatened in 1916.

Negroes of military service age quickly rushed to the colors after the declaration of war, the lure of the uniform exercising its customary potency. Negro college students left their classrooms to answer the call, and the American Negro Loyal Legion sent word to Washington that it could raise 10,000 volunteers on short notice. Army officials were not quite prepared for such a Negro eagerness to enlist, and, after a few weeks of uncertainty, the War Department issued an order to halt the recruitment of colored volunteers. As barbershop proprietor George Myers wryly told Vice-President Thomas R. Marshall, "It looked as if the Negro, like a burglar, would have to break into this war as he did the others."

Myers was right: the Negro was not to be bypassed for long. For if the volunteer service were closed to him, the draft system proved to be an effective equalizer. The Selective Service Act of May 1917, which required all men between the ages of 21 and 30 to register for the draft, was not discriminatory in itself, but its administration was in the hands of local draft boards, on which Negroes did not serve. Boards in the South invariably tended to call up a higher proportion of Negroes than of whites. Of all the Negroes registered in the draft, 31.74 per cent were called to arms, whereas only 26.84 per cent whites were. Of the more than one-third of a million Negroes summoned to military service, many thousands from the South would have been placed in the excepted or deferred classes had it not been for their color.

If most white southerners favored the drafting of the Negro, they were opposed to his receiving basic training in their communities. Many feared that training camps for Negroes might lead to trouble, and, indeed, there were unpleasant incidents. In Manhattanville, Kansas, a Negro sergeant was refused admission to a theater. The strong protests of his colored regimental mates and those of the Negro press forced General C. C. Ballou to have the theater owner fined. But Ballou also issued a strong order to the Negro troops directing them to refrain from any act that would cause "the Color Question" to be raised. "Attend quietly and faithfully to your duties," ran his order, "and don't go where your presence is not desired." A more serious incident took place at Spartansburg, South Carolina, when Noble Sissle was roughly handled for not removing his hat when he went into a hotel lobby to buy a newspaper. Sissle's enraged army mates, white and colored, were prevented from striking back by a hastily determined directive from the War Department, ordering the Negro unit to break camp and sail for France. A riot, the most tragic of the southern camp embroilments, occurred in Houston, Texas, when an unsuccessful attempt by a group of Negro soldiers to board a street car reserved for whites led to a street fight in which twelve civilians were killed. Severe punishments were given to the soldiers, thirteen receiving the death penalty and fourteen being sentenced to life imprisonment.

After their basic training camp the majority of Negroes were placed in noncombatant units—labor battalions and service regiments. Army officials believed that the Negro was peculiarly fitted for manual work because of his familiarity with it and because of his happy-go-lucky disposition. The Navy followed a similar practice of assigning its 5,300 Negroes to jobs that required more brawn than skill—mess-men, water tenders, gunner's mates, and coal passers. Negroes who could not read and write were hardly in a position to complain about being assigned to service and menial occupations, but such assignments were particularly galling to Negroes with academic degrees and to those who had left college in order to enlist.

Negroes with an education beyond that of high school felt that they should be trained as officers. Army officials, however, were not enthusiastic about commissioning colored men. Indeed, at the outbreak of the war there was only one Negro graduate of West Point, Charles Young, and he was only the third of his color to have finished at the Academy.

At the outbreak of the war, Congress authorized the establishment of fourteen training camps for white officers, and none for colored. Negroes protested this exclusion, forming a Central Committee of Negro College Men, which held conferences with Army officials and paid visits to members of Congress. The effort to make officer training available to Negroes received the strong support of Joel E. Spingarn, a national officer of the N.A.A.C.P., who broached the subject to General Leonard Wood and received his backing.

Finally the War Department authorized, on May 19, 1917, a reserve officers' training camp for colored men. The camp was established at Fort Des Moines, Iowa, and on June 15 the candidates began their training. Four months later, to the day, 639 Negroes became officers in the Army. As they came forward for the bestowal of commissions, many of them were moved, sensing something of the event's importance in revolutionizing Army policy.

The Fort Des Moines trainees comprised about one-half

of the total number of Negroes commissioned during the war. The quota of Negro officers was kept small. For example, despite a great shortage of physicians, the medical corps had only 100 Negroes at the close of the war. Many Negro physicians were drafted as privates, a practice which drew a sharp criticism from the National Medical Association, a colored group with a membership of 5,000, at its annual meeting in Richmond in August 1918.

One disappointed Negro seeker of a commission based his plea less on his qualifications than on his family. Newspaperman Ralph W. Tyler, in a letter to the Special Assistant to the Secretary of War, dated October 8, 1917, pointed out that in every one of America's wars, his family had been represented—his brother in the Spanish-American War, his father in the Civil War, his grandfather in the Mexican War, his great-grandfather in the War of 1812, and his great-great-grandfather in the Revolutionary War. "All served as privates," wrote Tyler. "The family, I think, has earned a commission by this time."

Negroes who received commissions were, on the whole, men of intelligence and ability. They were often called upon to demonstrate a special kind of fortitude. White privates and lower-ranking officers did not always salute them. The attitude of some white superiors was lukewarm; they honestly believed that Negro officer training was an experiment bound to fail.

Some superiors were supercilious. Y.M.C.A. worker Charles H. Williams told of a colonel who met a Negro captain whose face seemed familiar:

> "Haven't I seen you somewhere?" he asked. "Yes, sir," replied the man, "I was with you on the border; Captain French is my name, sir." "Oh, I do remember,"

said the colonel, "you are Sergeant French." "No, sir, I am Captain French." "Well," said the colonel as he walked away, "if I forget and call you Sergeant, don't mind."

* Did the Negro officer and combat soldier maintain high morale despite the many evidences of color discrimination? Such a question admits no ready answer. Undoubtedly thousands of Negro soldiers were bitter about their treatment, and hundreds sent complaining letters to Secretary of War Newton D. Baker and, after October 5, 1917, to Emmett J. Scott, who had been appointed as his special assistant in matters affecting Negroes. "To catalogue or specify all of the complaints that have come to the War Department," wrote Scott, "would be an almost endless task." But to grumble was part of the ritual of the boys in khaki, black or white. Moreover, to the Negro soldier discrimination was nothing out of the ordinary, for he had been a Negro prior to becoming a soldier.

In the infrequent instances in which Negroes performed poorly in combat, a number of special factors could be held responsible. Negro troops were not always placed under competent men; poor performance by high-ranking officers was tolerated in Negro troops as it would not have been elsewhere. Many commanders simply assumed that Negro officers and soldiers would be failures even before they had been tested. General Robert L. Bullard, for example, was convinced that Negroes, being slothful and superstitious, were emotionally unsuited for war. Some commanders issued orders forbidding Negro soldiers from mingling with the French people at social affairs, often subtly spreading the word that the Negro was vicious and depraved. Such attitudes would certainly not tend to raise the military efficiency of the Negro troops in his command.

The two Negro combat divisions were organized in ways that hardly made for esprit de corps. The Ninety-Second Division was late in getting to France because, unlike any other division that went overseas, it had no cantonment of its own. The fact that its various units had been trained in seven different camps is a valid explanation for the small difficulties it encountered during the early weeks of fighting. What was to have been the other Negro division—the Ninety-Third—never really materialized. One of its regiments arrived in France in December 1917 and the other three landed in April 1918, but all four were brigaded with the French troops.

Whatever their degree of discontent or resentment, the Negro troops did their job. The Ninety-Second Division arrived in France in June 1918 and seven weeks later moved to the front, where they remained until the end of the war, under enemy fire most of the time. The Division's artillery brigade became notable for its accuracy, and its engineer regiment did front-line work in the Meuse-Argonne offensive. "See It Through" was the regimental motto of the 367th Infantry. In the drive to Metz, the last action of the war, this regiment remained on the offensive until the Germans retreated. "This Division is one of the best in the A.E.F.," said General Pershing at Le Mans as the Ninety-Second passed in review before leaving France.

The Ninety-Third Division likewise made a good record, winning high praise from French commanders. The 371st Infantry was cited by Marshal Pétain as exhibiting the best qualities of bravery and audacity. The 372nd Regiment, brigaded throughout its service to the "Red Hand" Division of the French Army, was cited by Vice-Admiral Moreau for having shown "the finest qualities of bravery and daring exploits." The 370th Infantry won twenty-one American Distinguished Service Crosses and sixty-eight French War

Crosses. The entire 369th Infantry, first of the Negro troops to see action, won the Croix de Guerre for gallantry in battle; under continuous fire for a record-breaking period of 191 days, this regiment was given the honor of leading the Allied armies to the Rhine a week after the signing of the Armistice. The 369th could boast two soldiers, Henry Johnson and Needham Roberts, who performed one of the most sensational exploits of the war. While on sentry duty at a small outpost on May 14, 1918, these two privates were attacked by a party of from twelve to twenty Germans. Fighting back, although badly wounded, Johnson and Needham routed their attackers. For this feat the two Negroes were awarded the Croix de Guerre.

Headline fame was most unlikely to come to over two-thirds of the Negro troops because they were in the service of supply rather than combat units. But even though their jobs were backbreaking and humdrum, the labor battalions were indispensable. Someone had to get the fighting men to the front and then to furnish them with food, supplies, and ammunition. Negro worker-soldiers generally discharged their assignments in good spirits. The morale of the stevedore units seemed to be particularly high. Visitors at their camps were impressed by the rapidity with which they worked. One of these admiring visitors, Ella Wheeler Wilcox, wrote a poem in their honor, containing the lines:

> We are the Army of Stevedores, and work as we must
>   and may,
> The Cross of Honor will never be ours to proudly wear
>   away.
> But the men at the front could not be there
> And the battles could not be won,
> If the Stevedores stopped in their dull routine,
> And left their work undone.

Possibly one of the reasons for the relatively good morale among colored troops was the attitude of the Negro on the home front. Almost in spite of their strong sense of realism, Negroes were impressed by the wartime slogans calling for the self-determination of all peoples in a world made safe for democracy. Negroes believed, as had their forebears, that by taking part in the war they would have additional grounds for demanding better treatment after it was over.

Spurred by such hopes, Negro leaders and opinion makers gave full support to the war effort. Charles H. Wesley, educational secretary of the Army Y.M.C.A. at Camp Meade, wrote that Negroes were fighting "in order that innate racial superiority as championed by the Germans and as practiced by other races and groups may die a deserving death." The influential W. E. B. DuBois, in a *Crisis* editorial, urged Negroes to forget their special grievances and close ranks, shoulder to shoulder, with their white fellow citizens. The DuBois olive branch drew some fire, the *Pittsburgh Courier* pointing out that no other group with special grievances was being asked to forget them. Moreover, to do so was impossible: "The lyncher won't let us. The Jim-Crower won't let us."

Unquestionably all was not rosy in race relations on the home front. During a particularly distressing outburst of violence that took place at East St. Louis, Illinois, in July 1917, some forty Negroes and eight whites lost their lives. At a dramatic protest held in New York 5,000 Negroes with banners and muffled drums marched down Fifth Avenue in a silent parade.

But, in the main, Negroes preferred to follow the advice of DuBois. On an August Sunday in 1919, Madame C. J. Walker invited 100 prominent guests, white and colored, to Villa Lewaro, her estate on the Hudson, in order to confer about the Negro's role in the war. The assembled guests came to the conclusion that the Negro should continue to be loyal. Such a conclusion was predictable, and equally as predictable was the Negro's faith in America: "Would to God that all people were as loyal as mine," wrote George Myers to James Ford Rhodes on May 21, 1918.

In support of the war, Negroes formed circles for the relief of soldiers and their families. Various cities had their thrift clubs; the entire membership of the Philadelphia Thrift Club reported itself as having bought as many war bonds and savings stamps as possible. A Negro bank, Mutual Savings of Portsmouth, Virginia, was awarded first place among the banks of the country in the Third Liberty Loan Drive, having oversubscribed its quota nineteen times. Many individual Negroes held important positions on the home front: Alice Dunbar Nelson was a field representative of the Women's Committee of the Council of National Defense, and William S. Scarborough, president of Wilberforce, served as a member of the Ohio Council of National Defense, a sort of war cabinet of the governor.

The national government took a few steps to boost Negro morale. Emmett Scott's appointment as special assistant to the Secretary of War was meant to allay unrest among Negroes. At the time of his appointment, Scott was Secretary of Tuskegee Institute and had, in 1909, been a member of an American commission to Liberia. Scott proved to be a hard worker with administrative ability, though, as a former confidential secretary of Booker T. Washington, he was given to seeing the sunny side of things. After visiting an army camp, he generally reported that the men were enthusiastic and overjoyed to be serving their country; when he attended a mass meeting of civilians, he was sure to discover that cheerfulness and patriotism were the dominant sentiments.

Another government appointment was that of Ralph W. Tyler as a war correspondent to report news of interest to Negroes. This step was taken as a result of strong urging by the Negro press. The only Negro war correspondent accredited by the Committee on Information, Tyler's clear style and instinct for interesting items made him a good newspaperman. His reports came first to the Committee on Information, which turned them over to Emmett Scott for clearance, editing, and circulation. The Committee may not have cared for some of the topics selected by Tyler, but they knew Scott would strike out such items as the alleged discrimination against Negroes by the Y.M.C.A. and reports of friendly conversations between Negro soldiers and French housewives.

The last morale-building appointment by the government was that of Robert Russa Moton, the successor of Booker T. Washington at Tuskegee, who was to go to France and speak to Negro troops. Moton had the ear of the Wilson Administration: it was upon his recommendation that Scott got his appointment. In April 1918 Moton had headed a committee of Negroes who visited the White House on behalf of Liberia, a fruitful call resulting in a $5,000,000 loan to the Negro republic.

Moton's mission officially was that of "doing morale work among colored troops." But the appointment came two weeks after the war had ended, and it seemed designed primarily to impress upon Negro troops the necessity for good behavior. With the war's tensions removed, Negro soldiers might, it was feared, tend to overrelax.

Moton's trip was not a complete success. He did investigate some of the charges against individual soldiers unjustly accused of crime, and he did tell the white troops that upon their return home they had a responsibility to work for fair play for colored Americans. But in addressing Negro troops, he hardly struck a morale-building note. Sounding much like Booker T. Washington, Moton told the colored soldiers that as soon as they returned to America they should find a job and get to work. Save your money, he admonished, get hold of a piece of land, marry and settle down.

However sensible, this kind of talk seemed to admonish the Negro to behave as though the war had never taken place, as though race relations at home had not changed, and would not change. This the men who had borne arms did not wish to believe, and during the first days of their return from Europe, it did seem as if their hopes for a better America were sound. They received a tumultuous welcome. When the 369th marched through the streets of New York, the dense crowds cheered and waved flags, and high-ranking state and city officials were present on the reviewing stands. When the returning 370th arrived in Chicago, offices and stores were closed for the day. In full war equipment the regiment paraded down Michigan Avenue, bells and whistles sounding.

Some of the more quiet admirers of the Negroes in khaki expressed their sentiments in verse, among them Charles S. Jones:

> Back from their days of danger daring,
> Over the leagues of foam,
> Back from the scenes of their far wayfaring
> Our dusky boys come home.

Among the spectators who lined Fifth Avenue for the homecoming parade of New York's 369th Infantry was the editor of *The Outlook*. The sight of the marching Negroes put him in a reflective mood: "The services which these representatives of their race have rendered in the war to make the world safe for democracy ought to make forever secure for the race in this their native land their right to life, liberty, and the pursuit of happiness."

Certainly this was the way the Negro saw it, too.

8

From "Normalcy" to New Deal (1920–1940)

IN THE FIRST presidential election held after World War I, the Republican candidate, Warren G. Harding, campaigned on a platform calling for a return to "normalcy," a word he had coined. Harding meant that the country needed a rest from international involvements and from domestic reforms, a return to the good old days. The decisive victory won at the polls by Republican officeseekers seemed to prove that Harding had correctly appraised the mood of the voters.

In the elections of 1920 the vote of the Negro went almost solidly to the Republicans. This did not mean, however, that Negroes had any desire to return to "normalcy" in their status. They wanted to play a new role in the America that emerged from the war, not to return to the old one. But this would not prove easy.

Postwar America tended to swing to the right. The wartime emotions of group loyalty and hatred found an outlet in the persecution of those persons or parties held to be un-American. The spirit of intolerance took hold of many, particularly those who were frightened, or rural-minded, or who feared a changing America. The strong dislike for socialists frequently spilled over to include those who espoused the cause of the Negro.

Of all the expressions of postwar intolerance, the one that affected the Negro most was the rebirth of the Ku Klux Klan. The new Klan had been organized late in November 1915 near Atlanta, Georgia, by William J. Simmons. Until the end of the war, its numbers were small, but it then grew rapidly, until it had a membership of 100,000 by the end of 1919. The new Klan, unlike the old, did not confine its activities to the South but operated from Maine to California. Again unlike the old Klan, it was opposed to Orientals, Jews, Catholics, radicals, and immigrants as well as Negroes.

A person who incurred the hostility of the Klan would wake up one night to find a fiery cross burning on his lawn, and a day or so later he would receive a warning to leave the community. If such measures failed, sterner ones were employed (including, in extreme cases, stringing the victim from a tree). The officers of the Klan usually denied that the organization resorted to terror, but its secrecy and its use of masks and disguises in dress were open invitations to lawlessness.

For a few years in the mid-twenties, the Klan was powerful. Its revenues, coming primarily from the initiation fees and dues of more than 4,000,000 members, made it a wealthy organization, and one to be reckoned with in state and national elections. In 1925, with the government's permission, it paraded in the nation's capital, marching down Pennsylvania Avenue and past the White House. But its decline was soon hastened by the uncovering of extensive fraud by high-ranking officials. The Klan left its impress, however: its spirit and methods underlaid the race violence that erupted in the cities of the North immediately after the war.

In the year following World War I, the United States witnessed a series of race riots unprecedented in numbers and in violence. Of the more than twenty such disturbances that broke out in 1919 in cities from Omaha, Nebraska, to Longview, Texas, the most serious outbreak took place in Chicago. The incident that touched off the riot was the death of a Negro boy at a Lake Michigan beach in late July. Drifting on his home-made raft into a section of the beach customarily used only by whites, he had been met by a shower of stones and had fallen into the water and drowned. Throughout the city rumors inflaming both white and colored were fanned by animosities already smoldering. Mobs soon formed, roaming the streets on the night of the beach incident and for the next two days. Eventually the militia had to be called out. When order was restored, the dead numbered thirty-eight and the wounded totaled 537. The burning and destruction of property left hundreds of families homeless.

A shocked country urged Congress to take action. For the Chicago riot, like that in Washington itself a few weeks before, revealed that the Negroes had fought back with a new intensity, thereby making such outbreaks more costly than ever in lives and property. And thoughtful Americans were sobered by President Wilson's comment that in both the Washington and Chicago outbreaks "the white race was the aggressor" and that the stain cast "upon every one of the majority group in our land" was "the more censurable

because our Negro troops are but just back from no little
share in carrying our cause and our flag to victory."

The causes of the race riots were many, among them the
competition of whites and Negroes for jobs and the moving
of Negroes into neighborhoods hitherto occupied only by
whites. In the cities of the North the Negro's quest for jobs
and housing had become acute because the colored population had greatly increased. The North and West had over
470,000 more Negroes in 1920 than they had in 1910, the
migration resulting mainly from the economic dislocations
of World War I.

Since the war brought a halt to foreign immigration,
the pool of unskilled laborers and domestic servants that
had been coming from Europe by the boatloads shrunk. The
war also took out of the factories and put into khaki uniform
hundreds of thousands of skilled and semiskilled workers,
though the booming war industries demanded more workers than ever. Desperately in need of laborers, manufacturing companies turned to women and to Negroes. They sent
labor agents into the South, where the Negroes readily
responded to offers of a good job and free transportation.
Soon there was a wholesale migration of Negro workers
from the South, and they were followed by their clergymen
and physicians.

The Negro migration was so rapid and large that it created a problem for southern planters and manufacturers,
especially since their white laborers were also moving away.
Serious efforts were made to halt or slow down the departure of the Negroes. Laws were passed imposing heavy fines
on labor agents. At some railroad stations Negroes could not
buy tickets to the North. As in an earlier migratory movement, Negroes were told that those who left the South were

starving and freezing. Hard-hit states like Louisiana and Mississippi sent commissioners to try to lure the Negroes to come back, with all return travel expenses paid. But, as the commissioners found out, the overwhelming majority of Negroes had come North to stay.

To the black migrants, however, life was far from easy. After the intoxication of being out of the South wore off, the newcomers found that the sprawling, impersonal cities of the North were not quite the land of promise they had expected. Though they no longer saw "White" and "Colored" signs everywhere, they quickly became aware of segregation in churches and social clubs. The color line took visual form in the existence of a "black belt," a section of the city, characterized by rat-infested houses, poor health and sanitation facilities, high incidence of crime and juvenile delinquency, and policemen too quick with the nightsticks or guns.

Adding to the plight of the black newcomer was the worsening condition of the labor market. During the years following the war employment dwindled rapidly. As government purchases of supplies came to an end, war contracts, and the jobs that went with them, were concluded. The demobilization of 4,500,000 soldiers further glutted the labor supply. Many Negroes were laid off or fired. Those who remained on the payrolls were generally in such traditional occupations as road building, stockyard and longshore work, and railroad maintenance—"hot and heavy operations in the hot and heavy industries."

In domestic service the postwar outlook was not hopeful. The need for servants was lessened by the construction of modern apartments equipped with labor-saving devices. The service jobs that remained were now sought by whites who had been displaced by the new machines. Jobs that were once a Negro monopoly were passing into other hands.

In 1923 the management of the Hollenden Hotel in Cleveland informed George A. Myers, who had opened a barber shop in 1888, that upon his retirement, his all-Negro staff of thirty barbers and manicurists would be replaced by whites.

The Negro who had left the South was not disposed to return. But faced with unemployment, job ceilings, and ghetto-like living conditions, he might sometimes have wondered whether the city to which he had come was less a frontier of escape than a new imprisonment.

Out of the postwar disillusionment of the urban Negro and his groping to find a way out emerged the imposing figure of Marcus Garvey. Although he was but one in a long line of Negro dissenters, Garvey had special points of uniqueness. More than any other Negro leader he had a talent for reaching the masses, and his influence extended into both hemispheres. Born in Jamaica, Garvey came to New York in 1916, possessed of a dream of a black empire governed by black men.

A self-dramatizer as well as a man of amazing energy and persuasiveness, Garvey established himself in Harlem and literally catapulted himself into the limelight. Branches of his brainchild, the Universal Negro Improvement Association, mushroomed in Negro urban centers, and his well-edited weekly, the *Negro World,* effectively spread the Garvey gospel. With a sure sense of mass psychology, Garvey utilized plumed hats and cockades, street parades with brass bands playing martial airs, "African Redemption" medals, and the conferring of such titles of nobility as "knight" and "duke." At the height of his influence in the mid-twenties, Garvey had upwards of a million followers.

But the imagination of Negroes was excited by something more than his showmanship, his appeal to their vanity and craving for power. Garvey's simple message—pride in race—served to give meaning to their lives and worth to their personalities. When he told the Negro masses that they should be proud of being black, that the Negroes of Africa had carved a glorious page in history, he gave to them a deepened sense of self-respect and a pride in their historic past. In making the Negro feel that he was a somebody rather than a nobody, Garvey went to the extreme of becoming a black supremacist. In the African Orthodox Church he founded, angels were black and Satan and his imps were white, and the black worshippers could glorify "the Black Man of Sorrows" and the "Black Virgin Mother."

Garvey had no use for light-skinned Negroes: the blacker a person's skin, the better he was; unless he were of unmixed Negro blood, he was not a Negro. Garvey well knew that there were color lines within the color line, that many light-skinned Negroes held themselves aloof from those who were black and brown, to whom they felt superior, and he magnified and exploited the natural resentment of dark Negroes. Since a goodly percentage of Negro intellectuals were light-skinned, Garvey castigated the whole group, calling them liars, thieves, and traitors.

Garvey held that America was a white man's country and that the Negro must found an independent nation in Africa, the ancestral homeland. Styling himself the "Provisional President of Africa," he created a small army, the African Legion. The Back-to-Africa appeal was more lukewarmly received than any of the similar efforts that preceded it. But, though Garvey himself never got to Africa and his movement never transported a single returnee across the Atlantic, his African views gave to his followers a wider view of the world, shaking them out of their provincial outlook. And among Africans themselves, Garvey's name was to be exalted as one who foresaw the day of liberation.

Like all black nationalists, Garvey preached economic

self-sufficiency, contending that Negroes should have their own stores and factories. But in establishing and operating his numerous business enterprises, he followed nobody's advice but his own. He thought of himself as a financial titan, a misconception that proved his undoing. His business ventures were failures, the ill-fated Black Star Line, an all-Negro steamship company, showing a deficit of $500,000 after four years of operation. Brought to trial in 1923 for fraud, Garvey was found guilty and sentenced to five years in the Atlanta Penitentiary. Pardoned in 1927 by President Coolidge, he was deported as an alien. He never regained his former prestige and influence, but died obscurely in London thirteen years later.

Yet he made a lasting impression. When in May 1925, Garvey's star was sinking, a man outside the movement, A. F. Elmes, attested to its pull:

> Let it be observed that no man can stand in one of those teeming Liberty Hall audiences, see one of Garvey's ostentatious parades, hear Garvey's magnetic voice, read his *Negro World,* watch the sweep of his ideas, and then say there is nothing to it.

In 1910 Mrs. Ruth Standish Baldwin, a wealthy white woman, called a conference of the various groups working in the interests of the Negro in the city of New York. Out of this conference came the National League on Urban Conditions among Negroes, later shortened to the National Urban League.

The National Urban League, like the Garvey movement, was designed with the city Negro in mind. But the League was America-centered in program and interracial in personnel. Although its aim was that of improving the living and working conditions of Negroes in cities, it did not consider itself narrowly racial: "Let us work," said Mrs. Baldwin, "not as colored people nor as white people for the narrow benefit of any group alone, but together, as American citizens, for the common good of our common city, our common country." Starting off with a budget of $8,500 for its first year, the League by 1925 had increased this figure to $300,000.

Local branches of the League, numbering fifty-one in 1925, tailored their programs to meet the specific needs of their own communities. But all branches sought to assist newcomers by finding them suitable homes and jobs. At meetings held in the evenings in schoolhouse buildings, branch workers urged Negro workers to make good on the job, to be efficient. The branches urged both local employers to use Negroes in new capacities and young Negroes to train themselves so that when the doors of opportunity swung open they would be ready to go through. Local branches also sought to prevent crime and delinquency, setting up departments for wholesome recreation.

The national office published a monthly magazine, *Opportunity,* and conducted surveys and investigations concerning the Negro. To keep unemployment down, it issued monthly bulletins listing the cities in which jobs were available and those in which they were not. The national office also granted fellowships for the training of social workers. As was their hallmark, the League tried always to operate in a climate of interracial cooperation and good will.

In the postwar South the chief organization working to improve conditions for Negroes was the Commission on Interracial Cooperation. Founded in April 1919 when a small group of whites met in Atlanta, the Commission carried out its work through a network of loosely organized state and local branches composed of leading whites and Negroes. The Commission's aim, to use the language of its able director, Will W. Alexander, was "to make life here in the South richer and more efficient for all the people." While striving to create interracial good will, the Commission called attention to the Negro's needs in education, health, public welfare, police protection, and equal justice.

In the main an educational agency with a gradualist philosophy, the Commission published tracts and pamphlets, many of which described the Negro's contributions to American life, and strove to place such materials in schools, libraries, and legislative halls. With all its resources the Commission fought the Ku Klux Klan, and it waged an equally relentless fight against lynching, operating through its own agency, The Association of Southern Women for the Prevention of Lynching. The Commission's work met with some success in cities and in college and university centers. But its influence was small in the rural South, which, cut off from urban and national impulses, tended to remain in a cultural and social backwash, holding firmly to fixed notions concerning the Negro and his place.

The postwar restlessness of the colored American found expression in the so-called Negro Renaissance, a creative outpouring in literature, art, and music. Though like so much else in Negro life, this phase was part of a more general trend in American letters, the Negro Renaissance was distinctive in two major respects: as an effort to articulate the discontent of the Negro, it was also an evidence of "a renewed race-spirit that consciously and proudly sets itself apart," explained Alain Locke, midwife to the movement as well as its chief chronicler. Negro writers and artists made a deliberate effort to cease aping others and to produce work that might be racial in theme but that would also be universal in depth and appeal. They sought to be writers, not Negro writers. Although their themes would be Negro, they would be fashioned with high technical skill and designed for an audience not exclusively Negro. There would, however, be no catering to whites.

All the writers of the Negro Renaissance agreed on one canon: the use of dialect was taboo. Their objection was not so much to the dialect tradition as to the literary and topical limitations it imposed. In their opinion it was high time to bury a school of Negro expression which abounded in stock characters who were full of grins and grimaces and whose English was quaint and mirth-provoking. The Negro dialect school was not without literary respectability, having included such well-known whites as Joel Chandler Harris of "Uncle Remus" fame and Thomas Nelson Page. Masters at blending humor with pathos, these dialect writers were able craftsmen and at the turn of the century had been widely read. But they generally put a comic mask on the Negro, and what emerged from their pages was a caricature rather than a person.

In its heyday the Page-Harris school had its Negro practitioners, among them Paul Laurence Dunbar, the best-known of all Negro writers. In his poems, short stories, and novels, Dunbar had achieved a lyric utterance unequaled by any previous Negro. He was hailed by American critics, but, to his great disappointment, his dialect output rather than his legitimate English writings had brought him fame. Dunbar's use of dialect had stemmed in part from economic considerations, for Negro writers of his day believed that only by using dialect could they reach the bookbuying public, which was almost wholly a white public.

Disdaining economic considerations and unconcerned about the approval of whites, the Negro writer of the twenties was concerned above all with expressing his own feelings in his own way. In poetry the three foremost Negroes to emerge were Claude McKay, Langston Hughes, and Countee Cullen, each of whom bore comparison with the best of the moderns. McKay became best known for his hymns of social protest ("The Lynching" and "If We Must Die"), but he was also a gifted nature poet who could celebrate the color of a poinsettia seen ten years previously. Langston Hughes, although then barely in his mid-twenties, became a figure of importance in 1926 with the publication of a collection of verses under the title *The Weary Blues.* An experimenter in free verse, he struck a popular note in poems that were often short and had an air of informality. Unlike the outgoing Hughes, Countee Cullen was shy and withdrawn. Holder of a master's degree from Harvard, he revealed a wide acquaintance with the best traditional poetic forms; he was "endowed with a wide range of poetic skills," wrote Margaret Just Butcher, being "equally at ease as a lyricist, an epigrammatist, and a narrative poet."

In the field of the novel the twenties produced Jessie Faucet, Jean Toomer, and Rudolph Fisher, to name only three. In *There Is Confusion,* the first of her four novels, Miss Faucet dealt with problems of the color line, but her characters were respectable members of the educated middle class. "White readers don't expect Negroes to be like this," explained a publisher who had rejected the manuscript. Miss Faucet's themes and characters were akin to those employed by the most able of the earlier Negro novelists, Charles W. Chestnutt, whose five novels, the last of which was published in 1905, realistically depicted the lot of the mulatto.

Jean Toomer's fame rested upon *Cane,* considered by many critics as the single best literary work of the Negro Renaissance. Toomer's prose, like his poetry, touched a deeply human note, although his themes were Negro. Despite its merit, *Cane* had few buyers; a year after it had appeared, it had sold only 500 copies, reported its publisher,

Horace Liveright, in March 1924. Perhaps this was one of the reasons for light-skinned Toomer's withdrawal from Negro society to live with whites. Rudolph Fisher typified the Negro Renaissance, for he wrote of Harlem, then the cultural capital of colored America. In *The Walls of Jericho* he presented a many-sided view of Negro New York and its types.

In drama, as in fiction, the American public was slow in showing any interest in the serious portrayal of Negro life. Budding Negro dramatists like Willis Richardson faced not only white indifference but also the artistic limitations imposed by Negro audiences who, as a rule, did not like dialect, did not like unpleasant endings, and who insisted that all Negro characters must be fine, upstanding persons, barely a cut below the angels. But if the twenties produced no Negro playwright comparable to Cullen in poetry or Toomer in prose, the period did witness the production of a series of Negro problem plays by white dramatists of the calibre of Eugene O'Neill and Paul Green. And the plays of such pioneers gave Negro actors like Charles Gilpin and Paul Robeson unusual opportunities to perform in serious drama.

If the Negro playwright had no ready-made audience, the same could hardly be said of the Negro musician. Those who were interested in serious music might face an uphill fight; the mother of Roland Hayes advised him against a career in voice—"Negroes don't understand good singing," she said, "and white people don't want to hear it from them." But in popular music all avenues were open. This was not surprising, since the Negro himself had been a prime contributor to American popular music.

The Negro of the post–Civil War decades had contributed chanteys, folk ballads, and chain-gang, railroad, and hammer songs. At the turn of the century the work songs of the Negro were modified in subject matter and diverted into the field of entertainment in a new creation known as "ragtime" (music "with a ragged time to it"). The ragtime tunes originated with Negro piano players in the free and easy resort towns along the Mississippi. Such men "did not know any more of the theory of music than they did about the theory of the universe," but their ear for rhythm was impeccable. Out of ragtime soon came a variant known as the "blues," with its own poetic pattern and special note of sadness ("The mail man passed but / He didn't leave no news").

In the decade following World War I ragtime, now further evolved and bearing the name "jazz," came into its own. Its vogue was partly the result of a reaction against the strains and horrors of the war, but it turned out to be far more than a form of emotional release and escape. Expressing something of the restless vigor of the country that gave it birth, jazz struck a popular chord, becoming the musical idiom of America.

At night clubs and cabarets white musicians listened intently to the Negro originators of jazz and then proceeded to form bands of their own. This white movement into the new idiom was climaxed in 1924 when Paul Whiteman gave a concert of "classical" jazz. The interest of serious musicians and composers was aroused. In 1925 the new music won high praise from Leopold Stokowski and from Serge Koussevitzky, then beginning a distinguished career as conductor of the Boston Symphony. The influence of jazz was to spread to Europe, and beyond. "Jazz is on its way to becoming the music of the world," observed the Belgian musicologist Robert Goffin, in 1945. It is the music of freedom, he added, "the great art of democracy."

In the dance, as in music, the influence of the Negro was unmistakable. The nineteenth-century plantation dances were the progenitors of the Negro minstrel show, the first blackface performers patterning their acts on the crooning tunes sung by field hands to the accompaniment of a guitar or banjo and a series of peculiar shuffling dance steps. It is to be noted that not all minstrels were white men in black-face: there were Negro performers, such as James A. Bland, composer of "Oh, Dem Golden Slippers" and "Carry Me Back to Ole Virginny." When the dance patterns of minstrelsy moved to the cities at the turn of the century, they emerged as the cakewalk and "buck and wing" and "stop-time" dances. And after World War I the Negro impulse in the dance led to such innovations as the Charleston and the Black Bottom. "The influence which the Negro has exercised on the art of dancing in this country has been almost absolute," wrote James Weldon Johnson.

The "race-spirit" which infused the creative work of Negro writers and musicians resulted in part from their aware-ness of the historic role Negroes had played in America. In the twenties, as never before, Negroes began to realize that their roots were deep in the land of their birth, and that col-ored men and women had contributed significantly to Amer-ican history and culture. The scholar who did most to construct this new vision of the Negro past was Carter G. Woodson, the father of the scientific study of Negro history.

Trained at Harvard and the Sorbonne, Woodson in 1915 founded the Association for the Study of Negro Life and His-tory, and in the following year he brought out the first issue of *The Journal of Negro History*. The carefully documented articles carried in this quarterly not only became invaluable sources for history scholars and race relations workers but also furnished a mine of information for other students of Negro life and history. The work of Woodson as author, edi-tor, and publisher gave to the Negro a new appraisal of himself: "With the discovery of what the study of Negro life and history reveals for American life and history, old shames and embarrassments are being displaced by new prides," wrote Charles S. Johnson in 1928.

In the same year Alain Locke appraised the fruits of the Negro Renaissance: "We have a general acceptance of the Negro today as a contributor to national culture."

If the postwar years brought forth a new Negro in the arts and letters, this period was also marked by a new Negro independence in political party affiliation. In 1920 the Negroes had supported the Republicans, as had their fathers, but within a span of ten years they were ready to move in a new political direction. This direction was not to the extreme left, despite the wooings of the socialists and the communists.

The two most prominent Negro socialists of the early twenties were A. Philip Randolph and Chandler Owen. The *Messenger,* which they jointly edited and described as a "magazine of scientific socialism," was kept alive for half a dozen years by donations from labor and reformist groups. Despite the zeal and dedication of the editors, their paper and the Socialist Party made little impression upon Negroes. Although the entire Socialist program revolved around the workingman, the Party was able to make no special appeal to the Negro. Viewing the problems of society as primarily economic rather than racial, they saw the Negro primarily as a worker and only incidentally as a Negro. No matter how eloquent, their program was viewed by the Negro as a bit remote from his immediate needs. In the presidential election of 1928 W. E. B. DuBois might announce that he would vote for the Socialist candidate, Norman Thomas, but among Negroes there would be no answering echo.

The failure of the Socialists to win the Negro was carefully studied by the communists. Regarding the Negro as an asset, they felt he could help to spearhead the proletarian revolution in the United States and assist in the liberation of dark-skinned peoples ruled by the imperialist powers. To win Negro support the Communist Party operated on many fronts, devoting most of its efforts to practical measures rather than to indoctrination in Marxist theory.

The Communists sought to organize Negro workers and then to persuade white workers to accept them as equals. Going a step further, they organized the American Negro Labor Congress in 1925, which was designed to bring all Negro trade unionists together in order to strengthen the Party. In that year they also organized the International Labor Defense, a legal arm designed to defend Communists in the courts. The I.L.D. concerned itself particularly with Negro cases, whether or not litigants were Party members.

Another tactic to win Negroes was that of practicing social equality. Communists ate with Negroes, went on outings with them, and lived in the same apartment buildings, all in an effort to make the Negro feel a complete personal acceptance. Still another part of their program was designed to push Negroes to the fore by giving them responsible positions in the Party and running them for high office on the Party ticket in state and national elections.

Despite their strenuous efforts, the Communists made few Negro converts; by 1928 there were, estimates Wilson Record, not more than 200 Negro party members in the United States. Realizing that they must adopt a new line, the American Communists, upon the recommendation of the Sixth World Congress of the Party, launched in 1928 the idea of a separate Negro republic within the United States. For the next six years the Communist Party pushed the idea of self-determination for Negroes in a forty-ninth state.

But this idea was based upon an incorrect analogy with Russia, where different areas were occupied by different races with different languages and customs. The Negro was not different from any other American in language, culture, or historic traditions, and his chief objection to the idea of a forty-ninth state was its underlying assumption that Negroes did not and could not fit into American life.

Noting the coolness to their proposal of a black republic in the Deep South, the Communists sought to capitalize on the Scottsboro Case, which, because it seemed so obvious a miscarriage of justice, had a great emotional impact on Negroes throughout the country. On March 25, 1931, nine Negro adolescents were charged with the rape of two white women while on a freight train in Alabama, and two weeks later eight of the boys were sentenced to the electric chair. The N.A.A.C.P. hastened to furnish legal counsel for the accused, but the Communists cried out that the International Labor Defense was better equipped to represent the boys, since legal procedures alone would not be successful. Mass meetings and international propaganda must also be used, ran their argument, and in these techniques they had developed special skills. The I.L.D. persuaded the parents of the boys to let them handle the case.

For four years the I.L.D. fought the case in the courts while at the same time conducting a worldwide propaganda campaign portraying the Scottsboro boys as victims of racial injustice in capitalist America. In 1935 the Party, in one of its tactical shifts, decided to permit other groups to share in the case. The new Scottsboro Defense Committee was successful in July 1937 in winning the acquittal of four boys and in laying the groundwork for the eventual release of the others. In their joy the Negroes were quite willing to give the Communists some of the credit they claimed for the victory.

The Negro's sense of gratitude toward the Communists did not prompt him to join the Party, however. A presidential candidate poll published by *Opportunity* magazine in May 1932 showed that out of 3,973 Negroes polled, only 51 planned to support the Communist nominee. Negroes simply did not seem to be attuned to the Communist message, for reasons that are not hard to fathom. Typically American, the Negro was individualistic, not likely to submerge his personality in conformity to a party line from which there could be no deviation. Most Negroes took their cues from their clergymen or their secular leaders, both of whom had a middle-class outlook on the economics of property and each of whom had special reasons for disliking the Communists. Moreover, the Negro, again like other Americans of his day, was not class conscious—the very vocabulary of the Communists struck him as foreign. Basically, too, the Negro was a man of conservative mold. Because he protested against "Jim Crow," he was thought to be a revolutionary, but at best he was a "forced radical," and, even then, only on the issue of race. And, finally, Negroes were cool toward Communism because they were skeptical of utopias and somewhat suspicious of the intent of their promoters.

The basic conservatism of the Negro in accepting new theories of government did not extend to political party affiliation, for in the decade following World War I he made a major shift in party loyalty. Though in the presidential election of 1924, the Negro newspapers and voters again supported the Republican party, a change had been setting in, engineered in part by enterprising Democratic political bosses and machines in the northern cities. Democratic politicians had taken careful note of the large Negro migrations from the South and, knowing that these newcomers were Republican-minded, had busied themselves in seeking them out and urging them to register and vote. They gave Negroes small political jobs, such as watchers at the polls, and provided small favors, such as baskets of food or tickets to an entertainment.

By 1928 the Democratic wooing of the Negro began to show results. In the presidential campaign the Democratic candidate, Alfred E. Smith, did well among Negro voters, particularly in Harlem, where Tammany Hall had built a large Negro following. Smith did not win the election, but he disproved the notion that the Negro would automatically vote Republican.

The newly elected Republican president, Herbert Hoover, did little to retain his party's slipping hold on the Negro. He gave few federal appointments to Negroes. When his Administration arranged to send Gold Star Mothers to France to visit the graves of their sons, Negro mothers were segregated and given inferior accommodations. Hoover remained silent concerning the more than fifty lynchings of Negroes that took place during his Administration. In 1930 he nominated for the Supreme Court Judge John J. Parker of North Carolina, who ten years earlier had said that the participation of the Negro in politics was "a source of evil and danger to both races." The N.A.A.C.P. vigorously fought the nomination, holding mass meetings and sending petitions to congressmen, and Negroes were overjoyed when the Senate withheld confirmation of Parker.

In the presidential elections of 1932 Negroes overwhelmingly supported the Democratic standard bearer, Franklin D. Roosevelt, helping to make Hoover a one-term president. The vote of the Negro in 1932 meant one thing: he had become an independent in politics. One observer, journalist Arthur Krock, hailed the Negro's behavior as a "splendid revolt" which indicated that when the Negro voters went to the polls they put out of their minds Abraham

Lincoln and Jefferson Davis "who were not running in 1932."

Two years later, in the congressional elections of 1934, the defection of the Negroes from the Republican ranks showed no signs of having been arrested. Oscar DePriest, Negro Congressman from Illinois, was replaced by Arthur W. Mitchell, a Negro who only four years earlier had switched to the Democrats. "Lincoln is Finally Dead," mourned a DePriest supporter, the *Chicago Defender,* generously adding that the Democratic party was to be commended on running Negroes for so many elective offices throughout the North.

The main reason for the success of the Democrats in the presidential election of 1932 was the failure of the Hoover Administration to cope successfully with the great depression. Following the collapse of the stock market in October 1929, some eight months after Hoover had been inaugurated, the country went through three years of hard times unprecedented in its history. As the roster of unemployed mounted higher and higher, reaching 15,000,000 by 1932, the Negro was particularly affected. Whites were only too willing to become street cleaners, bellhops, and redcaps, ousting Negroes from such jobs. The unemployed, white and colored, tended to vote for Roosevelt in 1932 because in the election campaign he voiced deep concern for the "forgotten man" and pledged a "new deal" for the people.

Once in office Roosevelt took on the role of guardian of the national welfare, greatly expanding the activities of the federal government. Many of the New Deal programs were designed to assist the working classes and the poor, and Negroes bulked large in both categories. Roosevelt did not design his program with the Negro in mind (the New Deal actually had no fixed policy toward the Negro), but he was opposed to any racial discrimination implementing it. Many of the decentralized New Deal programs placed great power in the hands of local officials, however, who might not have deemed it wise or expedient to practice racial equality, regardless of the policy line formulated in Washington.

It was clear, however, that the Negro would stand to gain by each of the objectives of the New Deal—relief, recovery, and reform. Negroes made up 3,000,000 of the 18,000,000 persons on relief in May 1935. In direct relief— the giving of food allowances, clothing, and commodity surpluses—the Negro faced little discrimination, but in work relief, he received few skilled-labor or white-collar jobs. The Public Works Administration, under Secretary of the Interior Harold Ickes, stipulated that in slum-clearance projects a quota of skilled Negroes should be used. The low-cost housing activities of the P.W.A. greatly reduced the congested living conditions of Negro families in over twenty-five cities. Other relief agencies which assisted the Negro were the Civilian Conservation Corps, which had an enrollment of 16,000 Negro youths in May 1935, and the Works Progress Administration, under Harry Hopkins. Among the branches of the W.P.A. were the Federal Arts Project, which employed Negro actors and writers, and the National Youth Administration, which had a Negro Division headed by Mary McLeod Bethune.

Two aspects of the recovery program—the industrial and the agricultural—were of major concern to Negroes. The National Recovery Act authorized the setting up of codes for various industries, codes which determined such matters as minimum wages and the length of the work week. In the early days of the agency the matter of establishing a special low wage for Negroes was seriously considered. Supporters of this viewpoint claimed that most Negroes in the South were able to hold jobs only because they would accept a lower wage than whites, and that the wiping out of the pay differential would lead to the replacement of Negroes by whites.

Negro leaders, influenced by the Urban League, expressed solid opposition to the special-low-wage theory, holding that the Negro should contend for equal wages even at the risk of being fired. This point of view became the official policy of the N.R.A., and some Negroes in the South did lose their jobs. The displacement of Negroes because of the N.R.A. policies was not great, however, and the codes definitely weakened the tradition of a wage differential based on color.

As in industry, the most important of the New Deal measures in agriculture had some disadvantage to the Negro. The Agricultural Adjustment Act of 1933 authorized a reduction in the acreage of basic crops, including tobacco and cotton. Farmers who agreed to restrict crops were to receive payment from the government. In practice, however, the A.A.A. tended to dispose of thousands of agricultural workers, for many planters did not hesitate to evict tenants and fire field hands as they reduced their acreages. Even where tenants were not evicted, they did not always receive the checks which planters were supposed to pass on to them. The serious plight of the sharecroppers led them in 1934 to organize the Southern Tenant Farmers' Union.

During Roosevelt's second term in office the New Deal agricultural program was of more direct benefit to the small farmer and sharecropper. The Bankhead-Jones Farm Tenant Act of 1937 authorized long-term, low-interest loans to sharecroppers who wished to purchase land. In the first two years of its operation, 987 loans were made to Negro farm tenants. The Farmer Security Administration, avowedly designed to help low-income farm people, made it a practice to purchase submarginal lands from their poverty-stricken

holders, thus enabling them to buy more fertile plots elsewhere. During the years 1937–40 the F.S.A. made 50,000
rehabilitation loans to Negro farmers. With satisfaction the
Department of Agriculture announced in 1940 that a survey
of 50,000 Negro farm families showed that from 1936 to
1939 their average net worth had increased from $451 to
$752.

To Negroes, as to the country at large, perhaps the most
significant of the New Deal reform measures was the Social
Security Act, passed in 1935. This provided both old-age
insurance for workers and unemployment insurance for
workers, the latter to be administered in cooperation with
the states. The Act granted federal monies to the states for
public welfare services, including aid to the blind and crip-
pled, dependent mothers, and children and old people who
were destitute.

The fact that farm workers and domestic servants were
not included in the old-age insurance program was a particular blow to Negroes. But the impact of the entire Social
Security Act, with its point of view that the government had
a responsibility to the less fortunate, was of inestimable
value to a group which was at a disadvantage in the world
of work and in which the incidence of poverty was much
higher than the national average.

One of the most significant New Deal measures affecting Negroes was the Wagner Labor Relations Act of 1935.
By guaranteeing the right of collective bargaining and by
outlawing company unions, this Act greatly strengthened
organized labor. It gave particular approval to the militant
wing of the labor movement, which had not felt certain that
it had government backing in its drive to organize the great
mass-production industries, where many of the workers
were not unionized. These industries—steel, iron, automobiles, mining, longshoring, shipping, rubber and garment

manufacture—were the very ones in which large numbers of Negroes were employed.

Unskilled workers, long excluded from the crafts-dominated American Federation of Labor, turned eagerly to the Committee for Industrial Organization, founded in 1935 on the premise that unions should be organized along industrial rather than craft lines—that, for example, all garment workers, whether examiners, cutters, finishers, or pressers, should be in one union, regardless of crafts or skills. In 1936 and 1937 the Committee won the first of its many substantial victories, organizing the automobile workers and the steel workers and forcing the automobile and steel corporations to recognize the union. Expelled by the A. F. of L., whose membership it exceeded by the fall of 1937, the Committee in 1938 took the name Congress of Industrial Organizations.

From its beginnings, the C.I.O. followed a policy of equality for all workers, black as well as white. It may be pointed out that it was easier to incorporate Negroes into a new union than established ones, where racial discriminations had often become fixed. Many of the C.I.O. unions kept no records concerning members' race or color, and some insisted that the contracts they signed must contain clauses banning discrimination against members because of race or religion. Believing that white and colored unionists had a great deal in common, the United Mine Workers frowned on "Jim Crow" locals. As in other unions, the mine workers encouraged the election of Negroes to office in the various local lodges.

By 1940 there were 210,000 Negroes in the C.I.O. Many of them had acquired new skills, and all of them had a new consciousness of unionism, a new sense of identity with the white worker. The Negro would still face special problems in the mixed unions, and the major craft unions still barred him from membership. But now, thanks to the C.I.O., he no longer felt that in the ranks of organized labor he was little more than an outsider.

Though the Negro gave the lion's share of the credit for his economic gains in the 1930s to Roosevelt, in truth the President himself did not come to the foreground in racial matters. From Negroes he received the gratitude that more directly belonged to subordinates like Harold Ickes, who set a pattern for other cabinet officers by appointing William H. Hastie and Robert C. Weaver to responsible positions in the Department of the Interior. Roosevelt also profited from the great popularity of his wife among Negroes. In 1939 Mrs. Roosevelt, who was friendly with Mary McLeod Bethune, withdrew her membership in the Daughters of the American Revolution when that organization denied the use of Constitution Hall to contralto Marian Anderson. When, a year later, Miss Anderson received the Spingarn medal from the N.A.A.C.P., it was from the hand of Mrs. Roosevelt.

The popularity of the Roosevelt name among Negroes was reflected at the polls. In the presidential election of 1936 Roosevelt received from 70 to 80 per cent of ballots cast by Negroes, and in the campaign of 1940 he did almost as well. The winning of the colored vote was important, since the Negro by 1940 had come to hold the balance of power in some ten states outside the South.

In both 1936 and 1940 Roosevelt won smashing victories at the polls. However, his success in the latter campaign was not so much an approval of his New Deal measures as it was a vote of confidence in his foreign policies. For in 1939 war had broken out in Europe, with France and England arrayed against Hitler's Germany. Roosevelt made little attempt to conceal his sympathies, which became more evident when France capitulated in June 1940. As Roosevelt drew closer to England, it became only a matter of time before the United States would be drawn into the conflict. When Germany's ally, Japan, attacked the American naval base at Pearl Harbor on December 7, 1941, it marked the beginning of a global war.

America's entry into World War II would bring her face to face with a number of new realities, among them the wartime role of her own most numerous minority, the Negro.

9

War and Peace: Issues and Outcomes (1940–1954)

AMERICA'S ENTRY INTO World War II presented the Negro with no problems of divided loyalty or emotional adjustment. He had no historical identification with Germany, Italy, or Japan and even before Pearl Harbor had been anti-Hitler, having a natural distaste for the "master race" theories of the Nazis. Negroes remembered that when the 1936 Olympic games were held in Berlin, Hitler had left his seat every time a Negro athlete won an event, thus avoiding the necessity of meeting him.

When the United States entered the war, there was a distinct note of "wait and see" in the writings of some Negro journalists who remained cold sober as America put out more flags, and Negro leadership in general took the stand that unless the Negroes received better treatment they could not wholeheartedly and unreservedly support the war effort. Thinking only of the many indignities they had suffered, the rank and file of Negroes may not have carefully weighed the American way of life, with all its imperfections, against the freedomless system of the totalitarian powers. But Negroes of a reflective turn of mind supported the war in the belief that if America lost, the Negro stood to be the greatest loser. And Negroes high and low sensed that if they wanted to get something out of the war, they had to put something into it.

The Negro reacted to the coming of the war as a patriot with an ingrained touch of skepticism. Not having forgotten that his gains in World War I fell far short of expectations, he was wary of high-sounding phrases about freedom. Though President Roosevelt had used the words "arsenal of democracy" in reference to the Lend Lease Act of March 11, 1941, for example, in the early stages of building the vast stockpile of military supplies and equipment, the Negro workingman had little share. In principle the Roosevelt Administration was opposed to racial discrimination, but its attention and energies had shifted from the New Deal domestic reforms to a program of national preparedness for a role in a war-torn world.

In the fall of 1940, when the national defense program got started, 90 per cent of the holders of defense contracts used no Negroes at all or confined them to nonskilled or custodial jobs. The National Defense Advisory Commission recommended to contractors that they adopt equal employment practices, but the new war industries evoked an old standby: the hiring of Negroes was "against company policy." White workers were imported to industrial centers where qualified Negroes were looking for jobs. Though the National Defense Training Act, designed to provide vocational training for defense industries, carried an antibias clause, by March 1941 only 4,600 of the 175,000 trainees were Negroes.

Job discrimination in defense industry called forth strong protests by the Negro press and Negro welfare

groups. Liberal whites joined in, as did many of the northern newspapers. In many cities Negroes resorted to picket
lines. But the most effective step was that taken by A. Philip
Randolph, President of the Brotherhood of Sleeping Car
Porters. Unable by conference-table methods to induce the
Roosevelt Administration to take effective action against
employment bias, Randolph proposed nothing less than a
national Negro March on Washington, a direct action by
100,000 Negroes. In the spring of 1941 Randolph organized
the movement and set the date for July 1. It was an all-
Negro effort: "We shall not call upon our white friends to
march with us," said Randolph. "There are some things
Negroes must do alone."

The Roosevelt Administration was puzzled by this
threat, which was indeed something quite new in Negro
protest activities. The President attempted to have the
march called off, finally summoning its leaders to the White
House. At this conference Randolph stated that the march
would go on unless the President issued an executive order
prohibiting discrimination in defense industries. Roosevelt
exercised his skill and charm, but he was talking to men
who could not be dissuaded. One week after the conference,
Roosevelt came to a decision. Faced with the possibility of
an embarrassing large-scale demonstration in the nation's
capital, Roosevelt yielded, issuing on June 25 Executive
Order 8802, which officially reaffirmed the government's
policy of nondiscrimination in employment.

With Roosevelt's Executive Order the color bar in
employment began to bend. The Order directed that the
vocational training program be conducted without reference
to race, and it stipulated that all future defense contracts
should include nondiscrimination clauses. More important,
it established a Committee on Fair Employment Practice to
investigate violations of the Order. Through its field staff,

the F.E.P.C. processed complaints and held public hearings. The Committee was instrumental in opening new job opportunities for Negroes, particularly in aircraft plants and firms making airplane equipment, such as Lockheed-Vega and Glenn L. Martin. "By the summer of 1944," wrote Robert C. Weaver, "there were about 100,000 Negroes in aircraft, and they were about 6 per cent of the total." The Committee was even more gratified by the results of the trainee program; by October 1944 over 323,000 Negroes had received pre-employment and supplementary defense training. The acquisition of new industrial skills would inevitably lead to higher-level jobs.

President Roosevelt had been quick to extend the authority of the Committee to cover employment by federal bureaus and departments. In this sphere the results were gratifying beyond expectations. Negroes, particularly women, were brought into government service in mounting numbers. In the four years from 1938 to 1942 the percentage of Negroes holding federal jobs in Washington rose from 8.5 to 17, and over one-third of the latter were employed in clerical or professional occupations. Thanks to the Executive Order and an increasingly tight labor market, the Negro worker's outlook brightened with each passing month, a development which led many Negro civilians to become more and more enthusiastic about the war.

As the war went on, the status of the Negro on the fighting fronts also underwent a change. In mid-1940 the number of Negroes in the armed services was small, totaling 13,200 in the Army and 4,000 in the Navy. In October of that year the War Department announced its two guiding principles concerning Negroes: the proportion to be enlisted would correspond to their proportion in the population, and colored and white soldiers would not be intermingled. The Army thus reaffirmed its traditional policy of a separate regimental organization of Negro troops. The day after Pearl Harbor a group of Negro editors, headed by Claude A. Barnett, director of the Associated Negro Press, met with war department officials and urged them to create a mixed volunteer division—one open to all men irrespective of race, creed, color, or national origin. Perhaps the Army officials gave the proposal careful thought; at any rate they did not formally reject it until September 1943.

Although the Army retained its segregated pattern, it made changes in its draft procedures and officer procurement policies. In the operation of the selective service, there was little discrimination. Lieutenant Colonel Campbell C. Johnson, a Negro, was made an executive assistant to Selective Service Administrator Lewis B. Hershey, and Negro civilians held white-collar jobs in the selective service offices. By the summer of 1942, 1,800 Negroes sat on draft boards.

Needing Negro officers to handle the vastly increased Negro soldiery, the Army made what it regarded as a bold decision: Negro officer candidates should be trained in the same schools and classes as whites, even in training schools located in the South. At the Fort Benning School, Earl Brown, Negro staff member of *Life* magazine, noted that the white and colored candidates "march elbow to elbow across the wide expanse of south Georgia soil, sit together in classrooms, eat in the same mess hall, sleep in the same barracks, with no indication of racial prejudice." By the end of 1942 more than 1,000 Negroes had been graduated from officer training schools and had become second lieutenants. The War Department also trained white and colored women together in its Women's Auxiliary Army Corps at Des Moines. Of the first class of 440 women reporting in July 1942 for officer candidate training, thirty-nine were

Negroes. All of the candidates attended classes together, but the Negroes were given separate tables at meals and separate lodgings. After three months of training, thirty-six of the Negro WAACs were graduated, along with their white classmates.

The success of the mixed officer candidate schools for army officers had no influence on War Department policy in training air cadets. A flying school for Negroes was set up at Tuskegee Institute on July 19, 1941. Nearly eight months later—on March 7, 1942—five of these candidates received their "wings" and commissions from General George E. Stratemeyer. These first Negro pilots of the Army Air Corps formed the nucleus of a new unit, the 99th Pursuit Squadron. By the end of the year this unit numbered forty-three pilots, and a second Negro air squadron, the 332nd Fighter Group, had been activated. However, the recruiting of Negro pilots had been so halfheartedly conducted and their role so vaguely defined that William H. Hastie was led to resign his position as Civilian Aide to the Secretary of War on January 5, 1943.

In breaking from tradition concerning the Negro, the Navy went much further than its sister service. When the war broke out, the Navy followed a "messmen only" policy for Negroes, confining them, along with Filipinos, to the Steward's Branch. There were no Negro officers. Ignoring criticism, Navy Secretary Frank Knox, at a White House conference in October 1941, reaffirmed the official policy: Negroes, he said, would be recruited only in the messman's branch.

Six months later Knox was forced to yield, announcing on April 7, 1942, that Negro volunteers would henceforth be accepted for general services as well as for mess attendants. The chief incident that led to this reversal was the conduct of Dorie Miller, messman third class on the *Arizona,* on the morning of the Japanese attack on Pearl Harbor. When the general alarm sounded, Miller went on deck, helped remove the dying captain, and then manned one of the machine guns. He brought down at least four of the enemy planes before the sinking *Arizona* had to be abandoned. Miller was subsequently awarded a Navy Cross, pinned on him by Admiral C. W. Nimitz, and was the recipient posthumously of a Congressional Medal of Honor. But his feat on that historic day served to dramatize the Navy's "Jim Crow" policy and added to the nationwide tide of protest, thus forcing Knox's hand.

Knox's statement that Negroes would be used for general service turned out to be somewhat less meaningful than it sounded, however. The Navy announced that beginning June 1, 1942, Negroes could enlist for service other than messmen, but that they would not be placed on seagoing combat ships; instead, they would be limited to shore installations and harbor craft. Moreover, Negroes were to be placed in separate units. The Negro press and clergy sent up a chorus of protest over the "Jim Crow" aspect of the policy. But in June 1942 Negroes began to receive basic training courses at the Great Lakes Naval Training Station, their compound taking the name of the Negro naval hero of the Civil War, Robert Smalls. By the fall of 1943 Negro sailors had been trained in more than fifty different job categories. Haltingly, but unmistakably, the Navy had begun to chart a new course.

The movement toward integration in the Navy stemmed from two sources, the unenthusiastic behavior of the Negro seamen and the influence of naval officers like Christopher Smith Sargent. In addition to being segregated, Negro sailors found that they were assigned to the jobs of handling ammunition and loading ships. Their resentful attitude was evidenced by many widely separated incidents, including hunger strikes, demonstrations, and refusal to obey orders. In one of these incidents fifteen Seabees stationed in the West Indies were discharged for protesting discrimination in camp facilities and job ratings. In another incident a detachment of 250 Negroes refused to load an ammunition ship at Port Chicago in San Francisco Bay after an explosion had killed 300 of their fellow servicemen. The mutineers were sentenced to long terms, but eventually the convictions were set aside and the men were restored to duty on probation.

The Negro sailor's attitude toward unfair treatment speeded a better day for him, as did the efforts of bold and imaginative white officers. In the summer of 1943, after Negroes had begun to pour into the Navy in order to make up their quota of 10 per cent, the problem of their utilization fell to Lieutenant Sargent of the Manpower Policies Section of the Bureau of Naval Personnel. Determined to move in new directions, Sargent established a Special Unit which in February 1944 persuaded the Navy to man two seagoing craft with all-Negro personnel, except for officers. Two months later twenty-two Negroes became commissioned officers, an almost revolutionary step for the Navy.

With James V. Forrestal as Secretary of the Navy, Sargent's influence grew stronger. In August 1944 Forrestal approved the Special Unit's recommendation that Negroes be assigned to twenty-five auxiliary ships on which, up to 10 per cent, they would be mixed with whites. The experiment worked so well that it led to the next step, the assigning of Negroes to all fleet auxiliaries; on these ships Negroes and whites worked together and lived together. By the summer of 1945 all segregated Navy camps and schools had been abolished.

Before taking the final step, Forrestal appointed Urban

League executive Lester Granger, a fellow Dartmouth College man, to tour naval bases throughout the United States and the Pacific and bring back recommendations. When Granger returned from his 50,000-mile trip, Forrestal's mind was made up; on February 27, 1946, an official directive went out from Navy headquarters: "Effective immediately, all restrictions governing the types of assignments for which Negro naval personnel are eligible are hereby lifted."

The Navy also moved ahead in two other branches of its service. In May 1942 it accepted Negroes into the Coast Guard in capacities other than messman. One month later the Marine Corps began to admit colored volunteers, for the first time in 167 years.

In the enlistment of Negro women the Navy lagged far behind its sister service. Though the women's reserve of the Navy (the WAVES) was organized in the summer of 1942, it was not until late in 1944 that colored women were permitted to join, and then only after continuous pressure, led by a Negro sorority council. The women's reserve of the Coast Guard (the SPARS) was equally tardy, not enlisting Negroes until October 1944. The Marine Corps never took the step.

Unlike the Army or Navy, the Merchant Marine was integrated from the outset, keeping no files of seamen or officers by color or race. Fourteen of its government-built Liberty ships were named after outstanding Negroes, four after Negro seamen who had lost their lives, and four after Negro colleges. Among the Liberty ship captains were four Negroes, of whom the best known was Captain Hugh Mulzac, who by May 1944 had taken the S. S. *Booker T. Washington* across the submarine-infested Atlantic seven times. The color-free policy of the Merchant Marine resulted from its civilian nature: not a part of the armed forces, it was made up of seafaring men who belonged to a labor union whose constitution forbade discrimination.

• • •

The performance of the Negro in naval service compared favorably with that of whites, particularly during later stages of the war, when his opportunities were greater. By V-J Day the number of Negro officers had risen to fifty-two, and as a group they had no trouble in winning the respect that went with their rank. By war's end Negro seamen outnumbered steward's mates, 58,000 to 57,000.

In the Army the performance of the Negro was undoubtedly affected by the policy of segregation. The separation of Negro soldiers from whites suggested that not much was expected of them, or else it made them feel aggrieved, thus providing them with an excuse for not doing their best. Like their white counterparts, Negro soldiers voiced innumerable complaints. However, half of the complaints of the Negro dealt with race or color. In a survey of Negro soldiers in March 1943, the question was asked, "If you could talk with the President of the United States, what are the three most important questions you would like to ask him about the war?" In reply, exactly 50 per cent of the Negro soldiers posed a question about racial discrimination. When, at the same period, 3,000 Negro soldiers were asked, "Do you think that most Negroes are being given a fair chance to do as much as they want to do to help win the war?" 54 per cent said "No."

Racial discrimination adversely affected the morale of the Negro soldier, but other factors tended to offset this problem. Negro soldiers believed that their group was doing its share or more in the war effort, 87 per cent of them holding this view. Moreover, the expectations of the Negro had a wholesome effect on his attitude toward the war. "There was a tendency among Negro soldiers to expect or hope for an increase in rights and privileges, improved treatment, and better economic status after the war," writes Samuel A.

Stouffer and his associates in a highly scholarly study made on the American soldier at the request of the Army itself. In the main, the Negro soldier was oriented toward the future: "By virtue of our valor, courage, and patriotism, things will be better for the Negro," said one of them.

On the whole, the Negro soldier adjusted to army life in much the same ways as the white, with a few differences. "In expressions of pride in his outfit, sense of importance of his Army job, and interest in his job, the Negro soldier's attitudes were generally somewhat more favorable than the white soldier's," writes Stouffer. "In attitudes toward his physical condition and in the related attitude of general sense of well-being, the Negro soldier tended to be somewhat less favorable than the white soldier." Negro soldiers were ambitious for advancement: "at every educational level, Negro enlisted men were even more likely than white enlisted men to express the desire to become an officer or noncom." The average educational level of the Negro soldier was considerably lower than that of the white, although the Negro G.I. had received much more formal schooling than his father in World War I.

During the last three years of the war the proportion of Negroes in the Army hovered around 8 per cent, reaching its highest point, 8.74 per cent, in 1944. When the war ended in September 1945, there were 695,264 Negroes in the Army, 8.67 per cent of its total strength.

Though a higher percentage of white than Negro soldiers preferred overseas service and combat duty, beginning in March 1944 the percentage of Negro army strength serving overseas in fact outstripped that of whites, and by June, 1945, 74 per cent of the colored soldiers were at overseas bases, as compared with 67 per cent of whites. As to branches of the Army, Negroes were heavily overrepresented in the service forces, and underrepresented in the air corps and ground combat arms. In 1942 nearly one-half of the Negro soldiers were in the service branches and by mid-1945 three-quarters were in those branches.

Negro soldiers undoubtedly did what they were called upon to do. Since most of them were in the service branches, they could be found everywhere in the Army's far-flung operations—building the Alaska-Canada Highway, constructing the Ledo Road linking China to India, cutting a path through the Burmese jungle, building airports in Liberia, unloading ships in half a hundred harbors scattered over three continents, and moving crucial supplies of ammunition to the front lines at the beaches of Normandy. But if the Negro soldier's work in the service branches speaks for itself, his record in the combat units is not as easy to assess. The 92nd Division, composed entirely of Negro units, received 12,096 decorations and citations, including two Distinguished Service Crosses, sixteen Legion of Merit Awards, ninety-five Silver Stars, and nearly 1,100 Purple Hearts—a creditable record, which would seem to indicate that the unit was not lacking in fighting qualities. But the 92nd was destined to be remembered primarily because of reports as to its lack of efficiency in an Allied offensive begun in the Cinqualle Canal region in Italy in February 1945. Truman Gibson, Negro civilian aide to the Secretary of War, reported that some Negro groups had "melted away" during the action and that others had engaged in "more or less panicky retreats."

The reverses sustained by the 92nd in the February offensive could be attributed to the inferior schooling and inadequate military preparation of so many of the men. The Negro press placed the blame wholly on the Army itself, pointing to its "Jim Crow" policies. Certainly there was

much truth in this charge. Aside from stigmatizing the segregated group, the policy of separateness impeded its opera-
tional efficiency. The Negro air force units, for example,
often found themselves short of replacements during combat
operations. At the same time, nearby white units had more
pilots than they needed. Since the shorthanded Negro contingent could not draw on those units, however, Negro airmen frequently had to complete twice as many missions as
white airmen before they could be sent back to the United
States.

A conclusive proof that segregation was a morale factor
was the mixed-units experiment. Badly needing infantry
replacements in Europe early in 1945, the Army decided to
accept Negro volunteers to be organized as platoons for service as units in white regiments. Some 2,500 Negroes placed
in the infantry division of the First Army performed ably in
the hard fighting on the east bank of the Rhine. When, subsequently, the white officers who commanded them were
asked the question, "How did the colored soldiers in this
company perform in combat?" 84 per cent replied, "Very
well," and 16 per cent, "Fairly well." Not a single officer
checked any of the other categories in the questionnaire:
"Not so well," "Not well at all," or "Undecided."

The mixed-units experiment had its effect on the Army.
Late in 1945 the War Department appointed a board of generals to make recommendations about the use of Negroes in
the future. Among the thirteen proposals made by the board
(in the Gillem Report) were those calling for the grouping
together of Negro and white units, the assignment of Negro
trainees to communities that would be favorably disposed
toward them, and the expansion of opportunities for
Negroes as officers. The Gillem Report did not abolish segregation in the Army: "A Negro American soldier is still first

a Negro and then a soldier," remarked the *Crisis* in an editorial criticism. But it did represent a firm step forward, and an augury of things to come.

On the home front the war brought something old and something new to the Negro. If the old was painful, the new was hopeful and forward-looking. A familiar sense of indignation grew out of a combination of factors, the foremost being the Negro policy of the Army. "No injustice embitters Negroes more than continued segregation and discrimination in the armed forces," ran a statement released on June 17, 1944, by representatives of twenty-five leading Negro organizations meeting in New York. Home-front Negroes were also disturbed by the mistreatment of colored troops in communities where camps were located. The Negro press carried innumerable stories describing the hostile behavior of white civilians and policemen in southern towns toward Negro soldiers and WACS.

Some hostility toward the Negro was inevitable. In an America at war, the familiar patterns of Negro-white relations were upset, and one of the results was an increase of tensions, fears, and aggressions. In the South many white people found it convenient to blame someone for the new challenges in race relations, and they decided upon Eleanor Roosevelt. Viewing her as a symbol of outside interference, they claimed that she was the inspiration behind the "Eleanor Clubs" formed by Negro domestics whose motto was "A white woman in every kitchen." This allegation was scarcely more credible than the rumor that Negroes were buying up all the icepicks and would, during some convenient blackout, start an attack on the whites. The contagion of rumors spreading through the South during the war years was a sobering indication of the extent to which white southerners were misinformed about the Negro and unaware of his real attitudes, not to speak of his considerable strides in education.

Tense race relations also existed in the North. The most dramatic expressions of hostility were four major racial outbreaks—one in Harlem, one in Los Angeles (the "Zoot Suit" riot), and two in Detroit. The most serious took place during the week of June 20, 1943, in Detroit, where the racial feeling engendered by an increase in population of 50,000 Negroes and 450,000 whites, many of them from the South, in three years, plus competition for housing, created an explosive atmosphere. In the eruption which began on a hot Sunday afternoon, twenty-five Negroes and nine whites were killed, and the losses in property exceeded $2,000,000. In sorrow and shame, Detroit established a Mayor's Interracial Committee in an attempt to get at the roots of the trouble and to take the necessary next steps.

The Detroit riot had a profound effect throughout the nation. It shocked the American people into a realization that the status of the Negro had undergone a significant change that could not be ignored. As a result, cities and states throughout the North began to take a new interest in Negro-white relations. Public officials read the signs; by the end of the war seventeen governors and sixteen mayors had appointed commissions to formulate immediate and long-range proposals for the improvement of race relations.

One of the reasons for the changed status of the Negro was his greater economic security. In 1944, 1,000,000 more colored workers were to be found in civilian jobs than in 1940. During that period the number of Negroes employed in government service had jumped from 60,000 to 300,000. The employment of Negro women in industry quadrupled during the war years. Between 1942 and 1945 Negroes "secured more jobs at better wages and in more diversified occupational and industrial patterns than ever before,"

wrote Robert C. Weaver, a brilliant scholar, able administrator, and an expert on Negro employment and housing. In
1940 only 4.4 per cent of Negro male workers were in the
skilled category, whereas four years later the figure had
risen to 7.3 per cent. During the same period the ratio of
semiskilled Negro male workers almost doubled, rising
from 12 per cent to 22.4 per cent. In 1940 seven out of every
ten Negroes were concentrated in farming, domestic, and
unskilled work; in 1945 the proportion had been reduced to
five out of ten.

World War II, like its predecessor, brought about a shift
in the Negro population. About 333,000 Negroes left the
South, but, unlike the earlier migrants, some two-thirds of
them went to the Pacific Coast. The Negro population of San
Francisco in 1945 was five times greater than that of 1940;
in Los Angeles 76,000 Negro newcomers arrived between
April 1944 and April 1945. West Coast whites were familiar
with peoples of yellow skin, and now the war brought an
influx of more nonwhite Americans.

Both the home-front Negro and the Negro soldier were
hopeful that war's end would result in a better America for
them. This feeling had been expressed by a conference of
Negro leaders at Durham, North Carolina, in October 1942:

> We have the courage and faith to believe that it is
> possible to evolve in the South a way of life, consis-
> tent with the principle for which we as a Nation are
> fighting throughout the world, that will free us all,
> white and Negro alike, from want, and from throt-
> tling fears.

It was in this spirit that the Negro faced the postwar
world.

World War II shook the United States from its isolationist moorings, convincing the large majority of Americans that a new world order was necessary. Man had shrunk the universe while at the same time multiplying the capacity for self-destruction. Such a perilous equilibrium seemed to require a new dedication to international cooperation. The United Nations Organization, established in San Francisco in June 1945, represented the worldwide response to this compelling urge to insure peace.

Negroes had shown a keen interest in the founding of the United Nations, every major Negro newspaper sending a correspondent to San Francisco. Along with other selected organizations, the N.A.A.C.P. had been invited to send official observers, and they had chosen Walter White, executive secretary of the organization, W. E. B. DuBois, and Mary McLeod Bethune. The most prominent American Negro participant at San Francisco was Ralph J. Bunche, the State Department's acting chief of the Division of Dependent Territories. Negroes liked the charter provision of the U.N. in which the member states pledged themselves to promote "respect for human rights and fundamental freedoms for all without distinction as to race, sex, language or religion." They also gave wholehearted approval to the statement subsequently issued by the U.N., "The Universal Declaration of Human Rights," whose first article opened with the line, "All human beings are born free and equal in dignity and rights."

Negroes were among the strongest supporters of the U.N. They felt that it might play a role in bringing an end to the system of colonialism. In 1944, at a meeting in New York, the representatives of twenty-five Negro organizations had stated that political and economic democracy must displace the prevailing system of exploitation in Africa, the West Indies, India, and other colonial areas. The war brought to American Negroes a realization that the subjugation of dark-skinned peoples in distant lands tended to strengthen color prejudice everywhere, including their own country.

Negroes welcomed the U.N. because it would sensitize the world to the problems of race and color and provide an international sounding board for yellow, brown, and black peoples to press their case. American Negroes could use the U.N. to air their grievances—as indeed they did in 1947, when the N.A.A.C.P. presented to the U.N.'s Office of Social Affairs a 155-page document with the lengthy title "A Statement on the Denial of Human Rights to Minorities in the Case of Citizens of Negro Descent in the United States of America and an Appeal to the United Nations for Redress." Negroes knew that membership in the U.N. would make America more aware of her own unfinished business. Her moral position as leader of the free world would certainly be questioned if she were unfair in her treatment of a particular group of her own citizens.

The Negro's attitude toward the U.N. went beyond an interest in himself, however, and even beyond an interest in the cause of the colonialist peoples. Like his countrymen, he was acquiring a broadening view of the world. Negroes are among the most resilient of Americans, among those least likely to be chained to fixed assumptions. If the world moved toward new unities, the Negro would move, too. This widening horizon of interest and of service—this world view—was well exemplified by the grandson of a former slave, Ralph J. Bunche, who in 1946 became chief of the U.N.'s Division of Trusteeship, who a year later became the secretary of the Palestine Commission, and who in 1948 succeeded in settling the thorny Arab-Israeli dispute, for which, in December 1950, he was awarded the Nobel Peace Prize.

•   •   •

On the domestic front the most pressing problem faced by the postwar Negro was equality of job opportunity, though, fortunately, he was able to retain many of his wartime gains. With the cutback in war-related industries, Negroes tended to lose jobs more rapidly than whites: in the two years following the war Negro membership in the Marine and Shipbuilding Works of America dropped from 40,000 to 5,000. But during these years the country experienced an unprecedented peacetime boom, bringing relatively full employment. With labor in demand, industry had no problem in absorbing Negroes, discharged servicemen as well as laborers. As late as January 1948 the percentage of unemployed Negro males did not compare unfavorably with that of whites, 5.2 as against 3.8 per cent.

The national government contributed importantly to Negro employment after the war. The wartime F.E.P.C. established by President Roosevelt went out of existence in June 1946, but since that time every chief executive has issued an order proclaiming equality of opportunity in federally controlled employment and has established a committee to effectuate it. President Truman created a Committee on Government Contract Compliance. President Eisenhower created a Committee on Government Contracts (for contractual employment) and a Committee on Government Employment Policy (for federal employment). In April 1961 President John F. Kennedy created a Committee on Equal Employment Opportunity, charging it with the twofold task of bringing about equality of job opportunity in government contracts and in the federal government itself.

At the present time, it can be said that the government's efforts to achieve fair employment practices in the contracts it granted have not been very effective except in the lowest category of jobs. A few firms with government contracts have actively sought to employ Negroes in administrative positions, and others have hired one or two "token" Negroes in nontraditional positions. But other firms holding contracts from the government have refused to hire Negroes except in unskilled capacities and have excluded them from company-sponsored training programs. The Committee on Equal Employment Opportunity put more vigor into the efforts of the federal government. With the Vice-President as chairman and the Secretary of Labor as vice-chairman, this Committee was given broader duties and greater authority than any of its predecessors. The new Committee was aggressive, not waiting for complaints to be filed but putting large contractors on the spot by publicity.

The Committee on Equal Employment Opportunity made an effort to persuade the organized labor movement to wipe out racial discrimination within its ranks. Though it had no direct authority over the unions, it realized that the Negro worker faced a formidable barrier in the pattern of racial practices still remaining in some of the unions. These discriminatory practices included outright exclusion of Negroes, all-Negro locals, lines of seniority promotion which denied to Negroes equal seniority with whites, and the barring of Negroes from the union-controlled apprenticeship training programs.

The President's Committee, after months of behind-the-scenes negotiations, succeeded in November 1962 in winning over more than 100 of the 130 affiliates of the A.F.L.-C.I.O. which had merged in 1955. Lyndon B. Johnson, then Vice-President, signed with the more than 100 union presidents a document, "Union Program for Fair Practices," which pledged the unions to abolish racially segregated locals and to accept all eligible applicants regardless of race, color, or creed. The unions also pledged themselves to work for nondiscrimination agreements in all the contracts they made with management.

The Committee was highly pleased with this action by the unions. But there was no way to force them to carry out their avowed intentions. And, as had happened more than once, a powerful international union might get little cooperation at the local, workbench level.

The President's Committee also conducted a community relations program designed to influence the states and cities. The states had not been idle. New York had taken the lead, enacting a measure—The Law Against Discrimination—declaring equal job opportunity a civil right and creating a commission to prevent unfair practices in employment. By 1950 seven additional states had followed New York's example, and by 1962 a total of twenty-one states had passed enforceable fair employment practice laws. The President's Committee worked hand in hand with the state commissions on fair employment, visiting them, conferring with them, and inviting them to Washington to a Conference of Commissions Against Discrimination.

The Committee on Equal Employment Opportunity worked hard to insure fair play in government jobs. The federal government itself employed 292,836 Negroes, or 13.2 per cent of its total personnel in December 1962. But these colored employees held a disproportionate number of the hourly rate blue-collar jobs rather than the salaried white-collar jobs. And even in the latter, a large majority of the Negroes were concentrated in the lowest four grade levels, leaving relatively few Negroes in grades 5 up to 18, the last of which paid $18,500 yearly. A study of federal employment in nine cities in December 1960 revealed that 7.7 per cent of Negroes held supervisory positions, whereas 20.9 per cent of the whites did.

The elimination of discrimination from such a vast and complex organization as the numerous federal bureaus was a task of some proportions. But the work of the President's committees in the fifties and sixties—its varied approaches, including education, persuasion, and, as a final resort, the formal filing of a complaint—had some effect in expanding federal job opportunities for Negroes. Surveys of five cities conducted in 1956 and again in 1960 by the Committee on Government Economic Policy revealed that over the four-year span there had been a striking increase in Negro employment at the higher levels in the classified, white-collar categories.

As if to set an example of upgrading, the chief executives themselves appointed Negroes to high office. William H. Hastie was made governor of the Virgin Islands and later became a judge in the United States Circuit Court of Appeals, Third District; J. Ernest Wilkins was appointed Assistant Secretary of Labor; A. Leon Higginbotham, Jr., a member of the Federal Trade Commission and later a United States District Judge for the Eastern District of Pennsylvania; John Morrow, Ambassador to Guinea; Clifton R. Wharton, Ambassador to Norway; Carl T. Rowan, Ambassador to Finland and, under President Johnson, Director, United States Information Agency; Thurgood Marshall, Justice of the United States Circuit Court of Appeals, Second District; Robert C. Weaver, Administrator of the Federal Housing and Home Finance Agency, and Howard Jenkins, Jr., a member of the National Labor Relations Board.

To Negroes seeking work opportunities and careers in postwar America the military branch of the federal establishment had much to offer. For the first time in history, they were invited to join the Army when the country was at peace. Adopting a recommendation in the Gillem Report, the War Department decided that the Negro should be given a continuing role in the Army, with his numbers corresponding to the ratio of Negroes in the total population. This new policy immediately attracted many Negroes: during the six months after V-J Day, over 17 per cent of the volunteer enlistees were Negroes.

Negroes joining the peacetime army found a serious, if familiar, drawback—they were assigned to segregated units. A Negro civilian group formed, on October 10, 1947, a Committee Against Jim Crow in Military Service and Training, headed by former army chaplain Grant Reynolds. Eight months later President Truman issued an order calling for equality of opportunity for all servicemen, at the same time creating a Committee on Equality of Treatment and Opportunity in the Armed Services to advise him about implementing the new order. In May 1950 the Committee recommended that every vestige of segregation be removed in the Army, Navy, and Air Force.

The conflict in Korea hastened integration in the armed services. Racially mixed units fought side by side in the see-saw war in the Korean hills, with no apparent sacrifice of military efficiency. "White units showed little reaction when Negroes were sprinkled among their ranks," wrote Lee Nichols in 1954 in *Breakthrough on the Color Front.* "Some officers even reported heightened morale among their all-white units after Negroes were added." A progress report from the Office of the Assistant Secretary of Defense, dated January 1, 1955, and titled "Integration in the Armed Services," bore out the conclusion of United Press newsman Nichols: "Thorough evaluation of the battle-tested results to date indicates a marked increase in the overall combat effectiveness through integration." Two Negro participants in Korea—Sergeant Cornelius H. Charlton and Private William Thomas—were awarded the Congressional Medal of Honor, the latter posthumously.

In 1955, two years after the end of the Korean conflict,

the Department of Defense announced that every all-Negro unit had been abolished. The increased integration of the armed services meant that there would be additional opportunities for Negroes to move up in rank. By 1963 there were 3,000 Negro officers in the Army. The 2,200 Negro officers in the Air Force included eight full colonels and Major General Benjamin O. Davis, Jr., Director of Manpower and Organization, Office of the Deputy Chief of Staff for Operations, with headquarters at the Pentagon. The 300 Negro officers in the Navy included Commander Samuel L. Gravely, skipper of the escort vessel *Falgout* and Lieutenant Commander George I. Thompson, attached to the Bureau of Naval Personnel. In March 1963 both Gravely and Thompson were chosen to attend the Naval War College, an honor the Navy bestows upon its most promising officers.

In the reserve components of the armed forces the progress of integration did not keep pace with that of the active services. In the Reserve Officers' Training Corps, the National Guard, and the Army Reserve evidences of segregation still remained—partly because of the local and sectional nature of the first two and the social, clublike nature of the third. Moreover, the semicivilian character of the reserve components posed problems which many War Department officials considered beyond military jurisdiction and control. At any rate, that full integration of the Negro serviceman is still to be achieved was implicit in the action taken by President Kennedy in June 1962 in appointing a new Committee on Equal Opportunity in the Armed Forces.

In bringing about a significant change in the status of the Negro since World War II, the role of the federal courts has been second to none. As no other branch of the national government, the courts had wrestled with the important question: Now, in the middle decades of the twentieth century, what is the meaning of equality in the concrete life of the American people? Free from the party politics a President must play and from the pressures of jockeying and bargaining that Congress must live with, the federal judiciary, particularly the Supreme Court, can grapple more single-mindedly with the meaning of freedom and equality.

In the early thirties the Supreme Court began to show an increased concern about civil rights and individual liberties. It began to go behind the formal law as stated in order to discover whether it was being fairly applied. It began to look beyond the laws enforcing segregation to see whether the separate facilities provided for Negroes were in fact equal to those for whites. With such new considerations in mind, the Supreme Court in the 1940s made a number of significant rulings concerning discrimination in voting, in transportation, and in housing. In 1944 the Court decreed that in primary elections a political party could not exclude a voter because of race (*Smith v Allright*), in 1946 it ruled that a Negro passenger in interstate commerce was entitled to make his journey without conforming to the segregation laws of the states through which the carrier might pass (*Morgan v Virginia*), and in 1948 it ruled that restrictive covenants—private agreements to exclude persons of a designated race or color from the ownership or occupation of real property—were not enforceable by the judiciary (*Shelley v Kraemer*).

Beyond all other fields it was on public tax-supported education that the Supreme Court rulings had their most profound impact. In a series of cases from 1938 to 1950 the Court, still operating under the "separate but equal" theory of the Plessy decision, sought to make the states meet the test of equality. In *Gaines v Missouri* (1938) the Court ordered that a Negro applicant be admitted to the law school of the University of Missouri since there was no other acceptable way for him to get a legal training within the state. Ten years later the Court ordered Oklahoma to provide Ada Louise Sipuel with a legal education, and to "provide it as soon as it does for any other group." Two years later the Court ordered Oklahoma to desist from segregating G. W. McLaurin, requiring that he sit at a designated desk in an anteroom adjoining the classroom, apart from other students, to sit at a designated desk in the library, and to eat in the school cafeteria at a special time. In the Sweatt case, decided on the same June day in 1950, the Court ruled that a Negro applicant be admitted to the University of Texas Law School inasmuch as it was far superior to a hastily organized law school just set up at Texas State University for Negroes.

In all of these cases the N.A.A.C.P. had sponsored the litigation, hoping thereby to undermine segregation. The organization believed that the South would abandon its dual system of education because of the large sums of money that would be required if Negro schools were to be made equal to those for whites. But this hope of attacking segregation by a flank movement proved to be fanciful, for the southern states began to appropriate additional funds for Negro schools. The N.A.A.C.P. realized that by providing Negro schools and colleges with better buildings, better equipment, and better salaries for teachers and by changing the title "college" to that of "university," the South was in effect strengthening "Jim Crow" by establishing "gilded citadels of segregation" manned by Negro administrators and teachers who would have a vested interest in maintaining the status quo in racial education.

Realizing that its victories in the "separate but equal" cases were failures concealed in success, the N.A.A.C.P., at a top-level meeting in New York in 1945, decided to change directions. "We decided," said Thurgood Marshall, "to make segregation itself our target." To launch a direct, frontal attack on segregation in the public schools required careful preparation, but by 1950 the N.A.A.C.P. was ready. On May 16 of that year its legal counsel filed a suit in the federal court in Charleston, South Carolina, on behalf of sixty-seven Negro children asking that they be admitted to the public schools of Clarendon County without regard to race. This case, along with four similar ones, eventually reached the Supreme Court, all of them taking the name *Brown v Board of Education.*

The issue before the Court was momentous. It had to decide whether a state or the District of Columbia had the constitutional power to operate segregated schools on the elementary and secondary levels. On May 17, 1954, the nine Justices, three of them southerners, rendered a unanimous decision: segregation of children in public schools solely on the basis of race was unconstitutional. Completely reversing the Plessy decision of 1896, the Court declared that separate educational facilities were inherently unequal and hence deprived the segregated person of the equal protection of the laws guaranteed by the Fourteenth Amendment.

The Brown decision was immediately recognized as a revolutionary step in American race relations. The decision itself applied only to schools below the college level, but it had unmistakable implications for public institutions of higher education. And it had similar implications for any publicly operated facility—library, museum, beach, park, zoo, or golf course. Indeed, the Brown decision could be extended to any field in which segregation was imposed by state law. It did not apply to private groups and organizations, but it would undoubtedly cause many of them to re-examine their racial policies.

In fine, the Brown decision meant that America would have to look anew at its colored citizens. "The abiding subconsciousness of the Negro turned overnight into an acute and immediate awareness of the Negro," wrote James Jackson Kilpatrick, editor of the *Richmond News Leader.* And as the nation came to grips with this historic decision, it would come face to face with a Negro who seemed to have grown taller.

10

Democracy's Deepening Challenge
(1954–1963)

THE SUPREME COURT'S decision in the school segregation cases created a sense of crisis in the South. Ever since Reconstruction its social structure had been buttressed by both social and legal sanctions. Now the latter had received a body blow, one that threatened the whole social pattern of the South.

The immediate reaction was varied. In border states, such as West Virginia and Missouri, the response was calm, if unenthusiastic. In intermediate states, such as North Carolina and Oklahoma, the attitude was one of "wait and see." But in the Deep South, states such as Alabama and Mississippi, the reaction was one of shock and anger, which soon hardened into defiant resistance.

Gradually this spirit of resistance spread throughout the South, fanned by the familiar belief that civil rights meant social equality. The resistance movement was led by white supremacy groups, of which the strongest were the White Citizens Councils. The first of these was organized at

Indianola, Mississippi, less than two months after the Brown decision. Others were soon organized in other states. The White Citizens Councils were generally made up of business and professional people, leaving to the Ku Klux Klan the mobilizing of lower-income groups.

The rapid growth and strength of the resistance movement had its influence on politics in the South, forcing public officials to denounce the Supreme Court's edict. The full weight of the organized resistance movement became evident in March 1956 when nineteen Senators and eighty-one House members issued a "Southern Manifesto" praising "the motives of those states which have declared the intention to resist forced integration by any lawful means." To declare war on the Brown decision had become almost a matter of survival to southerners holding public office.

Spearheaded by the White Citizens Councils, the strategies of resistance took many forms. On the constitutional level, the doctrine of interposition—that a state can interpose its own authority if the national government oversteps itself—was resurrected. The Supreme Court was vigorously condemned, being charged with basing its decision not upon the facts of law but upon psychological and sociological theories whose purposes were centralist and whose inspiration was socialistic.

Another form of resistance was economic reprisal. A Negro who sought to enter his child in a "white" school might find it difficult to keep his job, to have his teaching contract renewed, to extend his mortgage, or to get credit at the bank. A Negro tenant who favored integration ran the risk of being evicted. Similar reprisals were visited upon whites favoring integration, who had to bear the additional burden of being socially ostracized by their own group.

Among the resistance techniques was that of closing public schools and replacing them with "private" segregated schools. The most headlined of the school-closing incidents came in Little Rock, Arkansas, where the public schools remained shut during the entire term 1957–58. In Prince Edward County, Virginia, the public schools closed in 1959, although private schools for white children were operated with the support of state funds.

To strike at Negro-improvement organizations was a method of curbing or slowing down integration. In some southern cities the Urban League branches were removed from the Community Chest, losing a crucial source of income. The N.A.A.C.P., as was to be expected, was attacked most strongly: states investigated its activities, requested its membership lists, prohibited public employees from joining it (on the ground that it had Communist ties), and enjoined it from providing legal counsel in suits challenging the validity of state segregation laws.

The White Citizens Councils disclaimed the use of violence, but some of the individuals and groups advocating more direct action found it a ready instrument of resistance. The admission of nine Negro students to Central High School at Little Rock in September 1957 was followed by rioting and mob violence, making it necessary for President Eisenhower to rush federal troops to the city. Similarly, President Kennedy five years later had to dispatch regular army troops to Oxford, Mississippi, to put down a riot when James Meredith arrived to enroll as a student at the University. Such places as the churches of civil rights ministers, homes like that of militant lawyer Z. Alexander Looby of Nashville, or schoolhouses where some integration had taken place, as in Clinton, Tennessee, were bombed. A worker for civil rights might be roughly handled or shot at. Two such workers were murdered: William L. Moore, a white freedom walker, and Medgar W. Evers, N.A.A.C.P. field secretary for Mississippi.

The resistance technique of violence tended to be self-defeating. If violence did not create a sense of sympathy for its victims, it aroused a feeling of vexation toward its perpetrators. Moreover, violence hurt the business life of a community, for large corporations would not locate plants there, making it difficult for a violence-prone municipality to float its bonds at a normal interest rate.

There were other factors in bringing about a change in the initial unyielding attitude of the white South toward mixed schools. Parents of school-age children were not happy about closing the schools or turning them over to "private" parties in order to avoid integration. Moreover, the voices of some whites of unusual courage began to be heard—among them Ralph McGill in Georgia, James McBride Dabbs in South Carolina, and Sarah Patton Boyle in Virginia—telling their kinsmen that they must lay some of the ghosts of the past if the South were to remain true to some of her finest traditions.

As it became evident to the white South that some degree of compliance with the Brown decision was inevitable, the policy of massive resistance gave way to one of partial compliance. In the integrating of the schools, the southern states had some leeway. In the second Brown decision, delivered in May 1955, the Court declared that desegregation might be brought about "with all deliberate speed"—that when a start had been made the courts might find "that additional time is necessary to carry out the ruling in an effective manner."

The chief devices used by southern states to limit school integration as much as was legally possible were the stair-step and pupil-placement plans. The stair-step plan of integration operated on a grade-a-year basis, beginning with the first grade, so that it would take twelve years to integrate a given school. Proponents of the plan said that it avoided the difficulties of beginning the process of integration on the upperschool levels, where the academic preparation of the Negro student might differ markedly from that of the white.

In communities using the pupil-placement plan, the Negro students were originally placed in Negro schools but were permitted to apply for a transfer. In considering a transfer request, the school board based its decision upon the availability of facilities and the academic ability of the applicant, plus his conduct, morals, health, home environment, and ability to adjust in a new situation.

To seek such a transfer required considerable trouble, and in some instances court action. But, in spite of the difficulties, many Negro parents enrolled their children in formerly all-white schools. Entering the white schools for the first time, the smaller Negro children in the grades were perhaps more curious than apprehensive or troublesome. Some of the young Negro girls, wearing red ribbons in their hair, might giggle a little self-consciously as they walked through groups of white children. In Dallas, a Negro mother, asked by a reporter about her entering son's views on integration, replied simply, "He's just a little boy."

Negro boys and girls of high school age, knowing more of the ways of the world, were more apprehensive about their debut into formerly all-white schools. They had to be forewarned that they would face many trying experiences, including hard looks, name-callings, and ostracism. Some of them returned to all-Negro schools, but others persevered.

The courage and fortitude of these student pioneers betokened a will to succeed and a heart to fight. To an increasing degree these characteristics had become evident in Negro life since World War II. The ruling of the Supreme Court in the school segregation cases had been a boon to seekers of civil rights, but in the latter-day struggle for full equality it was a landmark rather than a point of origin. It was a component in what had become a rising wind. America's Negro sons and daughters had become more purposive, with their heightened militancy finding manifold expression.

In seeking to create a better picture of himself, and thus to move up to a plane of equality, the Negro attempted to influence those in control of such powerful media as motion pictures, television, and radio. Negro moviegoers in the forties notified Hollywood that they resented the stereotyped role of the Negro as a slow-witted, eyeball-rolling, splay-footed buffoon, and that they were not especially enamored of the ivory-toothed grins of Little Farina and Sunshine Sammy. Negroes protested that they did not care to view colored maids and "mammies" on the screen, even though Louise Beavers had made a reputation in such roles and Hattie McDaniel had won an "Oscar" from the Academy of Motion Picture Arts and Sciences for her "mammy" role in *Gone With the Wind.*

In protest against the type casting of Negroes, the N.A.A.C.P. in 1945 established a Hollywood unit to advise screen writers and producers. The film industry began to listen, aware that it had some responsibility to refrain from promoting race prejudice. As a result, Metro-Goldwin-Mayer abandoned its plans to screen *Uncle Tom's Cabin,* and Twentieth-Century-Fox changed the name of the film *Ten Little Niggers* to *Ten Little Indians.*

Negroes were not united in their attitude toward the full-length all-Negro pictures like *Cabin in the Sky* and *Stormy Weather.* Such films were enjoyed by many colored moviegoers, since they carried names that were household words in the world of Negro entertainment—Ethel Waters, Bill Robinson, Lena Horne, Louis Armstrong, and Cab Calloway. But Negro leaders deplored such pictures, sharing the opinion of William Grant Still that all-Negro films, no matter how expensive and glamorous, tended to "glorify segregation." Hollywood soon abandoned such pictures, not only because they drew criticism but also because they did not draw very well at the box office.

During the fifties Hollywood tended to break away from the stereotyped Negro and began to portray the Negro in roles which explored various aspects of the color line. The most outstanding Negro performer in motion pictures was Sidney Poitier, who became a first-rate Hollywood star on the basis of acting ability alone, not as a singer or dancer. But, while the film industry might explore the race problem in pictures, it was reluctant to cast a Negro as a doctor, lawyer, or scientist in pictures with non-Negro themes.

In television and in radio the Negro also sought to win equality of status, but, outside of sports, he was seldom encountered in the programs or the commercials. As in the films, Negro reform groups succeeded in bringing about the burial of the Negro buffoon type, but they were not able to secure any significant number of replacement roles for colored performers. Here again the matter of buying and selling loomed as all important. Sponsors of programs were fearful that the use of Negroes would incur the disapproval of many white buyers, particularly in the South. On radio and television Negro leaders and spokesmen were increasingly asked to comment on Negro questions. But rare was the occasion when a Negro, no matter how competent, was asked to take part in a program on the arts or sciences.

In the legitimate theater it was easier to bring about a change in attitude toward the Negro and the wider use of Negro actors. The American theater took its cue from Broadway, and a play that was to be performed on the New York stage for a sophisticated audience was free to deal with the Negro in dramatic terms rather than stereotyped patterns. Beginning with *Detective Story* in 1948, Negro actors were featured in roles that were nonracial.

After 1950 plays about Negro life with predominantly Negro casts appeared on Broadway, including Louis Peterson's *Take a Giant Step,* Ossie Davis's satire *Purlie Victorious,* and Lorraine Hansberry's *A Raisin in the Sun,* which won the Critics Circle Award. Plays written and acted by Negroes appeared on off-Broadway stages, many of them the productions of "little theater" groups which made use of library auditoriums and church basements. In these Negro-run community theaters, Negro life was treated in fresh and imaginative terms.

A Negro production of notable quality for its blending of drama and music was Langston Hughes's *Black Nativity*. This song-play, wrote critic Robert Shelton, took "the volcanic energy of Negro gospel music and channeled it skillfully toward theatrical ends." Striking a note of universal appeal, *Black Nativity* met with great success in half a dozen European capitals.

The critical and popular acclaim given to the Hughes work rested in part on its vibrant rhythms. It was this familiar element in Negro music that enabled colored folk singers like Huddie Ledbetter ("Leadbelly") and Josh White and jazz men like Edward K. ("Duke") Ellington and Count Basie to continue their dominant roles in popular music. In the development of "modern jazz" during the period following World War II, Charlie Parker, Thelonious Monk, Dizzy Gillespie, and Miles Davis were pre-eminent. Many of these later performers, unlike their predecessors, were college-trained and had made a serious study of music. As part of the cultural exchange program, the United States government arranged foreign tours for Negro jazz groups.

Like the folk ballad singers, the gospel singers, and the

jazz men, the colored composers of serious music made use of Negro idioms in the large art forms they employed. The best known of these contemporary composers was William Grant Still, born in Mississippi and educated at Oberlin and the New England Conservatory. Still's work was steeped in the Negro idiom, as suggested by such titles as "African American Symphony," "Pages from Negro History," and "Fanfare for the 99th Squadron."

The role of the Negro musician in the mass culture of America was matched to some extent by that of the Negro in sports. It hardly need be said that in some sports Negroes had been prominent long before World War II. In boxing the roster of outstanding Negroes went back to the days of heavyweight Peter Jackson, who at the turn of the century was hailed as the "Black Prince of the Ring." Many other Negro champions made prize ring history, including heavyweights Jack Johnson and Joe Louis, the latter holding the title for a record twelve years. Henry Armstrong was the only pugilist to hold three titles simultaneously, in one year—1938—winning the featherweight, lightweight, and welterweight crowns.

Over the years Negroes had been outstanding in track. In 1912 Howard P. Drew, representing the University of Southern California, broke into the "fastest human" class. In the twenties, thirties, and forties a procession of Negroes emerged as winners in the Olympic games, including DeHart Hubbard in the broad jump, Eddie Tolan in the 100-meter sprint, and the incomparable Jesse Owens in both the broad jump and the sprints. In the 1948 Olympic games four United States Negroes won first places, including Alice Coachman in the women's high jump. Miss Coachman's feat would pale in comparison with Wilma Rudolph's winning of three gold medals in Olympic competition twelve years later.

287

Two sports—horse racing and bicycle racing—in which Negroes had once been prominent were later closed to them. At the turn of the century Negro jockeys were common, the greatest being Isaac Murphy, who rode three Kentucky Derby winners in the 1880s. But by 1912 a Negro jockey was no longer permitted to have a mount in the Derby, and the other major tracks had adopted similar policies of exclusion. In bicycle racing Marshall W. (Major) Taylor became the American sprint champion in 1898, when he was only twenty, and until he retired twelve years later he bore the title "The Fastest Bicycle Rider in the World." But after his day, Negroes were frozen out of this sport. This exclusion had no lasting importance, however, for bicycle racing had already begun to lose its great popularity in America.

Any restrictions against the Negro in the world of sports tended to pale in the light of his great gains after World War II—especially in professional baseball. Since 1920 Negro leagues made up of such teams as the Kansas City Monarchs, the New York Bacharach Giants, and the Homestead Grays had existed, but Negro players had not been admitted to the major leagues or the important minor clubs. Negro sportswriters, supported by many of their white counterparts, urged club owners to give tryouts to colored players. In 1945 Branch Rickey, Sr., head of the Brooklyn Dodger system, took the bold step, signing Jackie Robinson, formerly an all-around athlete at U.C.L.A.

Rickey could not have made a better choice, for Robinson proved to be an exciting performer and a deadly competitor. In 1946 at Montreal he led the International League in batting and in stolen bases. Brought up to the major leagues in 1947, he won the "Rookie of the Year" award, which he capped two years later by being selected as the National League's "Most Valuable Player."

In subsequent years this high award would be won by

other Negroes—Willie Mays, Don Newcombe, Hank Aaron, Ernie Banks, and Maury Wills (and Elston Howard in the American League)—but it was Robinson who had unlocked the door. For his abilities on the diamond he was elected in 1962 to the baseball "Hall of Fame" at Cooperstown, New York. But his greatest significance lay in the fact that he, as no other single person, placed the Negro in the public eye.

Moreover, the example he set was not confined to baseball. "If he hadn't paved the way, I probably never would have got my chance," wrote tennis champion Althea Gibson, twice winner of the singles at Wimbledon, England. Professional football and professional basketball followed baseball's lead in using Negroes in goodly numbers. Negro stars were to become commonplace in both. In football the greatest Negro name was that of Jimmy Brown, the versatile and powerful back of the Cleveland Browns. Professional basketball had such names as Bill Russell, Oscar Robertson, Elgin Baylor, and Wilt ("The Stilt") Chamberlain, the highest-paid player in the history of the National Basketball Association. The participation of the Negro in sports that attract hundreds of thousands of spectators has been a significant development in bringing him into the mainstream of American life, and thereby in the larger promotion of American democracy.

Developing out of the Negro's struggle to broaden the base of democracy, and giving literary expression to it, was a new corps of writers. Most of these were novelists, among them Richard Wright, Chester Himes, Ann Petry, Ralph Ellison, and James Baldwin. As a rule, these authors wrote in a vein of protest, evoking the experience of deprivation and travail, whether the locale be a ghetto in Chicago, a shipyard in California, or a storefront church in Harlem. If the topics they dealt with were somber, the reason may be found in the answer Richard Wright gave to a young woman who asked him whether his ideas would make people happy: "I do not deal in happiness; I deal in meaning."

For all the social content of their pages, these novelists were more than mere chroniclers of hate and frustration. The tragic mood they evoked sprang basically from an underlying belief in the great ideals for which their country stood—ideals which had been perverted by color prejudice. These Negro writers thought of their characters as authentic Americans, Richard Wright giving the title, *Native Son,* to his first novel.

Some Negroes wrote novels dealing primarily with non-Negro characters and themes, Willard Motley's *Knock on Any Door* being a typical example. But writers who possessed sufficient literary skills—such as Wright, Ellison, and Baldwin—were able to take racial themes, often rooted in personal experience, and invest them with a universal touch. The work of such writers was significant because of the conception and quality of their performance. Neither their humanity nor that of their characters was limited by its racial context. In the hands of Richard Wright a Bigger Thomas became Everyman, not simply a neurotic young Negro foredoomed to run amok in a hate-twisted land.

The ablest Negro writers believed that they might perform a valuable service by calling upon their countrymen to stop looking through race-colored glasses. To come to grips with the Negro—this was their message to America. Out of such a confrontation would come something new and better. "It is the Negro," said James Baldwin, "who can make America what America must become."

Negro writers did not spare the Negro himself, calling attention to his shortcomings. The sharpest and most learned of these attacks came from sociologist E. Franklin Frazier. In *Black Bourgeoisie* he portrayed the Negro middle class as lacking in intellectual culture and having no love for learning. Negroes who had some money were portrayed by Frazier as black status seekers whose highest ambition was to appear in the society columns of the colored press, perhaps with an accompanying picture showing them entertaining friends at their country estate or attending a debutante ball at a "downtown" hotel.

Frazier's sharp criticisms drew indignant denials, but his book was widely read in colored circles. Its appearance heralded not only the growth of the Negro middle class but also the new spirit of self-analysis and self-criticism among Negroes. The ability to look at himself critically was an indication of the growing maturity of the Negro. But in viewing himself objectively—in facing reality himself—the Negro did not think it too much to ask that others do the same.

In the fifties, particularly after the Court decision in the school segregation cases, the Negro's battle for equality moved at a much faster pace. New organizations came into existence, bringing to the fore new faces and new techniques. By far the best known of the newer leaders was Martin Luther King, Jr., a Baptist clergyman who became a national figure because of his role in the Montgomery, Alabama, bus boycott.

This movement started on December 1, 1955, when seamstress Rosa Parks boarded a bus in downtown Montgomery, took a seat in the section reserved for whites, and refused to surrender it to a white man who subsequently entered the bus. "When I asked her what had happened," wrote an interviewer later, "she said she did not move," that "she had made up her mind never to move again."

The arrest of quiet Mrs. Parks, a college graduate and church worker, stirred the Negroes of the city. In protest, they decided to boycott the bus line, forming an organization, the Montgomery Improvement Association, with King as president. Until success came a year later, King led the movement—raising money to carry it on, organizing voluntary car pools, keeping the spirits of the protesters high, and holding weekly meetings at churches so that he might give instructions of the philosophy of nonviolent resistance to evil as expounded by Thoreau and practiced by Mahatma Gandhi, King's model. When in December 1956 the Supreme Court, affirming the decision of a lower federal tribunal, declared that Alabama's state and local laws requiring segregation on buses were unconstitutional, it was a victory shared by thousands. But foremost among them was King.

The Montgomery bus boycott, and its leader, had received national attention. The success of the boycott brought wide fame to King and endeared him to Negroes everywhere. To them he became an oracle and a miracle worker rolled in one. Whether he would have it or not, leadership was thrust upon him.

King was not the sort to avoid a challenge. Leaving Montgomery and returning to Atlanta, he divided his time between his duties as associate pastor (along with his father) of Ebenezer Baptist Church and as president of the Southern Christian Leadership Conference. Founded in 1957 by 100 clergymen, the latter organization reflected the belief that the church should become a dominant force in the battle for civil rights. Its key personnel were ministers, a majority of them Baptists. The organization had an able executive director, Reverend Wyatt T. Walker, who in the spring of 1963 headed a paid staff of nearly fifty workers and supervised the operations of the loose union of eighty-five affiliates. As might be expected, the campaigns conducted by the Southern Christian Leadership Council had a distinctly religious tone, with an emphasis on nonviolence.

The strength of the S.C.L.C. centered in King, who remained the most popular of Negro leaders. People could not forget that he had been imprisoned twelve times, that he had been the victim of a near-fatal stabbing, and that he and his family had been constantly threatened. King was an eloquent public speaker, with a resonant voice and a florid style reminiscent of the great orators of the nineteenth century. Everything he said and wrote carried a stamp of sincerity and dedication. He was a man of this world. "I'm not concerned with the New Jerusalem," he said in 1960: "I'm concerned with the New Atlanta, the New Birmingham, the New Montgomery, the New South." But if he preached a social gospel and went out into the streets, he also had a reflective turn of mind, as may be gleaned from the pages of his books, *Stride Toward Freedom* and *Strength to Love,* in both of which he revealed himself a man of deep compassion. "One day we shall win freedom, but not only for ourselves," he wrote in the latter. "We shall so appeal to your heart and conscience that we shall win you in the process."

Although King was a man of unquestioned influence neither he nor the S.C.L.C. held the spotlight alone. In the Negro revolution of the fifties and sixties, there were other strong voices, other important organizations. One of these groups, the Congress of Racial Equality, was akin to the S.C.L.C. in that it held to a philosophy of nonviolent direct action, and its national director, James Farmer, was akin to King in his discipleship to Gandhi. CORE actually was older than King's organization, going back to 1942, when Farmer—with the help of the pacifist Fellowship of Reconciliation, of which he was race relations secretary—established a Chicago Committee on Racial Equality. Out of this grew the national organization CORE, an interracial urban movement with headquarters in Chicago until 1946 and in New York since then.

CORE's growth was slow until the middle fifties, when it began to recruit students in increasing numbers and to move into the South. By the spring of 1963 the organization had a paid staff of thirty-five and an annual budget of over $700,000, most of which came from the dues of its 70,000 members. Part of CORE's growth may be attributed to its use of new action techniques to combat discrimination. CORE trained many of the southern student leaders in the proper method of staging a "sit-in."

Strictly speaking, the "sit-in" technique was not new. Since Reconstruction days Negroes had protested segregation by taking seats in white sections of theaters and streetcars. Indeed, the Louisville "ride-in" campaign of 1871 had received nationwide attention, ending only when the horse-drawn streetcars permitted mixed seating. What was new about the "sit-in" technique in 1960 was the manner in which it captured the imagination of southern Negroes, especially college students.

The contemporary "sit-in" movement began on February 1, 1960, when four students from North Carolina Agricultural and Technical College at Greensboro sat down at the segregated lunch counter in a Woolworth store and were refused service. Keeping their seats, the students opened their textbooks and began to read their lessons. The counter was closed down, but the next day the students came back. A local Negro dentist, learning of their action, telephoned to CORE in New York, and within hours a corps of trained field workers were on their way to Greensboro. They conducted institutes in which the student "sit-ins" were schooled in the techniques of nonviolent protest—the refusal to laugh, strike back, or curse, the ability to bear everything without whining or anger.

As students in other cities heard about the Greensboro demonstrations and decided to stage "sit-ins" of their own, the movement soon took on massive proportions. Within eighteen months, as reported by the Southern Regional Council, 70,000 persons had taken part in student "sit-ins." The results were equally impressive, no fewer than 101 southern communities having desegregated one or more of their eating places.

The "sit-in" movement stirred the conscience of the South and of the nation. The sight of well-dressed and well-behaved young men and women not being served was bad enough, but many of them, and their white associates, were spat upon and dragged from their seats. More than 3,600 of them went to jail during the first six months of the demonstrations; many refused bail, preferring to stay in jail until the day of their court trial. While in jail some went on hunger strikes, others volunteered for solitary confinement, and all of them sang the new songs about such upsetting things as freedom and love and equality, recurring often to their theme song, "We Shall Overcome."

Although the "sit-in" movement received considerable assistance from CORE and other groups, it remained student-centered and -led. The effort to coordinate the movement led to the founding of the Student Non-Violent Coordinating Committee, with headquarters in Atlanta. This group, dubbed SNICK, received some of its support from the Northern Student Movement, a group dedicated to helping Negro student, North and South.

Since the "sit-in" demonstrators were young people testing segregation in eating places, it remained for another and more elderly group, the "freedom riders," to test segregation on buses and in bus stations. Although the Interstate Commerce Commission in 1955 had ruled against the segregation of interstate passengers, and the Supreme Court had decreed in 1956 that segregation on public buses was unlawful, the practice had not stopped. In May 1961 the

Congress of Racial Equality decided to challenge "Jim Crow" in travel.

CORE selected a party of thirteen to make the trip, including national director James Farmer and six whites. Leaving Washington on May 4, these pioneer "freedom riders" traveled through Virginia, the Carolinas, and Georgia without serious trouble. In Alabama they met with violence: outside of Anniston one of the buses in which they were traveling was burned, and when they reached Birmingham the riders were attacked as they got off the bus, one of them requiring some fifty head stitches. Unable to get bus transportation out of Birmingham, the group took a plane to New Orleans, their destination point.

Though the riders had been unable to make the complete trip by bus, their mission was not a failure. Their courage and their ordeal in Alabama evoked expressions of sympathy from church groups and the public press. Other groups of riders quickly formed, undeterred by the threat of violence or the likelihood of being jailed. They encountered some violence, although no more bus burnings, and some were arrested. But increasingly it became easier for Negro passengers to sit anywhere in buses and in bus stations.

Although CORE had sponsored the first group of "freedom riders," the bus-travel movement, like other civil rights efforts, had the wholehearted support of other Negro-improvement groups. Among the five major organizations—the N.A.A.C.P., the Urban League, CORE, the S.L.C.U., and SNICK—some rivalry for power and financial support was to be expected. Actually, far less time and effort were spent on organizational confusion than was typical among reformers. Recognizing that their aims were identical and that their task was urgent, many-sided, and formidable, the groups tended to work together more and more.

The two "old-line" organizations—the Urban League

and the N.A.A.C.P.—showed a resilient capacity to move with the times. While the League did not organize demonstrations or advocate other activist methods, it expressed its support for those who did. Its national board of trustees urged President Kennedy to protect the lives and the rights of the "freedom riders" in the summer of 1961. Recently the League has advanced the argument that the Negro, having suffered denial for so long a time, now needs a period of special consideration. As put by Whitney Young, Jr., the League's able executive director: "As the colored American for more than 300 years has been given the special consideration of exclusion, he must now be given special treatment by society, through services and opportunities, that will insure his inclusion as a citizen able to compete equally with others."

The N.A.A.C.P. showed no signs of relinquishing its predominant role in the battle for equality. In court cases involving civil rights it continued to furnish most of the legal counsel, in 1962 bearing more than 90 per cent of the financial burden. In the spring of 1963 its Legal Defense and Educational Fund was handling 125 court cases, some of them costly. After the "sit-in" movement had begun, the organization did pay more attention to the formation of youth councils and college chapters, its youth memberships increasing from 23,512 in 1961 to 37,913 in 1963. The N.A.A.C.P. has taken pains to make clear that its attack "has been from all angles, at all targets, at all times, with all weapons, over all the years."

Like the N.A.A.C.P., the other organizations working for Negro equality found it necessary to attack from many angles. Job rights, housing rights, and voting rights were seen to be interwoven, and to be closely related to other rights, such as equality in public schooling and public accommodations. A brief look at the areas of jobs, housing, and voting will indicate both their related character and their contemporary importance.

After World War II, as has been noted, the executive branch of the national government, along with many state governments, made an effort to establish fair employment practices. But in the sixties the Negro worker still faced special problems. Negro women found it particularly difficult to push back artificial employment barriers. Industry was loathe to appoint Negroes to administrative or managerial jobs; in the ten years from 1948 to 1958 Negro managers and officials climbed only 0.2 per cent. The income gap between the white and Negro worker did not narrow. In 1951 the average Negro's income was 62 per cent of the average white man's, but by 1962 the Negro was receiving only 55 per cent of the income received by the white. In 1960 the average wage for the white worker was $5,137, whereas for the Negro worker it was $3,075.

As always, the greatest threat to the Negro worker was joblessness. The persistently high unemployment level in the American economy during the sixties has affected the Negro. In March 1963, 12 per cent of the Negro population was unemployed, whereas for the population as a whole the rate was 5.6 per cent. Moreover, the world of work was increasingly haunted by the specter of automation, adding to the Negro's danger of being reduced to the ranks of the chronically unemployed.

Negro-improvement organizations had sought in various ways to get more jobs for colored workers. In many of the larger cities, North and South, the Negroes conducted "selective patronage campaigns," urging customers not to buy from firms which do not hire or upgrade Negroes. This purchasing-power theory of unemployment was not new, for Negroes in the thirties had conducted "double duty dollar" and "don't buy where you can't work" campaigns. But in the sixties such efforts were far more successfully conceived and planned and were led by Negro clergymen with large congregations. Moreover, the buying power of the Negro had increased. For all his deprivation, the Negro in 1962 had an income of $23 billion a year, thus forming a sizable component of purchasing power in the market place. And, finally, the selective patronage efforts were successful because the merchants against whom they were directed found a new mood of cooperation and determination among Negro buyers.

Another technique recently used more than ever by seekers of jobs for Negroes was mass picketing and demonstrating at construction sites where few or no Negroes are employed. The ranks of the demonstrators often included clergymen, white and colored. In some instances the demonstrators were not satisfied with carrying signs and singing songs: they blocked the roads in attempts to prevent both workers and materials from getting through.

Though the Negro's high level of unemployment and lower average income had a marked effect on the kind of housing he could afford, his residence was also determined by the color of his skin. As the United States Civil Rights Commission pointed out in 1959, housing "seems to be the one commodity in the American market that is not freely available to everyone who can afford to pay." By the beginning of the sixties, segregation in housing had become a universal fact of Negro life.

In the North the confining of the Negro to certain neighborhoods had not begun until the twenties, following the Negro migrations from the South. As whites began to adopt racial zoning policies, a Negro who tried to move into a "white" district increasingly faced the kind of experience that came to Dr. Ossian H. Sweet in 1925. Upon returning from several years of study in Vienna and a period of research on radium effects under Madame Curie's direction,

Sweet purchased a home in an all-white neighborhood in Detroit. On the second night that a crowd of stone-throwing demonstrators gathered outside the home, they were met by an answering burst of gunfire that killed a white man. The occupants of the house were arrested and brought to trial. They were eventually acquitted, the N.A.A.C.P. having engaged Clarence Darrow and Arthur Garfield Hayes to defend them.

After the Sweet case, more subtle ways were found to confine Negroes to separate neighborhoods. Real estate group—builders, brokers, and mortgage lenders—who wielded great influence in determining where people should live adopted a policy of racial homogeneity. White renters or buyers were shown properties in "white" areas only, and Negro renters in "Negro" areas. Until recent years the federal government itself was a staunch supporter of segregated facilities, the Federal Housing Administration recommending, in an early underwriting manual, that "properties shall continue to be occupied by the same social and racial class."

Federally supported renewal projects imposed a particular hardship on colored tenants and home owners. Nearly three-quarters of the families removed by slum clearance and redevelopment projects have been Negroes. "Urban renewal means Negro removal," ran a wry quip. In some instances where the neighborhood selected for renewal had been stable and integrated, the displaced white families were offered a wide choice of selection, while their Negro counterparts could go only where the shrinking supply of "colored" housing was available.

Segregated housing also operated to the disadvantage of the Negro by fostering a "two-price" system in which he paid a higher price than a white renter or purchaser for the same housing. To meet the higher prices, Negro families often had to double up or take in lodgers, increasing the population density of the neighborhood. Moreover, segregated housing tended to produce segregated schools.

To combat housing discrimination, Negro groups sponsored a policy of "open occupancy" in the real estate market—the freeing of sales and rentals from racial restrictions and the integration of public and private housing. Negro organizations have sought to dispel whites' fears about living next door to a Negro, including the belief that property values decline when a Negro moves into the neighborhood. This belief owed its chief strength to "block-busting" real estate manipulators, white and colored, whose profits were greatest when people were panicked into selling.

The policy of open occupancy received support in many quarters. In November 1962 President Kennedy issued an executive order barring discrimination in the sale or rental of federal housing as well as housing financed through federal assistance. By February 1963 eighteen states had passed open occupancy laws, and fifty-five cities had followed suit. Every major church group in America has taken a stand for fair housing practices, and in many communities voluntary groups of "citizens for integrated living" have been at work. And the successful operation of more than 100 interracial community developments in the early sixties was a measurable step toward an open market in housing.

The achievement of fair employment and fair housing practices was closely linked to the Negro's power at the polls. Since the Negro's greatest gains were won in those cities and states where his vote was important, it was not surprising that "white supremacy" advocates in the South concentrated their efforts on maintaining discrimination at the polls. The white primary had run afoul of the Supreme Court in 1944, but an effective substitute had been found in the registration hurdle.

A Negro desiring to vote had to run an obstacle course strewn with technical roadblocks. To begin with, the applicant might have to play a game of "hide and seek" before he even found the registrar. Once found, the latter might employ a number of discriminatory techniques, such as requiring identity "vouchers" from would-be Negro applicants or requiring them to take a lengthy written test, which they would fail for no apparent reason. A registrar might engage in a massive slowdown in processing the applications of Negroes, or he might never notify them as to his decision.

At Tuskegee, Alabama, where a sizable number of Negroes managed to register, the state legislature changed the town's boundaries in order to minimize the Negro vote, but this gerrymander was declared unconstitutional (*Gomillion v Lightfoot,* 1960). Aside from registration procedures, the most effective deterrent to Negro voting in the densely Negro-populated regions in the South was economic pressure. When Negroes depended upon white landlords for goods and credit, they feared the loss of both if they asserted their rights. Such was the case in Fayette and Haywood counties in Tennessee, where vote-minded sharecroppers received eviction notices.

Nonvoting among Negroes was not caused solely by political discrimination and intimidation by whites. Many Negroes of low income and little schooling, North and South, showed no interest in voting. To overcome such political apathy, Negro organizations and community leaders waged registration and "get out the vote" campaigns. This crusade for the franchise was based on the contention that the ballot was a means by which the Negro could correct injustices. "One of the most significant steps a Negro can take is the short step to the voting booth," said Dr. King.

The increased efforts to make the Negro rank and file politically aware were not lost on the seekers of public office. The Negro's voting strength was a vital factor in forcing Congress to address itself to the problem of racial discrimination, thus somewhat belatedly following the lead of the Supreme Court and the chief executive. In 1957 Congress passed a Civil Rights Act designed to prevent the denial of voting rights, and set up an investigative agency— a Commission on Civil Rights. Three years later Congress reaffirmed its interest and concern by passing a second Civil Rights Act.

In the political campaign of 1960 the Negro's power would be demonstrated in the election of five Negroes to the House of Representatives, and in furnishing the successful presidential candidate, John F. Kennedy, with the crucial margin of votes necessary for his narrow victories in Illinois, Michigan, and South Carolina. After 1960, with the waning of the poll tax and with the Supreme Court–ordered reapportionment of state legislatures, long dominated by a rural, status quo point of view, the Negro vote would become more important. In April 1962 Negroes comprised 17.6 per cent of the voting age population of the twenty-five largest cities in the land.

The question of the proper role and status for the Negro in American life dated back to 1619 when the Dutch man-of-war landed its twenty "Negars" at Jamestown. But in the 1960s it took on two new and major proportions, scope and urgency.

In the 1960s, as never before, the Negro became an object of nationwide attention. No longer did he arouse only a sectional awareness, for by 1960 the Negro population was more widely distributed than ever before. During the 1950s a total of 1,457,000 Negroes left the South, a record number for any ten-year period. During those years the rural southerner had not fared well, with machines replacing the man and the mule. Other technological advances cut the need for farm labor, and the crop acreage was reduced. To the Negro the only solution was migration. And, unlike the white rural workers, most of whom went to southern cities, the Negro surplus workers, except for a meagre 7.5 per cent, left the South completely. In the cities of the North and West the sharp rise in the number of Negroes meant that note must be taken not only of these recent arrivals but of the entire colored population, old and new.

In the sixties the national conscience became more aware of the Negro. Church and religious groups joined in the fight for racial equality. "The Church of Jesus Christ can make no compromise with discrimination or segregation on the basis of race," declared the National Council of Churches of Christ in July 1963. This was not the first time this group of churchmen had spoken out on behalf of justice, but increasingly such statements would be carefully pondered by the public. A more receptive audience awaited other religious groups whose voices had been raised for human brotherhood and equality, including the American Jewish Committee and the Catholic Interracial Council, under the leadership of Father John La Farge.

Not limited even to its national scope, the role of the Negro in American society in the sixties had its significant influence in lands across the seas. The United States had been plunged into the international spotlight as a result of becoming the leader of the free world, which inevitably exposed it to the kind of searching scrutiny implicit in a statement by Attorney General Robert F. Kennedy on April 21, 1963: "If we say that a Negro is not as good as a white person, I don't see how we can then go to any part of the world and say we have a system different from the Soviet Union." This point of view was echoed a month later by Secretary of State Dean Rusk, who stated at a foreign policy conference that the United States was running in the international race against the Communists "with one of our legs in a cast" because of racial discrimination at home.

The nonwhite peoples of the world were quick to take note of America's domestic practices concerning her Negro citizens. The image America created among yellow, brown, and black peoples everywhere would be influenced by racial policies and practices within her own borders. And, in a larger sense, America's treatment of her own Negroes would be regarded as an index of her moral capacity to lead the free world. The American Negro became the touchstone of Western man's ability to transcend color prejudice in the building of tomorrow's world.

In the sixties the Negro question assumed a new urgency, for the nation's awakening to its responsibility to its colored citizens was brought about in large measure by Negroes themselves. Their pressure for change had almost a "now or never" quality. It is not that Negroes were listening to a different drummer; it was rather that they were calling for a much faster beat, as befitted a more urgent hour.

More Negroes than ever before were city dwellers, and their sense of economic power mounted despite their disadvantages. The gains they had made had not matched their rising level of expectation. And the progress toward equality had been, they felt, far too slow: 100 years had passed since the Emancipation Proclamation, but they were still not wholly free; ten years after the Supreme Court's ruling in the school segregation cases, over 90 per cent of the Negro children were still going to all-Negro schools.

The Negro of the sixties had a keener sense of the many and varied opportunities he had missed but which he might have shared had his skin been white. To obtain these opportunities he was willing to run risks. He was less reluctant to offend the feelings of white people of the "go-slow," "look-how-far-you-have-come" type. As his loss of fear became more marked, he pressed harder for equality of opportunity because he saw himself as an equal. His self-image had taken an upward turn. He no longer regarded himself as a lesser, inferior person. That in his own mind he stood equal was the impelling force behind the Negro's demand that he be served like anyone else in hotels, theaters, and restaurants.

One of the components of the Negro's new self-image was his changed attitude toward the land of his fathers. Just as American Negroes were no longer ashamed of their color, so they were no longer ashamed of having originally come from Africa. "I am confident," wrote Ralph Bunche in 1961, "that I reflect accurately the views of virtually all Negro Americans when I say that I am proud of my ancestry, just as I am proud of my nationality." Negroes took note of the impressive number of newly independent African nations—twenty-nine from 1950 to mid-1963—that had emerged on the world scene. They saw pictures of the diplomats from these self-governing countries speaking at the sessions of the United Nations.

Not satisfied with sharing a pride in the newly independent black nations, some American Negroes sought to identify with it. In 1957 a group of intellectuals and artists, including the musician-composer Duke Ellington and the poet Langston Hughes, founded the American Society of African Culture, with the aim of "presenting black African sculpture, dance, music, art and literature—the high culture of the African Negro as it has existed in Africa, in the

United States and in Latin America," to use the language of John A. Davis, the organization's president.

Noting the changes that had taken place in Africa and in their own country since the end of World War II, most Negroes felt that the future was not hopeless. They had not given up the American dream. But this attitude of guarded hope was not shared by one group, the Black Muslims.

Aimed at the unemployed, lower-income, and lesser-educated Negroes who were most likely to succumb to despair, the Black Muslim movement was both religious and secular: Its followers held that Allah had commissioned as his messenger Elijah Muhammad, born in Georgia over sixty years ago as Elijah Poole. During the 1930s Elijah Muhammad established his headquarters at Chicago. The movement—the Nation of Islam—had radiated to some thirty states by 1963, with a membership of over 50,000 (perhaps well over that figure, the actual numbers being kept secret). Bent on becoming economically self-sufficient, the Muslims made it a point to be industrious and thrifty, for their goal was to set up their own stores. They succeeded in rehabilitating those followers who had been drunkards or drug addicts, and they gave to their entire membership a sense of dignity and self-worth.

The Muslims were a self-segregating group. Suspicious and distrustful of whites, they wanted a complete separation from them. As a sort of "back pay" for services rendered, they asked that a portion of the United States be set aside for exclusive Negro occupancy. The Muslim belief that whites and Negroes could never get along together was one that most Negroes found hard to accept. Negroes who had worked in civil rights movements, or who had ever seen such movements in operation, were well aware of the large measure of support they received from whites. Indeed, in the sixties many of the civil rights organizations felt a sense of satisfaction that they had become increasingly interracial in character.

Negroes could understand the forces that gave rise of the Black Muslim movement, and they could sympathize with the constructive elements in its philosophy. But what the overwhelming majority of Negroes wanted was their full rights as American citizens. They could not agree with the Muslim point of view that this was not possible.

To most Negroes outside the Muslim movement, the vision of the founders of this republic was still a vital force. Americans to the core, they believed that freedom and equality for all could be achieved in their native land. This belief they would not easily surrender, for it had been their lodestar.

This belief had been one of their significant contributions to the making of America. In enlarging the meaning of freedom and in giving it new expressions, the Negro had played a major role. He had been a watchman on the wall. More fully than any other American, he knew that freedom was hard-won and could be preserved only by continuous effort. The faith and works of the Negro over the years had made it possible for the American creed to retain so much of its deep appeal, so much of its moving power.

A conclusive demonstration of such faith and works took place on August 28, 1963, in the "March on Washington for Freedom and Jobs." Sponsored by more than 400 national organizations, the March turned out to be an event of which America could "properly be proud," in President Kennedy's words. Over 200,000 Americans—white and black, Christian and Jewish—assembled for a nearly mile-long march from the Washington Monument to the Lincoln Memorial. Here they listened to moving speeches from liberal whites and from Negro leaders, including A. Philip

Randolph, Roy Wilkins, and Martin Luther King (the lone absentee among the leaders was James Farmer, lodged in a Donaldsville, Louisiana, jail for having taken part in a demonstration in Plaquemine). These speakers conveyed a common note of urgency, as if to underscore the word "Now" which appeared on hundreds of placards. If the speakers transmitted something of their own fervor and determination, they also struck a broadly patriotic note, for in their thinking the March was a reaffirmation of the Constitution and the Declaration of Independence.

An effort that brought together all the major civil rights organizations, plus many church groups, the March was a climax and beginning. It served notice that America's Negroes were no longer willing to wait generation after generation for rights that other citizens took for granted. And it brought America face to face with her full responsibilities as a nation. The days of decision had come—this was the historic meaning of the March. America must needs address herself to the unfinished business of democracy, and time was of the essence.

11

A Fluid Front (1963–1970)

How would the nation react to the urgent challenge embodied in the March on Washington? For one thing, the news media began to give much more coverage and space to the black American. Magazines and journals vied with the daily papers in featuring the Negro, probing his discontent if not his psyche. Public opinion surveys prodded many whites to indicate their views on the Negro. To some this sense of insistent urgency in Negro-white relations was stimulating, but to many it was upsetting.

Painful or not, there it was. The various branches of the federal government quickly responded. During the closing months of 1963, President Kennedy threw his full support behind a new civil rights bill. Kennedy's assassination in late November 1963 stunned the country, leaving Negroes with an especial sense of loss. But his successor, Lyndon B. Johnson, served immediate notice that no memorial to the fallen leader could be more fitting than a strong civil rights bill.

A Fluid Front (1963–1970)

President Johnson stamped himself as a leader in civil rights, surpassing by far any of his predecessors. In the election of 1964 he chose as his running mate Senator Hubert H. Humphrey, himself a long-time supporter of the Negro. In the process of an easy win over Barry Goldwater, the Republican candidate, Johnson won some 95 per cent of the black vote. Negro voters enabled Johnson to carry four southern states—Arkansas, Florida, Tennessee, and Virginia—that otherwise would have gone to Goldwater. If Johnson's response stemmed from this support at the polls, it also mirrored his personal convictions. In a commencement day address at Howard University in June 1965, he pledged to "dedicate the expanding efforts of my administration" to helping the black American win his way in our national life.

Johnson appointed Negroes to positions never previously held by anyone of their group. In 1965, Thurgood Marshall became Solicitor General of the United States, followed two years later by his appointment as an Associate Justice of the United States Supreme Court. Robert C. Weaver was named Secretary of the Department of Housing and Urban Development, which, although a new agency, had 13,000 employees at the outset and in its first year ranked seventh in gross expenditures among the eleven cabinet departments. Carl T. Rowan, former ambassador to Finland, became director of the United States Information Agency, thereby taking a seat on the National Security Council. In line with his efforts to give women a more prominent role in public life, President Johnson appointed Patricia R. Harris as ambassador to Luxembourg, the first Negro woman to hold such a diplomatic post of this rank. In 1967, Johnson reorganized the District of Columbia government and appointed Walter E. Washington as the capital's chief executive, in essence its mayor.

"Each official of the government must understand that every program for which he is responsible must be administered to insure equal opportunity for all Americans," said Johnson on September 24, 1965. Thus all federal departments and agencies were charged with observing civil rights laws and regulations. Assisting them were seven federal agencies specifically charged with finding facts, conciliating the parties in dispute, and enforcing the law. In addition to the Commission on Civil Rights, these agencies included the Civil Rights Division of the Department of Justice and the Office of Federal Contract Compliance of the Department of Labor. As if to set an example, these agencies recruited their staffs without regard to race, color, or national origin. The Community Relations Service, under the Department of Commerce before being transferred to the Justice Department, was headed by presidential appointee Roger Wilkins.

The Community Relations Department and an Equal Opportunity Employment Commission were established by the Civil Rights Act of 1964. Spurred by two presidents, Kennedy and Johnson, this comprehensive measure dealt with voting, public accommodations and facilities, and discrimination in jobs. The most immediate effect of the act was the desegregation of some hotels, restaurants, and theaters in the larger cities of the South. But many dining places simply removed their "White Only" signs and declared themselves private clubs and therefore not affected by the law in question.

The accommodations section of the Civil Rights Act was attacked as being unconstitutional. One of the cases coming before the federal courts involved an Atlanta restaurant owner, Lester Maddox, who brandished a gun while refusing to serve three Negroes. The Supreme Court, in a unanimous decision, upheld the Civil Rights Act, rejecting the claim that to forbid race discrimination in public accommodations was a denial of personal liberty.

As the Civil Rights Act was making its initial impact, Congress was putting the finishing touches on another important measure, an act devoted exclusively to voting. Such a law had been requested in March 1965 by President Johnson in an address in which he characterized the Negro as "the one whose courage had awakened the American conscience." Black people did indeed deserve much of the credit for the voting rights act.

In this black thrust for equality at the polls the leadership had fallen to Martin Luther King. Upon his return from Sweden, where on December 10, 1964, he had been awarded the coveted Nobel prize for peace, King had gone to Selma, Alabama, to assist in the voter registration campaign. Sheriff James G. Clark had led in the work of keeping the black vote very low. Beginning in January, King had the county Negroes marching to the courthouse where they sang, chanted, and prayed. Two months later King scheduled a march from Selma to the state capitol at Montgomery, fifty miles away. This attempt on March 7, 1965, was turned back by Sheriff Clark's men assisted by state troopers. Their use of night sticks and tear-gas bombs aroused indignation throughout the country. This sense of outrage was stimulated a few days later with the death of a supporter of the march, the Reverend James J. Reeb.

Two weeks after the first attempt, the civil rights workers, with the national spotlight on them, held another march, spurred on by King's exhortation to "Walk together, children." This time the marchers were protected by the Alabama National Guard, called into federal service by Johnson. After five days of hiking and singing, the group reached Montgomery, where a crowd of 25,000 assembled on the steps of the state capitol. It was a historic moment, although marred before midnight by the assassination of Viola Gregg Liuzzo, like Reeb a white advocate of the cause.

The dramatic events at Selma spurred Congress to pass a voting rights bill, Johnson signing it on August 6, 1965. The three civil rights laws since 1957 had not provided direct federal action in enabling Negroes to vote. But the new measure, affecting six southern states and part of a seventh, plus Alaska, provided for federal examiners to monitor elections. The second central feature of the bill called for the registration of those who could not read or write provided that they were qualified otherwise. The act also directed the Attorney General to challenge the legality of poll taxes in elections for state and local offices, the recently ratified Twenty-fourth Amendment having eliminated such taxes in the election of congressmen, the president, and vice-president. A year later the Supreme Court would respond by holding the poll tax unconstitutional in state elections.

The abolition of the literacy tests had a far-reaching effect. The officials in five southern states served notice that they would challenge the act but in general there was a full cessation of reading and writing tests. There was a significant increase in black voting and running for office in the South. During the four months after the passage of the act more than 175,000 southern Negroes were registered, over half of them as a result of the work of the Southern Christian Leadership Conference. Other black groups bent on political activity included the Lowndes County Freedom Organization, organized following a plea by Stokely Carmichael, and the Mississippi Freedom party, whose best-known figure was Fannie Lou Hamer.

In the two years after the passage of the voting rights act the Negro registration in Mississippi went from 6.7 to

59.8 per cent, and in Alabama from 19.3 to 51.6 per cent. In this span the number of Negro officeholders rose to over 200, more than double the previous high. In Macon County, Alabama, Lucius D. Amerson became the first Negro sheriff since Reconstruction. In Arkansas black votes helped Winthrop Rockefeller win the governor's chair. In Selma the recently registered Negroes brought about the defeat of Sheriff Clark for re-election.

Something of the spirit of these new voters was expressed by Selma's Mrs. Cornelius Pox who in spite of her eighty years got in line early to await the opening of the polls. "I feel all right," she said, in response to a reporter's question. "I am glad to do it this side of Judgment."

The enactments of Congress in civil rights and voter registration were important steps toward equality of opportunity. But the deeply rooted problems they attacked were far from being routed. Any significant rise in the status of the black American was bound to meet with some resistance. For example, the voting rights act, despite its substantial increase in registrants, and not all of them black, still fell considerably short of its goals.

In many instances Negro registration lagged due to a lack of federal registrars. In Birmingham such officers were appointed only after daily mass marches by the S.C.L.C. Negroes felt that the Johnson Administration was relying too heavily upon voluntary compliance by southern communities. A black registrant might find his name omitted from the official voter list or his ballot disqualified on technical grounds. A black office-seeker might find that the office he sought had been abolished or had been changed from an elective position to an appointive one.

In some parts of the Deep South the black office-seeker or voter faced harassment or violence. A rifle visibly displayed from a truck parked near a registration site might have its effect on a person of less than heroic mold. Negro registration in Lowndes County, Alabama, undoubtedly would have been greater but for the killing of Jonathan M. Daniels, a young white theology student and civil rights worker, by a part-time deputy sheriff. This form of veiled threat undoubtedly influenced the county elections in 1966 in which the Negro candidates lost although Negro voters were in a majority.

In some instances the Negro registration was kept down by a lack of political organization. In the southern states the major parties, Republican as well as Democrat, still practiced racial discrimination within their organizations or were unconcerned about equal suffrage. Sometimes it was the Negro himself who was indifferent. In some instances the ingrained habit of not voting, of having no role in civic affairs, was too strong to shake. And economic dependence deterred many poor blacks from claiming their political rights.

Full enfranchisement was not the only goal that eluded the southern Negro in the sixties. The economic pinch had lost little of its grip. In the rural areas the cycle of black poverty and dependency remained unbroken. The mechanization of farming, particularly the mechanical cotton picker, tended to force blacks off the land. The remaining Negro farms, small and poor, needed assistance.

Federal programs, under the Department of Agriculture, had been started to aid the rural southerner. This mission had been accomplished in the case of many white farmers. But their black counterparts received little help from the state or the federal government. The Department of Agriculture employed very few Negro agents, particularly in the Farmers Home Administration program, which meant that Negro farmers seeking a loan had to face an all-white, prejudicial board of county commissioners. In 1965, the Civil Rights Commission reported that their analysis of the four major programs of the Department clearly indicated a failure "to assume responsibility for assuring equal opportunity and equal treatment to all."

Continued poverty, reinforced by the pattern of discrimination, led many Negroes to leave the land. In the three decades following the end of World War II more than 3,000,000 colored people moved from the South to the North. These uprooted blacks, like those who had preceded them, made their way to the big city ghettos. By 1966 more than two-thirds of the Negro population had become urban dwellers, of whom one-half were concentrated in twelve cities. The influx to the cities would furnish a potential base of power for black politicians and new and more fiery black spokesmen. But the newcomers to the ghetto soon found that they had simply exchanged one poverty cycle for another.

The federal government had announced a war on poverty headed by R. Sargent Shriver, director of the Office of Economic Opportunity. But black joblessness did not lessen. Despite Shriver's efforts and the war in Vietnam, the Negro unemployment ratio remained the same, twice as great as that of whites. The reasons were familiar—a combination of advancing technology and a pattern of job discrimination. "Of the many groups now being exiled from the economy because of automation, the Negro is taking the cruelest blows," wrote Whitney M. Young, Jr., in the spring of 1966.

Racial inequality in employment proved particularly persistent, the gap between the white worker and the black worker narrowing but little. Many of the unions in the A.F.L.-C.I.O. continued to bar blacks from membership and excluded nonwhite youths from their apprenticeship training programs. Not until the early months of 1968 did the number of blacks in the registered apprenticeship programs take a significant spurt. Few Negroes held positions of power in union councils. In the South many unions maintained separate seniority lines, thus limiting Negroes to promotion only in the relatively low-skilled and lesser-paid occupations.

Some Negroes were hit harder than others. The teenage unemployment rate among Negroes was as a rule more than double that among whites. Black women were concentrated in dead-end jobs, and even there they were paid 25 per cent less than white co-workers. In the professions, notably law, the black aspirant found peculiar roadblocks. In the top-ranking jobs in business and industry a black face was a rarity. "The key to the executive suite is still tagged mainly for the white, Anglo-Saxon Christian," reported the Equal Employment Opportunity Commission in January 1968.

A relatively new factor in the Negro's frustrating quest for jobs was the businessman's flight from the city to the suburbs. Black workers could not quickly or cheaply reach jobs located beyond the city limits. Moreover, the housing patterns of the suburbs were even more restrictive than those in the city, thus preventing Negroes from living nearer to the newly opening jobs. This changing location of the job market was one of the reasons that Negro groups pushed for open housing on a statewide basis.

A final deterrent to be noted in Negro employment was lack of skills and low motivation. This in turn was often due to inferior schooling. Most of the all-black schools in the South and their counterparts in the inner cities of the North were inadequately staffed and financed. Quality education was the exception rather than the rule. In the ghetto schools the drop-out rate was high, swelling the ranks of the job-seekers and the habitually unemployed.

• • •

Poor schooling and housing, unemployment or underemployment, led to two dramatic developments in the mid-sixties—riots in the streets and the cry of black power. The years immediately before 1965 had not been free of racial violence but the country was shocked by the outbreak in August of that year in the Watts area of Los Angeles. The incident that lit the fuse was the arrest of a young Negro charged with reckless and drunken driving. Rumors soon spread about police brutality, and the swelling crowd began to throw stones at passing automobiles driven by whites. After a day of rising tension there was a wholesale outbreak of window smashing, looting, and arson. The California National Guard was called out to 60 per cent of its total strength. The six-day rampage resulted in 34 deaths and property damage approaching $40,000,000. Like others of its kind, the outbreak had begun as a spontaneous explosion of anger. But its roots were deeper. Black unemployment in Watts had reached a staggering 30 per cent. To economic deprivation must be added a mutual hostility between the police forces and the colored community.

Watts was contagious. Catching its mood almost instantaneously were the ghetto residents of large cities like Chicago and smaller ones such as Hartford, Connecticut. But these outbreaks were minor compared to Watts and to those which broke out in the following summers. More than forty riots or race disturbances took place in 1966, the great majority of them during the months of July and August. In five cities, Cleveland, Chicago, Dayton, Milwaukee, and San Francisco, the National Guard was summoned. In the Hough section of Cleveland four blacks were killed during the five nights of disorder. As in Chicago the police guardsmen met with sporadic sniper fire.

Racial outbreaks reached a new high in 1967. Nearly 150 cities underwent civil disorders, of which 75 were classified as major riots. The total number killed reached 83, the number arrested ran to more than 16,000, and the property damage to over $660,000,000. The two most costly in lives and money took place in Newark, New Jersey, and Detroit, both in mid-July. In the former a Negro taxi driver was beaten by two patrolmen, and the word was quickly spread throughout the black community. Coming at a time when Newark's whites and blacks were divided over local issues, this incident mushroomed into violence when several Molotov cocktails were hurled at a police station. The next day brought widespread looting and arson. Before order was restored three days later, 23 people had been killed, 21 of whom were black.

A few days after Newark had resumed an uneasy peace, an even greater riot erupted in Detroit. A police raid on a Negro speakeasy set things in motion. For four days and nights the turbulence continued. President Johnson federalized the Michigan National Guard and sent in a task force of paratroopers. The riot's death toll reached 43, of whom 10 were white. Detroit set off a chain reaction of disorders within the state and beyond its borders as urban America experienced its most trying summer in black-white relationships.

Before the National Guard was pulled out of Detroit, President Johnson appointed a commission charged with investigating the riots—finding out what happened, why it happened, and what could be done to prevent its recurrence. Headed by Otto Kerner, Governor of Illinois, this Commission on Civil Disorders set to work with zeal and dedication. After months of study, it presented a solid report which drew wide and continuing attention. Among many other things, the Commission commented on the typical rioter. He was, it pointed out, not a hoodlum or riffraff. He was young;

he was better educated than his Negro neighbor and, added the Commission, "he was proud of his race."

Among blacks this feeling of racial pride took root in the mid-sixties as never before. To be black was not a cross to be borne but a medal to be worn. This proud acceptance of oneself was a psychological achievement of major proportions, showing itself in many ways.

This heightened sense of self-worth led many blacks to stop using the word "Negro," which they found to be a relic of the Atlantic slave trade and hence paternalistic if not downright insulting. No longer "Negro" or "colored," they were black. The new pride led to an increasing interest in knowing the Negro's role in the American past. Thus given a new push, black history found its way into the schools and colleges. Business firms which made use of Negro historical figures in promoting their wares were amazed at the response. Sensing the full portent of their role in the American past, the black reading public raised questions about history's missing pages and distorted viewpoints.

This sense of black identity was reflected in the concept of "soul." Although more characteristic of the inner city than of suburbia, soul was not to be easily defined. Obviously it included popular music, a rhythm and blues man like James Brown winning the title Number One Soul Brother. But whether soul was a term to characterize the song styles of black history, a kind of southern cooking and dish, or a personal life style of staying loose, it was unashamedly and insistently black. The new concept hardly embraced hair arrangement, but many Negroes began to sport the "natural" look, no longer buying hair straighteners. In costume and dress there was a sprouting of African-inspired fashions, reflecting a pride in the ancestral homelands of the Negro American and their recent emergence as independent nations.

The combination of racial pride and economic depriva-
tion gave birth to the dramatic slogan, "black power."
Repeatedly chanted by Stokely Carmichael, chairman of the
Student Nonviolent Coordinating Committee, at a Jackson,
Mississippi, rally in June 1966, it caught the attention of
the country. Eventually most Negro groups came to the conclusion that the slogan was acceptable and even admirable.
"Black power" could be made to describe the protest cries
and self-help efforts of Negroes since the days of Richard
Allen. But the slogan as it emerged as a rallying cry in the
summer of 1966 did carry some newer connotations, and
these quickly became evident.

Black power stood for a lesser emphasis on integration
and more attention to a predominantly, if not exclusively,
black leadership in matters relating to race and color. White
liberals who had worked in civil rights movements were
expected to give up policy-making positions and turn their
attention to combating racism among their fellow Cau-
casians. The emphasis on black control and white withdrawal looked much like a policy of racial separation and
self-segregation. Some blacks defended such a policy on the
grounds that it was a temporary expedient, enabling them
to develop enough confidence and power to deal with whites
on a peer basis. Other black spokesmen, viewing whites,
including Jews, largely in an adversary relationship, viewed
a separatist, "go-it-alone" policy as a permanent thing. But
separation and black nationalism, whatever the duration,
was viewed in some quarters as withdrawal from the battle,
an excuse for not trying, a cloak for defeatism. "Separatism
is not the way of the future," said Roy Wilkins in December
1968.

The concept of black power inevitably conveyed to some
the idea of physical force. The language of Stokely Carmichael and his successor, H. Rap Brown, certainly did not

suggest that one turn the other cheek. The coming of the concept of black power seemed to bring with it a great upswell in the rhetoric violence and vilification. And indeed some young men, angry and anxious to prove the manhood of the black people, did reject the moderate approach, viewing its spokesmen as little better than a new breed of Uncle Tom.

The newer black militant groups believed in "defensive" violence. The Black Panther Party, organized in Oakland, California, in 1966, held that an armed confrontation may be the only way out. "We feel it necessary to prepare the people for the event of an actual physical rebellion," said Huey P. Newton, the founder of the party, himself given a two to fifteen-year sentence in the gunshot death of an Oakland policeman. In May 1967 a group of twenty-six Black Panthers carrying firearms entered the state capitol at Sacramento while the legislature was in session, pushing their way past the sergeants-at-arms. Another newer group sharing the Panthers' philosophy was the Revolutionary Action Movement.

Groups like the Panthers went beyond the traditional American black protest that focused its attention wholly within the United States. The newer militants viewed racial conflict as being international in character, and hence they identified themselves with the struggles and aspirations of darker peoples in lands across the ocean. "The kind of unity I would like to see among black Americans," wrote LeRoi Jones in 1966, "is a unity that would permit most of them to recognize that the murder of Patrice Lumumba in the Congo and the murder of Medgar Evers were conducted by the same people." To this school of militants, white America was in essence an imperialist power holding its colored inhabitants in colonial bondage. These militants found inspiration in the writings of Jomo Kenyatta and Frantz Fanon, the latter pointing out in his work, *The Wretched of the Earth,* that the task of the revolutionary is to mobilize colonial peoples and then lead them against their oppressors.

Black intellectuals and the rank and file shared a common esteem for Malcolm X. A former convict and one who had been thoroughly familiar with the seamy side of life, Malcolm was a fiery symbol of black anger. His condemnation of white America was merciless. His magnetic personality was matched by a stirring oratory. "We didn't land on Plymouth Rock, my brothers,and sisters—Plymouth Rock landed on *us!*" These words to a ghetto audience in Detroit could hardly fail to evoke a deep response. Malcolm was killed on February 21, 1965, while making a speech in Harlem, three alleged Black Muslims being charged with the shooting. But death simply enhanced his fame, his numerous admirers annually observing the date of his assassination.

The phrase "black power" gained some of its thrust because Negroes were becoming more visible than ever before in such popular fields as sports and entertainment. In ice hockey, as in horse racing, blacks numbered fewer than five. Likewise in golf and tennis the low participation of Negroes changed but little, although in the latter the feat of Arthur Ashe, Jr., of Richmond, in winning the men's singles title in the first United States Open Tennis Championship in 1968 was noteworthy. But in professional football, baseball, and basketball, the picture was different. In 1968, Negro players made up 26 per cent of professional football, 30 per cent of major league baseball, and 44 per cent of professional basketball. At the 1968 Olympic games held in Mexico City, black Americans set seven world records in field and track and won three medals in boxing. At the victory ceremony following the 200-meter run, Tommie Smith and John Carlos raised black-gloved fists symbolizing their protest against racism in America

Television viewers, sports lovers or not, began to see more nonwhite faces. Some of these appeared fleetingly in spot commercials. But some blacks had important supporting roles in weekly shows. A few were stars who had previously established themselves as entertainers, notably Sammy Davis, Jr., Bill Cosby, and Diahann Carroll. In motion pictures Sidney Poitier emerged as a major box-office attraction. Needless to say, the newer actors were different from those of an earlier day. Mr. Poitier was hardly reminiscent of Stepin Fetchit. Ruby Dee, in form and substance, differed from Hattie McDaniel. The powerful all-black 1968 screenplay, *Up Tight!* dealing with ghetto unrest, had little in common with *Cabin in the Sky*.

In opera and the theater the black presence was not to be denied. Leontyne Price, Grace Bumbry, and Shirley Verrett sang leading roles in opera. Black repertory theater companies, presenting plays with a Negro audience in mind, sprang up in a dozen cities. The Free Southern Theater, a touring group, was founded in New Orleans in 1964. Dedicated to plays that were relevant to Negroes, a Free Southern Theater performance was followed by a general discussion between actors and audience. In New York the Negro Ensemble Company, operating on a $750,000 Ford Foundation grant, attracted a talented corps of performers and created an outlet for black writers, directors, and technicians. Other somewhat similar groups included the Harlem-based New Lafayette Theater, the Studio Watts Workshop in Los Angeles, the Black Arts Theater in New Haven, Connecticut, the Concept East Theater in Detroit, and the Black Arts Spectrum Theater in Philadelphia. Looking inward, talented young playwrights like Ed Bullins based their themes on the black urban poor. Frederick

325

O'Neal, a performer with wide experience in the theater, black or otherwise, became president of the interracial Actors Equity Association in 1964.

The Negro American dance was interpreted anew by such groups as the Alvin Ailey American Dance Theater. To Mr. Ailey, a dancer, choreographer, and actor, his "dance theater" was designed to celebrate the "trembling beauty" of black music and dance which, he wrote, "has touched, illuminated and influenced the most remote preserves of world civilization." Mr. Ailey's company of fifteen dancers drew its music from folklore, including spirituals, work songs, and blues, and from contemporary composers such as Duke Ellington, Miles Davis, Dizzy Gillespie, and Talley Beatty. At the Harlem School of Arts youngsters were taught the ballet by Arthur Mitchell, organizer and director of the Brazilian Ballet Company and bearing an international reputation as a classical dancer. Embracing the arts in general, along with other significant forms of expression, a Black Academy of Arts and Letters was founded in March 1969, its chief purpose to study and foster the arts, letters, and culture of black people.

The audience for black culture was widened by the black student movement, itself a black power expression. In interracial colleges Black Student Unions and Young Afro-American Associations made their appearance. Until the mid-sixties the small number of Negro students on white campuses had tended to be individualistic and unobtrusive. But the substantial increase in the number of colored students and their heightened sense of racial worth brought them together. Black student spokesmen requested, if not demanded, that college administrations make race-related reforms, including more emphasis on the culture and history of Negro Americans.

The all-embracing concept of black power left its touch

on theology, giving rise in Detroit to the Shrine of the Black Madonna. Its pastor, Albert B. Cleagle, Jr., held that black religion must "reinterpret its message in terms of the needs of the Black Revolution." Hence to Cleagle a figure like Jesus was primarily a liberator bent on leading "a Black Nation to freedom." Cleagle would retitle the familiar hymn, "Fairest Lord Jesus," to "Darkest Lord Jesus."

To organize Negroes in all walks of life behind the concept of black power, Adam Clayton Powell in 1966 convened the First Annual Conference on Black Power, with Washington, D.C., the meeting site. At the second conference a year later at Newark, New Jersey, the attendance had grown from 100 to 1,000. The third conference, held at Philadelphia in September 1968, attracted 4,000. The theme of the Philadelphia conference, "Unity Through Diversity," was symbolic of the black Americans who attended.

Black visibility was hardly the same thing as black power. But neither term, nor the difference between them, was of particular interest to many busy Negro leaders. Working for more and better jobs for blacks, working through the church and politics, theirs was a quieter and more traditional revolution.

They faced man-sized obstacles, particularly in expanding the job market. "Employment discrimination appears at every level and in every sector of American industry," wrote Clifford L. Alexander in February 1969 from his firsthand knowledge as chairman of the Federal Economic Employment Opportunity Commission. Poverty's tenacious grip was dramatized by a Poor People's Campaign which brought to "Resurrection City" in Washington, D.C., over 6,000 campers, three-fifths of them black, from May 12 to June 24, 1968.

In housing, the pattern of segregation had increased in

eight of the largest twelve cities during the seven years preceding 1968. The Housing and Urban Development Act of
1968 and the fair housing provisions of the Civil Rights Act
of 1968 were forward steps in meeting the housing needs of
those with low incomes. But they fell far short of providing
an open and adequate housing market. Moreover, an economy-minded Congress failed to appropriate sufficient funds
to administer its fair housing enactments effectively.

In the schools the process of integration was slow,
despite the rulings of the courts and the election in 1968 of a
Negro woman, Elizabeth D. Koontz of Salisbury, North Carolina, as president of the National Education Association,
the nation's largest teacher organization. By 1968 the percentage of black students attending integrated schools in
eleven southern states had risen to 21.3, a new high. But the
freedom of choice plan, however good it sounded, tended
toward the perpetuation of the all-Negro school, often poorly
equipped and not accredited. The limited southern advances
in integration were offset by setbacks in the North. School
boards in the North proved adept at setting school boundaries so as to keep all-white schools as they were. Moreover,
the separate schools policy had the support of a black
spokesman like Roy Innis, National Director of the Congress
of Racial Equality.

To the setbacks in the Negro's struggle for full equality
the spring of 1968 brought the loss of Martin Luther King.
He was shot and killed while standing on a motel balcony in
Memphis, Tennessee, where he had gone to give support to
the striking garbage collectors. King's tragic death was
widely mourned, befitting a figure who bore the imperish-
able quality of the truly great. "We've got some difficult days
ahead," he had said on the day before his assassination.
"But it really doesn't matter with me now, because I have
been to the mountaintop."

A Fluid Front (1963–1970)

King's death led to outbreaks in 126 cities. This consequence, although perhaps to be expected, had an irony that many would not miss, being contrary to King's belief in nonviolence. Within a few days before his passing he had asserted that he was "not going to kill anybody, whether it's in Vietnam or here. I'm not going to burn down any building." However, his death by a bullet was viewed by some people as a refutation of the nonviolent approach, especially when it was followed two months later by the assassination of Senator Robert F. Kennedy, a figure beloved by blacks. If King's death cast a doubt on the effectiveness of nonviolence, it could not discredit the theories of black self-reliance in economics and politics. On these fronts King's passing removed a figure of major proportions. But his absence would be filled in some measure by the inspiration of his memory.

In running the obstacle race in employment, Negroes practiced selective buying and self-help, neither wholly new but both on a larger scale than ever before. The "operation breadbasket" technique was a request made to white business firms operating in the black community that they hire and upgrade black workers. Failure to do so would result in a boycott. Such selective buying campaigns were most effective as a rule.

Self-help projects included those of limited scope, like Operation Bootstrap formed in Los Angeles in 1965 with money from a black businessman. Its aim was to give job skills to the hard-core unemployed. A more ambitious undertaking took seed in New York, the National Economic Growth and Reconstruction Organization (NEGRO). This company raised money by selling bonds, some for as little as $25.00. By late 1967, after an existence of three years, it had over $3,000,000 in assets and was operating a clothing factory and a construction company. In Philadelphia, the Reverend Leon Sullivan launched an Opportunities Industrialization Center which won widespread commendation for its success in training the habitually unemployed and placing them in jobs. By February 1969, O.I.C. had branches in seventy cities.

As in Philadelphia, many of the black self-help programs elsewhere were led by clergymen. Black churches took the lead in sponsoring business enterprises, opening job-placement centers and conducting day-care nurseries for inner-city children. Some churches operated independently, such as the Wheat Street Baptist Church in Atlanta under William Holmes Borders. Some churches worked in concert, forming councils or alliances, such as the Interreligious Foundation for Community Organization in New York. To an increasing number of black clergymen the church had become a base of operations to improve man's life in this world. Religion was not only metaphysical, said Jesse Jackson, one of Martin Luther King's associates in Chicago, it was also "physical—economic, political and social."

Black self-help unaided could hardly hope to cope with the problem of unemployment—"how can you pull yourself up by your bootstraps if you haven't got boots?" Assistance to Negroes came from the white church, big business, and the federal government. Predominantly white denominations lent a helping hand. Church councils began to put Negroes on their policy-making general boards. In 1964 Edler G. Hawkins of New York was elected Moderator of the United Presbyterian Church in the United States of America. Economic assistance was given to Negroes through an interfaith organization known as Project Equality. Its members pledged themselves to eliminate job discrimination in their churches and synagogues and to purchase goods only from firms that were equal opportunity employers.

Business firms, shocked by the riots and fearful of the economic consequences of increasing urban decay, found ways to help the residents of the inner cities. Some firms contributed money or equipment to Negro self-help organizations, both the Ford and Burroughs companies giving such assistance to the Negro-controlled Career Development Center in Detroit. Aerojet-General set up an independent Negro-managed subsidiary in August 1966, the Watts Manufacturing Company, which launched its operations with a $2,500,000 contract to produce tents for the Defense Department. Early in 1969, the Xerox Corporation pledged itself to buy $500,000 in products over a two-year period from Fighton Incorporated, a company owned and managed by Negroes in Rochester, New York.

Other corporate businesses established job-training centers in ghetto areas. The Equitable Life Assurance Society, which had placed Negroes in twenty of its district managerships throughout the country, set up a job-training program for high school drop-outs. Moreover, some firms began to reappraise their job-testing and recruitment procedures. They began to question whether their employment tests tended to measure cultural awareness rather than ability and whether there were some abilities that were not measurable. With these things in mind, Detroit business executives hired over 50,000 unskilled workers during the six months from August 1, 1967, to February 1, 1968. In inner-city Boston, the Avco Corporation established a printing plant whose employees were Negroes and Puerto Ricans coming exclusively from such classes as former convicts, mothers on welfare, the hard-core unemployed, and workers holding part-time marginal jobs.

Assistance to black workers and entrepreneurs came from the federal government. Late in 1968, the Department of Labor granted $9,100,000 to the National Urban League for a program to train 7,000 hard-core unemployed in twenty-six cities. Leon Sullivan's Opportunities Industrial Center in Philadelphia was heavily subsidized by federal funds. Fighton Incorporated, the Rochester-based company, obtained a $444,677 training grant from the Department of Labor. The Small Business Administration, a federal government agency established in 1958, began to give more attention to the black entrepreneur, setting up a program to advise and assist him. From March 1, 1967, to April 30, 1968, the Small Business Administration made seventy-seven loans to black operators, in amounts ranging from $30,000 to $325,000. The South West Alabama Farmers' Cooperative Association, formed in 1966, received $400,000 from the Office of Economic Opportunity. Comprising one thousand families, this farmers' organization produced and marketed their crops—cotton, okra, cucumbers, and peas—through their own cooperatives.

Help from the federal government, like help from other quarters, stemmed in part from the ghetto outbreaks. But government help to Negroes also reflected the political power wielded by black voters, particularly those in the northern cities. With the increase in the black urban population, Negro politicians increasingly sought higher elective office. Black ballots contributed relatively little to the election of Edward W. Brooke to the attorney generalship of Massachusetts in 1962 and to the United States Senate four years later. The statewide Negro vote in Massachusetts was small. But in 1967 the victory of Carl Stokes in Cleveland and Richard Hatcher in Gary, Indiana, as mayor of their respective cities was made possible by a Negro electorate. Stokes received 96 per cent of the black votes and Hatcher received 95 per cent. But white support was crucial to the success of both, Stokes and Hatcher receiving 19 per cent and 12 per cent respectively of the white ballots.

The roster of Negro officials reached a new high in 1967, north and south. The black voter looked forward to doing better in the presidential year of 1968. As the November elections drew nearer, Roy Wilkins urged the 1,700 branches of the N.A.A.C.P. to get out the black vote. But many Negroes found it hard to get enthusiastic about the presidential contest. The Republican candidates, Richard M. Nixon and his running mate Spiro T. Agnew, left them lukewarm. The Democratic candidates, Hubert H. Humphrey and Edward S. Muskie, had excellent civil rights records. But they were saddled with the most unpopular issue—the war in Vietnam—that had arisen in national politics since the depression days of Herbert Hoover.

The war in Vietnam left most Americans, white and black, disaffected. Vietnam, formerly part of French Indochina, had been partitioned into two states following the defeat of the French in May 1954 by Vietnamese forces. With the expulsion of the French, a civil war ensued between South Vietnam and Communist-led North Vietnam. The United States supported South Vietnam, on the grounds, as stated by President Johnson, that "we have made a national pledge to help South Vietnam maintain its independence." Moreover, the Johnson Administration felt that America had a stake in preventing the extension of Soviet or Chinese power in Southeast Asia. In August 1964, following an attack on an American destroyer by three North Vietnamese torpedo boats, the involvement of the United States was greatly escalated, hundreds of thousands of American troops being sent into combat. But after four years of fighting the United States had failed to overthrow the Hanoi regime in North Vietnam or to silence its guns.

The American public had become increasingly disenchanted with the war in Vietnam, a mood shared by Negroes. They did not, as in earlier wars, loudly charge the armed forces with racial discrimination. For by 1964 the Army had removed practically all of its obvious color barriers, leaving the civilian establishment behind in the practice of racial equality. Even the pin-ups were integrated, wrote black newspaper correspondent Thomas A. Johnson, whether in a neat hotel in Saigon or a red-earth bunker in Khesanh. But Johnson also noted that some bars tended to be predominantly white and others predominantly black. And the Negro was still held back in seeking command positions, making up only 5 per cent of the 11,000 officers in the spring of 1967.

The Negro critics of the Vietnam war centered less on the treatment of the 50,000 black servicemen than on such things as the high rate of Negro combat casualties, the aims of the war itself, and the war's effect on domestic programs to relieve poverty and want. Negro criticism was voiced over the rate of black induction and the death toll. Sixty-four per cent of the Negroes examined in 1967 and found acceptable were drafted, whereas only 31 per cent of the white acceptables were drafted. In the same year, black troops made up 11 per cent of the total American fighting force in Vietnam but in army combat units the black component doubled that number. Negroes killed in action in 1966 constituted 22.4 per cent of the total and for the preceding five years the quota of black deaths was very nearly as high.

It is to be noted that the Negro acquitted himself well in Vietnam. Military service offered him, as it had his black predecessors in other wars, a chance to disprove the stereotype of racial inferiority and to demonstrate his manhood. "The American Negro is winning—indeed has won—a black badge of courage that his nation must forever honor," wrote a *Time* war correspondent in May 1967. Down to 1968, the Negro re-enlistment rate in the army was three times that of whites.

But Negro valor on the battlefield did not still home-front criticism of the war itself. Many black Americans, like their counterparts in World War I and World War II felt that this country was fighting to achieve a democracy in other lands that had not been achieved at home. Moreover, to some Negroes a war waged in Southeast Asia had overtones of race and color, with the United States, however unconsciously, playing the role of an imperialist power bent on imposing its will on darker peoples.

Criticism of the war was particularly strong among the draft eligible, younger blacks. In a visit to Howard University in 1967, General Lewis B. Hershey, director of the Selective Service, was booed off the rostrum. The prize fighter Muhammad Ali (formerly Cassius Clay) refused to be inducted into the armed services, a step which in April 1967 led the World Boxing Association to withdraw its recognition of him as the heavyweight champion. In January 1966 the Georgia legislature refused to seat Representative-elect Julian Bond because of his views against the war, a punitive action that the Supreme Court overruled a year later.

Many Negroes opposed the war because of its effect on the poverty program and civil rights, diverting attention from both. The staggering costs of the Vietnam struggle obviously reduced the appropriations available for the war on poverty, despite President Johnson's assertions to the contrary. To Martin Luther King, as to many others, the Vietnam venture was a "demoniacal destructive suction pump" drawing men and skills and money away from the task of rehabilitating the poor.

• • •

If the Vietnam war was harmful to the poverty program, it was fatal to President Johnson. His unpopularity had grown with every escalation of a war that would not seem to end. As the presidential campaign of 1968 drew nearer, Johnson realized that even if he won his party's nomination, he faced defeat at the polls. On March 31, 1968, he announced that he would not seek re-election. With Johnson on the sidelines, the Democrats selected Vice President Humphrey to lead them against the Republican nominee, Richard Nixon.

The contest that followed failed to arouse in black people the same fervor they had felt for Robert F. Kennedy, whom many had hoped to see at the head of the Democratic ticket. A small number of Negroes talked of "sitting out" the presidential contest. But the great majority of black voters decided Humphrey was certainly a far better civil rights candidate than Nixon and hence that they stood to lose more than to gain by ignoring the presidential race. Moreover, they were solidly opposed to a third major candidate, George C. Wallace, of the American Independent Party, a former Alabama governor who had become a symbol of segregation. Negro interest in the presidency was further stimulated by the candidacy of two write-in aspirants, Eldridge Cleaver, a minister of information for the Black Panther Party, and Dick Gregory, a former night club entertainer who had become an apostle of human rights. In the election Nixon won a close victory over Humphrey, with Wallace a distant third with 13.5 per cent of the total vote. Cleaver and Gregory received 195,000 and 150,000 votes respectively.

To Negroes the disappointment over the outcome of the presidential election was softened somewhat by the election of nine blacks to the House of Representatives, a new high. One of these newcomers was Mrs. Shirley Chisholm of Brooklyn, a member of the New York State Assembly, who became the first black woman to win a seat in Congress. Negro Democrats, moreover, could take some satisfaction in helping their party retain control of both houses of Congress, the Republicans making but small gains on Capitol Hill even though they had won the White House. And most Negroes, regardless of party affiliation, were pleased over the seating of Adam Clayton Powell in the new Congress. The preceding House had voted to exclude him because of alleged misuse of public funds. Powell returned to Congress, however, shorn of his position as chairman of the influential Education and Labor Committee.

"The race dilemma will be the President's toughest problem," wrote *Time* magazine four days after Nixon took office. Undoubtedly a still awesome job in race relations loomed ahead. For, as Negroes knew well, if some others did not, some freedom was not full freedom. But the task ahead was not the President's alone—it fell upon everyone. Sensing their responsibilities, black Americans had increasingly given evidences of a purposefulness and an inner strength that should have been as exhilarating to whites as it was to blacks themselves. One who took a closer look at the colored American would have discovered that he was in the grip of the same purpose as his fellow countrymen. Indeed the passionate rhetoric of the black militant and much of the riot behavior of the slum dweller alike find their motivation in a desire for equal justice and equal opportunity, themes as American as one could wish.

12

Widening Horizons (1970–1986)

DURING THE DECADE and a half from 1970 to the mid-1980s, Afro-American life reflected a series of sweeping and significant changes, whether in political participation, the striving for economic independence, or in a heightened sense of self-worth and oneness. The role of blacks in politics, whether on a local, state, sectional, or national level, took a marked swing upward. Spurred by voter registration drives conducted by social and civic groups, blacks went to the polls in unprecedented numbers, their stepped-up efforts resulting in a path-breaking increase in the number of black elected officials. In communities with sizeable black populations, white office-seekers sought to woo their votes. Seeking greater economic independence, black businessmen and -women engaged in a widening range of enterprises outside of the traditional strongholds of banking and life insurance to include commercial activities and industrial production. Blacks felt that a strong business class furnished unassailable proof that blacks were producers as well as consumers.

Black-owned businesses would make up only a minuscule percentage of all firms, but they left no doubt as to the ability of blacks to master the managerial and technical skills necessary for success as entrepreneurs.

In whatever station or walk of life, blacks of this period were characterized by a deepening sense of racial pride and exaltation, a newer awareness and appreciation of their role as culture-bearers. In black circles there was an explosion in the production of plays and poetry, music and dance, painting and sculpture, among other art forms. More and more blacks discovered the beauty, power, and wisdom of black folk expression, now regarding it a source of racial pride rather than of racial embarrassment and shame. Among blacks there was a growing conviction that their past was deeply rooted, richly endowed, and imperishably vibrant. In turn, we may note these broad developments in political life, in economic endeavor and outreach, and in cultural explosiveness.

Beginning in the early 1970s, black Americans increasingly turned to the political arena, viewing the ballot box as a key component to their economic advancement, to a fuller attainment of their civil rights, and to a deeper sense of racial self-esteem that would, in turn, ignite a renaissance of black culture in its multiple expressions. As Richard Hatcher, mayor of Gary, Indiana, pointed out in a 1972 speech to the newly formed National Black Political Convention, "The 1970s will be the decade of an independent black political thrust. Its destiny will depend upon us." Addressing his congressional colleagues in February 1971, Representative William Clay defined the new black politics as one that called for a revision of the old concept that "what is good for the nation is good for minorities." In contrast, said Clay, the new black politics must be based on the

339

premise that "what is good for minorities is good for the nation."

Showing a greater sense of political independence and maturity, blacks in increasing numbers made their way to the polls. Voter mobilization and registration drives took on a new impetus, spurred on by a variety of organizations, including fraternal lodges, civil and social groups, Greek-letter sororities and fraternities, and church groups whose pastors were politically conscious. "Politics controls as much of our lives as religion does," according to William Jones, president of the National Black Pastors Conference. Thus it would be misleading to say that blacks of the 1970s and 1980s were moving "from protest to politics," inasmuch as the kind of politics they played was itself protest oriented, a weapon in the warfare.

The single person most responsible for raising the political consciousness of blacks was the Baptist clergyman, Jesse Jackson. Well-informed, articulate and dynamic, a spellbinder among spellbinders, Jackson shared the belief that the church should concern itself about social issues. Bent on improving the quality of life in black communities, in 1971 Jackson organized People United to Save Humanity (P.U.S.H.), which directed its efforts to a comprehensive program of racial uplift and improvement. Participation in politics fell within Jackson's scope and in November 1983 he announced that he was a candidate for the office of president of the United States in the forthcoming election. His vigorous and exciting campaign, and the extensive media coverage he drew wherever he went, prompted many blacks to register and become voters.

Typical of the prevailing black political strategy of this period, Jackson's campaign for the presidency was characterized by a reaching-out, integrationalist approach. Jackson sought to enlist the support of a "rainbow coalition," one that cut across lines of race, color, ethnic background, and sex to embrace all who felt that they had been locked out. A decade earlier, in 1974, Jackson had pointed out that the building of a mass movement to halt discrimination required cooperative efforts: "blacks in cooperation with Mexican Americans, Puerto Ricans, American Indians, Asian Americans—all the diverse segments of the population which has experienced much of the 'benign neglect' that has been our experience." Speaking in May 1980 in Washington, D.C., at a conference for "Jobs, Peace and Justice," Jackson again sounded this theme: "We must find a new focus. We must do it as a coalition."

Such an integrationalist approach in politics would enable blacks to win elections even when their group was outnumbered at the polls. In Virginia, for example, Lawrence Douglas Wilder was elected lieutenant governor in 1985, the first black to win a statewide election in any of the former Confederate states since Reconstruction times. In his campaigning Wilder aggressively sought the white vote, explaining that "my strategy is to go for as many people as possible and show that I can be a voice for any and all of them." In the 1980s there would be little talk of a separate black political party.

In their successful campaigns for the office of mayor, black candidates, including those in such major cities as Los Angeles, Atlanta, and Philadelphia, succeeded in garnering impressive quotas of white voter support. In addition, in many communities in which there was a sizeable black vote but no black candidate in an election, black voters played a decisive role in determining which of the white candidates would emerge victorious. Such instances contributed to the black voter's growing sense of political importance, and to making the black public more politically minded.

The newer black political thrust owed much to black

women, whether in register-and-vote drives, behind-the-scenes activities, or in leadership roles. The National Black Women's Organization, founded in 1972, asserted that inasmuch as black females bore the double jeopardy of race and sex they should "develop a politics that was antiracist, unlike those of white women, and antisexist, unlike those of black and white men."

The increasing visibility of black women in politics was reflected in their winning of elective office, whether at the congressional level or the state and local. By 1976 Shirley Chisholm had been joined in the U.S. House of Representatives by three additional black women: Yvonne Braithwaite Burke of California, Cardiss Collins of Illinois, and Barbara Jordan of Texas, this foursome making up 25 percent of the female membership in the House.

Reaching for the stars, path-breaker Shirley Chisholm announced her candidacy for the presidency in 1972. Despite her reputation as an "unbought and unbossed" legislator, her campaign was haphazardly organized and poorly financed and did not attract the kind of support from either women or blacks that she had counted on. In seeking national office Chisholm was preceded by Charlotta A. Bass of California, who in 1952 had run as the Progressive Party's candidate for the vice presidency. Bass waged a spirited campaign, but she and her party fared very poorly at the polls, many voters holding that a vote for the Progressive candidates would be a vote "thrown away." The campaigns of Chisholm and Bass were not without some effect, however, prompting more blacks and women to become more politically conscious and to raise anew the question, Why not?

In getting elected to state office black women had some success. By 1984 no fewer than seventy of them were serving as state legislators, their numbers having a fourfold increase in the span of twenty years. These gains were modest but somewhat encouraging, especially to older blacks who remembered that it was not until 1938 that the first black female, Crystal Byrd Fauset, had won a seat in the Pennsylvania legislature. A hopeful note was sounded by astute participant-observer Maxime Waters, who in 1984 predicted that there was "a great future" for black office-seekers, that the next ten years would see a marked increase in the number of women elected to office, and advising black women of "the need to be ready."

The increased participation in politics by blacks of both sexes and their coalition-building efforts across the color line made for a rapid multiplication in the number of black elected officials, their numbers rising from 1,860 in 1971 to 6,056 in 1985. Such an increase sounded impressive, but these 6,056 blacks constituted only 1 percent of all elected officials nationwide. In 1985 more than a score of southern counties with black majorities had no black who had won public office. Some whites were reluctant to vote for a black, no matter how well qualified. In many communities throughout the country the black vote was diluted by such devices as gerrymandering and at-large elections. In some instances, however, the black community had only itself to blame; of the 19 million eligible to vote nationwide in 1984, only 12 million had registered, the other one-third still sitting on the sidelines.

Although in many locales the black vote would remain little more than symbolic, its total impact had to be taken into account. The efforts by blacks to place their stamp on the political process was not without its multiple results, its varied fruits. These may be noted by touching upon black political participation at the local and state levels, followed by a review of the blacks in Congress.

In 1967 Carl Stokes of Cleveland became the first black elected to the mayor's office in a large city. Less than twenty years later, in 1984, the roster of black mayors in the United States had reached 225. The large majority of these were mayors of small- and medium-size cities and towns, with more than half of them located in the rural, black-belt South. Of the twenty Mississippi towns with black mayors in 1982, none was located in a major city and six of them had fewer than five hundred inhabitants. Eleven of these mayors, however, served in the nation's largest cities and eleven more of them were to be found in cities with a population of over one hundred thousand.

In these major cities the black mayors were influential, power wielding. They certainly made a difference in black life in their respective locales. While not neglecting their responsibilities to their constituency, they tackled problems of special concern to blacks—problems of crime and juvenile delinquency in black neighborhoods, of strained relationships between blacks and the police, of high black unemployment, of trying to promote better opportunities for blacks to compete in the world of business and finance and in the professions. In these large cities with black mayors there was a lessening of racial discrimination in providing public services in black neighborhoods or in denying blacks equal employment opportunities in the allocation of city-controlled appointment jobs.

As in big cities elsewhere, black mayors wielded power on the state and national levels. They had a hand in nominating and electing candidates for state office. They likewise influenced the selection of delegates to national political party conventions, and in the selection and election of the member of Congress who resided in their municipality.

In local communities throughout a given state, blacks were elected as sheriffs, constables, and justices of the peace, among many other public offices. While their influence was not to be compared with that of the big-city black mayors, they too helped to make it easier for blacks to move into the political mainstream.

In politics at the statewide level blacks were making their presence felt. They won election to such statewide offices as state attorney general, state school superintendent, secretary of state, speaker of the state legislature, state superintendent of education, state comptroller, and state supreme court justice. Blacks were also becoming more noticeable in state legislative assemblies. In 1950, for example, no black served as a state legislator in the entire South. In 1979, some thirty years later, Mississippi alone had seventeen black state legislators—fifteen in the house of representatives and two in the senate. In some state assemblies blacks were numerous enough to form caucuses through which they could bargain for their vote.

In winning gubernatorial office there were no black breakthroughs. In 1971 Charles Evers, mayor of Fayette, Mississippi, ran for governor, his vote much lower than he had expected. In 1981 Kenneth Gibson, then serving his third term as mayor of Newark, New Jersey, lost in his campaign for the Democratic gubernatorial nomination, finishing a respectable third in a crowded field of hopefuls. In his 1982 campaign for the governor's seat in California, Thomas Bradley, the popular and highly regarded mayor of Los Angeles, won his party's nomination but lost by a close vote in the general election.

To blacks as a whole the most important political development of the last two decades was the launching in 1969 of the Congressional Black Caucus. Made up of the black members of the House of Representatives, its avowed aim was "to promote the public welfare," which was to be accomplished by "developing, introducing, and passing progressive legislation designed to meet the needs of millions of neglected citizens." This proved to be no idle boast. Firmly organized for action in 1971, the Congressional Black Caucus soon made its influence felt, both in the halls of Congress and at the White House, its proposals and actions winning national attention.

As other lawmakers who came to Washington, each of the congressional blacks had to be attentive to the demands of his/her particular district. While keeping their own home fires burning, however, these congressional blacks felt called upon to represent the broader national black community. The relative number of Afro-Americans who sat in Congress was so small that a black member automatically took on unusual proportions, acquiring a national constituency— the black community at large. This inclusive awareness of the problems and needs of minority groups tended to give these blacks in Congress a deeper sensitivity as to long-lasting social ills and an urge to overcome them.

By the mid-1980s the Black Caucus, its membership having increased from six in 1966 to twenty-one in 1984, had successfully sponsored a number of measures that were of importance to blacks. These included an extension of voting rights legislation, an expansion of youth employment programs, including a well-funded job training bill, and set-aside measures assuring minority-owned businesses of receiving a fair share of federally funded contracts. The caucus led the successful movement to pass a constitutional amendment giving full congressional representation to the predominantly black District of Columbia, although its sponsors were well aware that its ratification by thirty-eight states was unlikely. By 1985 Black Caucus members were chairpersons of seven House committees and fourteen subcommittees, including the very powerful House Budget Committee under the guidance of William Gray III, a clergyman from Philadelphia.

Of the many disappointments the Black Caucus had to face, none compared with the realization that all too often the measures they had fought to enact were not being effectively carried out. Blacks were not unprepared for such foot-dragging responses, however, having learned from past experience that policy enactment was one thing and policy implementation was another. Certainly this would be the case in matters relating to civil rights and equal opportunity, such measures sure to encounter the three standard hurdles; namely, the president and his personal staff, the federal bureaucracy in charge of administering the government offices, and the federal courts, especially the Supreme Court. Thus a voting rights act designed to safeguard minorities against discrimination in election practices, such as the one enacted in 1965 and its extensions in 1972 and 1976, did not go into operation automatically but required implementation, which might be lax, halfhearted, or minimal.

The first and foremost of the hurdles facing civil rights and equal opportunity measures was the office of president. In handling such legislation, three of the four presidents following Lyndon Johnson had attitudes either lukewarm or cool, and only one, Jimmy Carter, was regarded by blacks as being sympathetic.

In his campaign for the presidency in 1968, Richard Nixon, Johnson's successor, received heavy support from conservatives and white southerners, a factor further conditioning his already reserved attitude toward equal rights for minorities. Early in his first term he received a lengthy memorandum from Daniel Moynihan, the White House adviser on urban affairs, its essence contained in the key sentence, "The time may have come when the issue of race could benefit from a period of 'benign neglect.'" Nixon's subsequent behavior would indicate that he concurred. Blacks in turn demonstrated their coolness toward him, the members of the Black Caucus absenting themselves from the halls of Congress when he came before the body to deliver his 1971 State of the Union address. Over Nixon's veto, Congress passed the bill extending the life of the Voting Rights Act. In March 1970 the liberally inclined Edward Brooke of Massachusetts, the only black in the U.S. Senate and the only black Republican in Congress, charged the Nixon administration with pursuing "a contrived, calculated, designed" policy of neglecting the black community. Blacks found Gerald Ford, who finished out Nixon's second term, to be more approachable and accessible, but they soon found out that he shared Nixon's coolness to such programs as fair housing regulations and equal employment measures.

In campaigning for the presidency against Ford in 1976, Jimmy Carter pledged his support for equal opportunity and equal justice. In the contest against Ford he won an estimated 90 percent of the black vote, forty-five black organizations having banded together to get out the vote on his behalf, a support that proved to be crucial to his election. In general the Carter administration played a supportive role in the enforcement of federal laws forbidding discrimination against minorities. Although blacks felt that he might have fought harder in the cause, they hailed him for the unprecedented number of blacks and women he appointed to high office, his naming of thirty-eight judges, doubling their number when he took office. To the dismay of the great majority of blacks, Carter was defeated in seeking a second term.

The incumbent, Ronald Reagan, who would win re-election in 1984, was bent on "revitalizing the private sector," while simultaneously withdrawing or reducing federal government programs designed to help the needy and hardpressed. Not a champion of minority groups, Reagan did not favor policies that gave preferential treatment to those who claimed they had been the victim of discrimination. No advocate of civil rights legislation, Reagan had misgivings about programs requiring that women, blacks, and other minorities be given a fair chance in competing for jobs in federally funded projects. Reagan's critics were not slow in charging that his policies aided the rich at the expense of the poor.

The cries of protest came from many quarters. Julian Bond, the nationally known Georgia state legislator, said that the Reagan people intended "to turn back the civil rights clock until it became a sundial." John Jacob, president of the Urban League, accused Reagan of practicing "voodoo politics." In more measured tones the American Civil Liberties Union, in a report issued in February 1984 and pointedly entitled, *In Contempt of Congress and the Courts: the Reagan Civil Rights Record,* characterized the Reagan administration's civil rights record as "a radical and shameful assault on law enforcement in the United States."

The viewpoints of the president had a significant effect on the federal bureaucracy—the officials and staffs of the federal administrative agencies. Not wishing to incur his displeasure, the bureaucrats took his attitude in consideration in making their decision as to whether to promptly and fully implement a law or to delay and underfund it. As a 1973 report issued by the U.S. Commission on Civil Rights pointed out, "Minorities still lacked the economic and political power to influence or motivate a reticent officialdom."

More criticized by liberals and minorities than any other federal agency, the Department of Justice was attacked for its stand against affirmative action as a remedial tool, and for its failure to enforce the Voting Rights Act. This department was consistently understaffed and, as Georgia Congressman Andrew Young explained in 1976, "One consequence of understaffing is under-enforcement." Almost a decade later, in May 1985, the N.A.A.C.P. served notice that it was filing a suit against the Justice Department, charging it with an ongoing and increased activity in its efforts "to retard, roll back, and circumvent civil rights gains justly won over the years." Later that year *New York Times* reporter Anthony Lewis reproached Attorney General Edward Meese and William Bradford Reynolds, the Justice Department's civil rights chief, for having "been working to sabotage the country's civil rights laws—to abandon the whole effort at healing the wounds of the nation."

In the process of drafting regulations to carry out acts of Congress, the bureaucracy itself often played an independently vital role. Some laws, especially those in the field of civil rights, were vaguely worded or their language was ambiguous. In verbally clarifying such enactments and then proceeding to make them functional, the bureaucrats left their stamp upon them.

Civil rights legislation supported by the president and properly implemented by the bureaucracy still had to face another possible roadblock—the federal courts, particularly the Supreme Court. From 1953 to 1969, the period in which Earl Warren was chief justice, the Court was liberal on the whole, upholding affirmative action measures, voting rights, school desegregation, along with busing to achieve it, and the 1968 Fair Housing Act. This scenario changed when the Warren Court came to its end.

While running for the presidency in 1968, Richard Nixon pledged that his appointees to the federal bench would be "strict constructionalists" of the Constitution. Within three years after his election Nixon had the undreamed-of opportunity to name four of nine Supreme Court justices, among them Chief Justice Warren Burger, a consistent conservative in his legal viewpoints and interpretations of the law and the Constitution. The membership of

the Burger Court fell into shifting combinations and coalitions of conservatives, moderates, and liberals, with Thurgood Marshall invariably voting with the pro–civil rights
contingent. But whatever the ideological combinations
within the Burger Court, the decisions it rendered generally
reflected the go-slow and restrictive approach favored by
the Nixon, Ford, and Reagan administrations.

This backward-bending posture of the Court was highly
disappointing to minorities and their supporters but
increasingly it seemed to match the mood of the public in
the 1980s. Liberals were further dismayed by the likelihood
that Reagan, by his power to appoint the swelling number of
federal judges at the various levels, might be bent on shaping the federal bench along conservative lines for years to
come, and thereby cutting back more fully on civil rights.

In the twenty years following the passage of the Civil
Rights Act of 1965, political action as a means of attaining
civil rights had not met with the success its advocates had
envisioned. But if to Afro-Americans the great expectations
of the civil rights legislation were only partly realized, the
effort had a broad-ranging effect throughout the country,
one that extended to other minority groups, including
Native Americans, Hispanics, Asian Americans, and white
women, among others. Impressed by the protest strategies
and techniques brought into play by the civil rights organizations, these underprivileged groups proceeded to dupli-
cate them so that they too might make their presence felt in
the political arena. Blacks had been instrumental in pointing the way.

Blacks realized that politics alone would not solve all
their economic and social problems, even if all three branches
of both the federal government and the state government
were liberal as to civil rights and their implementation.
While welcoming the valued support of others, blacks real-

ized more and more that they had to rely primarily upon themselves, coming to grips with their own internal needs, problems, and pathologies. They must move beyond finding fault and assigning blame, and proceed to strengthen and expand self-help programs in their communities. Blacks nodded in assent to the admonition voiced by John Jacob at the 1984 Black Family Summit Conference in Nashville, "There is a lot we can do about our own problems ourselves."

In the economic realm one of the most promising fields in which blacks could demonstrate their self-help capacities was by developing a strong black business class. Such a class would show that blacks were producers of goods and services, not consumers only. Black-owned businesses would help reduce the chronic unemployment in black circles, and black entrepreneurs would serve as role models for upwardly mobile young blacks. This sense of racial responsibility prompted the black National Bankers Association to urge its members in a 1986 report "to recommit their resources to improving the lot of minority communities and to building coalitions with other minority organizations."

Numbering 231,203 in 1977, black-owned businesses rose to 339,239 in 1982, although it is to be noted that of this 1982 total 95 percent were small businesses with a single proprietor. This substantial rise in black self-employment resulted in part from the growth of black purchasing power, which in 1968 was estimated at $30 billion and had expanded in 1978 to $70 billion. Of the one hundred Negro businesses grossing the highest sales in 1978, over three-quarters (77) had been founded after 1968. Bent on reaching these black buyers, a growing number of white advertisers sought the service of black advertising agencies and made use of the black media.

Despite the spurt taken by black business in recent years, it still faced grave problems, some of them new, others deep-seated. Almost ironically, some of the new problems encountered by black entrepreneurs came as a result of their successes. In the production of hair and skin preparations and cosmetics, for example, blacks soon lost their monopoly, white companies having been attracted by these lucrative fields. In the publishing industry the black newspapers and periodicals faced a circulation and sales challenge from white-owned newspapers, the latter devoting more and more of their space to black news articles written by their own reporters, some of whom were black. Finding it harder to retain their more promising recruits, black businesses were placed in the unenviable role of becoming a training ground for white firms. Many such firms, however, started to furnishing the training themselves, signing up black men and women "to fill positions that are vital to our future growth," as one of them put it.

The new generation of black business people faced the old problem of getting funds, of capital formation. The black community itself had relatively little accumulated wealth to draw upon, and black entrepreneurs did not find it easy to borrow money, to float loans. Blacks welcomed the efforts, noted above, of government agencies to help minority-owned enterprises. Blacks also sought to enlist the aid of white corporations, launching "fair share" programs designed to get these firms to award purchase contracts to minorities, and to place minorities on their boards. The latter aim tended to languish. As explained in December 1985 by Andrew Brimmer, a former governor of the Federal Reserve Board and a leading black economist, "When the vast majority of directors meet in corporate boardrooms to select the managers and set the policies that shape economic activity, blacks generally are missing." This oversight should be corrected, added Brimmer, since "there is a long list of qualified blacks from which corporations can draw."

The difficulties experienced by blacks in the business world paled beside those of the black landowning farmer, 99 percent of whom were located in the South in the mid-1980s. They faced a somewhat grim future, as indicated by their steadily decreasing numbers from year to year. In 1984 there were only 148,000 blacks living on farms out of a total black population of approximately 28 million. Black farmers predominantly are small-scale operators and, like their white counterparts, they found themselves in a losing battle against the larger, more mechanized, and better financed giants in the field, the agribusinesses.

Meeting with racial discrimination in the private sector, black landowning farmers found it hard to obtain credit on reasonable terms from banks and other lending agencies. Black farmers had to cope with discrimination by the federal government, most notably in the wide-scale programs operated by the Department of Agriculture and its lending arm, the Farmers Home Administration. Blacks besought the government to grant them a just and proportionate share of the publicly owned lands that were periodically distributed. To combat discrimination and become more efficient, black farmers and their supporters formed a number of self-help organizations, regional and national, including the Emergency Land Fund, designed to promote the retention and acquisition of farm lands, and the Federation of Southern Cooperatives, embracing 130 farming and marketing cooperatives. Their supporters believed that the well-being of the independent black farmer was beneficial to blacks in general, a viewpoint shared in 1984 by Joseph Brooks, president of the Emergency Land Fund; to wit: "In effect, landownership in the rural South confers on blacks a measure of independence, security, and dignity that is crucial to elevating the status of the whole black community."

This sense of racial responsibility and stewardship had

its effect on blacks in the professions, especially among lawyers, a group from whom leadership was expected. Black judges and lawyers—the bench and the bar—worked for a color-blind system of justice, William Hastie, a highly regarded federal judge, defining his career as "a struggle toward an equalitarian legal order." The ages-long cry of black citizens for equal justice in the American legal system prompted black lawyers to form such organizations as the National Bar Association (N.B.A.) in 1925, the National Conference of Black Lawyers in 1969, the Judicial Council of the N.B.A. in 1971, and the National Association of Black Women Attorneys in 1972. The common aim of such organizations might be summed up in the charge by Judge George Crockett, Jr., at the founding convention of the Judicial Council, in which he expressed the hope that the council "would provide means by which its members could exchange information and prod their profession to rid the legal system of racism and classism."

As in the legal profession, blacks in medicine shared the goals common to their chosen field, plus an added one— in this instance, the eradication of racial discrimination in medical institutions and the expansion of minority representation in the forming and implementing of national health care policies. "The pathology of society is as much a function of the medical man as the pathology of human disease," wrote Henry Favil in 1909, a point of view echoed over half a century later by a fellow black physician, Carlton Goodlett, who held that "we need the best-trained mind, not only to respond to the physical and psychological ills of their patients, but to lend their genius and creative insight to the social ills of the body politic." This goal had originated with the predominantly black National Medical Association, an organization founded in 1895 and filling a void until 1968 when the American Medical Association, the gateway to the profession, admitted its first black to membership.

However more keenly aware they might be of the racial discrimination in the medical profession, socially minded blacks in health care in the 1970s and 1980s faced an uphill battle. In part this was due to the proportionately dwindling numbers. By the mid-1980s, blacks comprised less than 3 percent of the total physician pool, and the sharply rising costs of attending medical school made for a decline in black enrollments, blacks falling to less than 6 percent of the total 1983–84 entering class, a drop from the 7.8 percent of the entering class in 1974–75. This shortage of medicos was especially harmful to the inner-city black communities with their environmental health hazards of pollution and over-crowded housing. Compounding the health problems of these districts was the high percentage of dwellers who had no health insurance whatsoever in a period of upwardly spiraling costs for medical treatment.

If blacks in the professional world were underemployed— not put to their fullest use—blacks in the work-a-day world faced the grim problem of unemployment. In the mid-1980s the jobless rate for blacks reached its highest point in two decades, averaging 17 percent from 1981 to 1986. The industries that employed blacks, such as automobile, steel, and textiles, were being automated, as computers replaced people in the work force. In the public service sector, blacks seeking jobs as waiters and hotel workers found themselves competing with recently arrived Vietnamese, Cubans, and Haitians. Some labor unions to which blacks belonged con-tinued to discriminate against them—excluding them from policy-making discussions, failing to treat them equally with whites in promotion practices, and placing them in the "first-fired" category when employees had to be discharged. Jobs continued to move away from the central cities where blacks lived, relocating in the predominantly white suburbs. Year after year during the 1980s, the black unemployment rate was at least twice as high as that of whites.

To the youthful poor black "the idealism of work was stunted by the reality of no work." As a consequence of such long-extended joblessness, many blacks tended to stop trying, thus dropping out of the work force and becoming part of the "hidden unemployed" to whom being out of work had become a way of life.

Unemployment was the number one problem in the black community, adversely affecting family life, housing, and health, while at the same time fostering a subculture of crime and making for a climate of violence. During the 1970s, and down to the mid-1980s, the median income of the black family was never higher than 55 percent of its white counterpart. The declining employment rates among black males led to a shrinking pool of marriageable spouses, resulting in the rise of female-headed households, their numbers increasing from 20.6 percent in 1960 to 44.1 percent in 1980. The two-parent family remained the norm for upper- and middle-income blacks, with lower-class blacks making up the great bulk of the father-absent households. A growing concern in the black family was the increasing rate of pregnancies among unmarried teenagers. According to a report issued in 1985 by the National Urban League, teen pregnancy was "a problem of monumental proportions," one "that will affect three generations—the teen parents, their children, and the grandparents." Teenage pregnancies, with or without marriage, undoubtedly made for unstable families and for high unemployment, which in turn made for a higher degree of welfare dependency, of "going on relief."

A more long-standing problem in the urban black community, that of the lack of decent housing, remained acute and pressing. Despite federal, state, and local laws and ordinances forbidding racial discrimination in housing, the practice remained pervasive, although a few neighborhoods, such as Forest Park, Illinois, thirty miles from Chicago, could boast of combating white flight by combining open housing with racial stability. Segregation against nonwhites persisted even in federally subsidized housing, the agencies of the national government shirking their responsibilities in enforcing fair-housing enactments. In maintaining housing segregation, builders and real estate brokers used a variety of techniques, beginning with discouraging a tabooed applicant.

While the responses of the blacks of the 1970s and 1980s were more time-honored than ground breaking, the cultural response of this recent generation was unprecedented in the depth and scope of its manifestations—its racial appreciation of a goodly heritage in a variety of forms of expression, literary, artistic, and musical, and its ongoing production of similarly gifted works of its own creation—all to the end of illustrating a more illuminating sense of racial self-awareness, of bearing gifts not only to themselves but to all who might like to share therein.

To better their economic lot the great majority of blacks of this generation did not ask for handouts or charity but for equal opportunity. They had, as has been noted, advocated affirmative action programs. They had organized boycotts against firms that did not employ blacks or carry goods produced by black manufacturers, and in many cases they had succeeded in winning concessions from major corporations by threatening them with a boycott. With some success, too, the N.A.A.C.P. in 1981 launched Operation Fair State, its objective to persuade large corporations to hire and promote more minorities and to sublet some of their business operations to black entrepreneurs. And, as in earlier generations, some blacks solved the employment problem by joining the armed services. In 1982 blacks accounted for 33 percent of Army recruits and 22 percent of the Marines, much above the 12 percent in the general population. Black women, according to a 1985 Department of Defense study, comprised 42 percent of all the enlisted women in the Army in 1984.

Double-digit unemployment and economic discrimination left their mark on blacks of this generation. Like others before them, they found that color prejudice was still to be found in the laws, behavior, and attitudes of their white countrymen and women. Hence, and not surprisingly, in 1976 when the United States celebrated its bicentennial, many blacks felt that they had been excluded from the revolution all along. As Judge William Hastie observed in an address at historic Independence Hall in Philadelphia on April 5, 1976: "A nation's beginning is a proper source of reflective pride only to the extent that the subsequent and continuing process of its becoming deserves celebration." Two years later another black legal luminary, Thurgood Marshall, voiced a similarly pointed appraisal; to wit: "Measured by any benchmark of comfort or achievement, meaningful equality remains a distant dream for the Negro."

Blacks were well aware that the struggle for equality of opportunity would be long, that seemingly there would always be one more river to cross, but that they must not weary in the good work. However, as a phase of the struggle they now sought to a new degree to promote racial solidarity and progress by looking afresh at their own cultural inner world over the years—their own artistic creativity, inventive genius, and intellectual achievements. They devoted far more of their energies in demonstrating the ways in which their group had enriched the common culture and thereby had broadened the base of human freedom in a myriad of ways. They would give new depth, meaning, and precision to the expression "black is beautiful."

In their expressions, as in their viewpoints, blacks revealed that they did not think in lock step. Speaking in a multiplicity of voices and accents, the black community had never been monolithic. "In black culture," wrote John Langston Gwaltney in 1980, "there is a durable, general tolerance, which is amazingly free of condescension, for the individual's right to follow the truth, wherever it leads." Blacks were persons as well as types and in America, land of individualism, who could count the number of ways of being black? Afro-American culture was diverse and resilient, reflecting its richly varied expressions. Among blacks the sense of community and collective action to combat discrimination had gone hand in hand with individual self-assertion, particularly as to the forms and styles of cultural expression. However drab and monotonous inner city life might appear to the outsider, the black experience was never static, as its cloud of witnesses could bear testimony.

Within a group given to experimentation, to being on the cutting edge, divergencies and conflicting viewpoints were to be expected. Hence, whether in politics, economics, or cultural expressions, Afro-Americans had their array of conservatives, moderates, liberals, and radicals. For example, blacks had their company of conservative scholars who believed that affirmative action programs were a mistake, that racial prejudice and discrimination were declining in significance in the making of public policy, and that women should keep a low profile in public life. Led by the Association of Black Sociologists, these viewpoints were challenged by other scholars who held that they were a "misrepresentation of the black experience." The gamut of intraracial differences even extended to skin-color and hair-texture preferences, many Afro-Americans, though in decreasing percentages, according a higher status to the lighter-skinned than to the darker-hued, to those with "straight" hair than to those with kinky.

More than anything else, however, the difference among blacks resulted from a more strongly developed sense of self-identity. Blacks of this generation were more tolerant of differences within the group and hence more prepared psychologically to work cooperatively in common causes. A greater sense of group responsibility, of doing more for themselves, became the order of the day. As stated in the 1985 annual report of the National Urban League, "We would suggest that the strongest message coming out of Black America in 1984 was that it became increasingly aware of its own strengths and increasingly willing to act independently to achieve what it considers its own best interests." Moreover, to be on their own was hardly a new experience to black Americans, particularly in activities and spheres which did not threaten white interests, such as in cultural pursuits and expressions.

As a consequence of their renewed pride of race, Afro-Americans were unshaken by the attempts to pump new life into the theory that blacks were innately inferior. Blacks deplored the fact that these theories as to their genetic inferiority could and would be used by white supremacy groups like the Ku Klux Klan and others. As a group, however, blacks felt no misgivings as to the unsoundness of such viewpoints which in their opinion represented a discredited creed that increasingly would fall of its own weight—its falsity of premise and its disapproval by the high majority of the academic community.

In combating racial stereotypes against them blacks faced a much more formidable force in tackling the mass media. The press, radio, and television were powerful influences in shaping the beliefs and images that whites held about blacks. Blacks felt that the white media often misrepresented their group, meting out to them a harsher and more unsympathetic treatment than to whites in similar situations or walks of life. "The media too often project us as being impotent when, in fact, we are important; project us as liabilities when we are, in fact, assets," said Jesse Jackson in May 1980, explaining that blacks were portrayed as more violent than they were and less intelligent, hard working, and patriotic than they were.

Blacks charged that not only were they misrepresented in the media but that they were also underrepresented. Blacks comprised less than 3 percent of the work force of the white daily newspapers as of the early 1980s, including only three nationally syndicated black cartoonists. In commercial television in 1984 blacks accounted for 8 percent of the on-air professionals but in the managerial categories—the levels where important decisions were made—the picture was bleak, the three national networks having only seven vice presidents out of a total of six hundred, and only four black station managers out of a total of 1,181. Black-owned media, whether print or electronic, could hardly brighten the outlook. Of the fourteen hundred national magazines sold over the counter in 1980, only five were black-owned, and in 1983 of the 10,134 commercial radio stations, only 171, less than 2 percent, were minority-owned.

In part the white media's gingerly and selective treatment of blacks reflected a dependence upon large advertising sponsors who shied away from media that dealt forthrightly with controversial and emotion-laden issues of race and color. As this media well knew, such issues would tend to be upsetting, and hence not cost-effective, in the predominantly white middle class community with its high purchasing power. In its quest for life-or-death advertising revenues, the media took pains to avoid any sponsor barriers.

Publicly owned radio and television stations were not as susceptible as the commercial media to the pressures of corporate and advertising-agency sponsorship. Hence they could produce shows and programs that were more issue-oriented, more geared to minority concerns and to youthful audiences with little purchasing power. Thus in 1983 educational television could produce a ninety-minute motion picture on Medgar Evers, the slain civil rights worker. Educational television could run a long-lasting weekly, *Sesame Street,* geared predominantly to an inner-city, preschool audience. The first black-controlled educational television station was WHHM, Channel 32, founded in 1975 at Howard University in Washington, D.C.

The public media, however, could not escape the problem of raising money to operate, the public finances they received not matching their needs, present or perceived. Stations found it necessary to conduct periodic on-the-air appeals for memberships, subscriptions, and donations.

If commercial television could be charged with ignoring racial problems in the programs it presented, it made a much better showing in the exposure it gave to blacks in noncontroversial, nonthreatening fields. These included the realm of sports and that of entertainment—song, dance, and light comedy of a buffoonish sort. The same television audience that did not care to learn about blacks who were underprivileged or protest-minded were, on the other hand, quite willing to be amused by black comedians, to be aesthetically moved by black artists, or to be stirred by the exploits of black athletes.

To an unprecedented extent black athletes in the 1970s and 1980s received national media attention. Whether professional and paid or collegiate and of amateur status, black players were prominent, their exploits in the sports arena of history-making proportions. In basketball they dominated the courts. Whereas in 1955 only 7 percent of the athletes in the National Basketball Association were black, that figure had multiplied tenfold to 74 percent by 1982. Black basketball drawing cards of this generation included Kareem Abdul Jabbar (Lew Alcindor), Julius Irving, and Ralph Sampson. Professional football had its share of exciting black performers, including running back O. J. Simpson of the Buffalo Bills and the San Francisco 49ers. Professional baseball, too, had its black record breakers, among them Lou Brock, who in 1979 stole his 935th base, and Henry ("Hank") Aaron, who by hitting his 715th home run in April 1974 broke the record set by the legendary Babe Ruth, considered the most celebrated record in American competitive sports. Black professional boxers of the period included the colorful and popular world welterweight Sugar Ray Leonard.

In fields other than sports the white media's portrayal of blacks continued to be minimal in content and perspective. In the words of a conference entitled, "Blacks and the Mass Media," held at Aspen, Colorado, in August 1984, "So-called general audience programming on television is synonymous with white audience programming—created by, about, and primarily for whites, between the ages eighteen and forty-nine, with above average income." One small ray of hope for a more positive and inclusive portrayal of blacks in commercial television was the phenomenal success, dating from its first appearance in September 1984, of *The Cosby Show,* an excellently acted, warm, and witty half-hour weekly production revolving around Dr. Cliff Huxtable (Bill Cosby) and his family. As situation comedy the show's primary aim was entertainment. But, as Cosby took pains to point out, each of the show's episodes was also designed to be instructive and informative, its appeal reaching out to become racially inclusive.

The success of *The Cosby Show* would not go unnoticed by media executives. Blacks realized, however, that just as Cosby himself had worked diligently and sacrificially to launch his television weekly they too would have to work with increased dedication to bring to light the inner world of the Negro people, to preserve and cherish their cultural heritage and integrity. Spurred on by an ever-deepening sense of racial pride, Afro-Americans must make known their contributions to the national culture, and they must make it known to all Americans because whites as well as blacks would be deprived by not knowing, by not having armed themselves with information. "Lack of knowledge is darker than night," runs an old African proverb, and one that blacks of the 1970s and 1980s took to heart. They realized that access to knowledge was access to power, whether in political or economic circles or in the cultural life of a people or nation.

To blacks the getting of an education (i.e., the acquisition of knowledge) was an age-old and overriding goal. Afro-Americans endowed education with redemptive powers in their quest for freedom, whether freedom from racial oppression, from ignorance, or from poverty. "Education is the passport to the future," counseled Malcolm X. "How will blacks make real progress?" This question was to a nationwide cross section of blacks by a *Time*–Louis Harris poll in 1970. "Getting more blacks better education," was the response of 97 percent of the interviewees, with only 2 percent expressing no opinion, and 1 percent voting in the negative.

As they sought an education, lured by the magic wand of learning, blacks were hardly surprised to encounter race-related problems. On the elementary and secondary school levels, the troublesome issues of busing to achieve racial integration in the public schools would not go away, engaging the attention of the three branches of both federal and state governments throughout the period. Its advocates claimed that such busing was necessary because black schools had poorer facilities—buildings, libraries, and laboratory space—than the neighboring white schools.

Busing to achieve racially integrated schools found little favor with three of the four presidents of this period, Richard Nixon, Gerald Ford, and Ronald Reagan. In March 1970 Nixon stated that he was against the busing of students "beyond normal geographic zones." In 1971 he announced that his administration's efforts to enforce court-ordered busing would be minimal. In March of the following year, in a Special Message on School Busing, he urged Congress to prevent the courts from issuing any new orders requiring the transporting of students to achieve racial integration. In 1972 he also proposed that $2.5 billion be appropriated to improve inner-city schools as an alternative to the busing of pupils. Later that year he fired the chairman of the Civil Rights Commission, the distinguished Father Theodore Hesburgh, whose uncompromising advocacy of immediate busing did not sit well with the White House. President Ford, taking his cue from his predecessor, stated in 1974 that he had "consistently opposed forced busing," an accurate appraisal of his stand.

Jimmy Carter, Ford's successor to the presidency, was the only chief executive of the period to support busing. In 1980 he threatened to veto a bill prohibiting busing, Congress bowing to his will. In President Reagan busing found no such friend. Under the Reagan administration the Department of Justice lent its support in suits against busing in school desegregation cases, and Reagan approved measures that would have prevented federal judges from upholding busing. His administration supported proposals to grant tuition tax credits to parents who sent their children to private schools, to grant tax exemptions to schools that practiced racial discrimination, and to encourage legal attempts to stop busing for the desegregation of the schools. The irony of these attempts to reverse the Supreme Court's *Brown v Board of Education* decision of 1954, wrote research psychologist Kenneth Clark in 1982, "is that not only black Americans but all Americans will suffer if the foundations of our democracy are to be destroyed on the altar of racism." Unfortunately, however, in many communities in which the black schools and the white schools were combined there was an initial but significant loss of black administrators, principals, and department heads.

Hand in hand with the question of integrating the schools was the question of integrating the instructional materials used in the schools, including the textbooks, the audiovisual aids, and the library exhibits and displays. In the public schools down to the mid-1960s, the role of Afro-Americans had been generally ignored, except for references to them as slaves or to the problems they created when they weren't slaves. Otherwise they had no history, it seemed, and certainly no art, no literature, no life of the mind. Beginning with the late 1960s, however, forward-looking public school systems with sizeable black enrollments began to address this neglect.

Using their own staff, plus an outside consultant or two, such school systems fashioned new programs of study which incorporated Afro-Americans into the mainstream of United States history and culture. These schools also brought out integrated textbooks, and their example was quickly followed by commercial publishers sensing a trend. This new and more inclusive interracial approach helped black students to develop a better self-image and sense of identity, and it gave to white students a newer awareness of the cultural pluralism of their country. Moreover, the fairer treatment accorded to blacks in the school curriculum had a wholesome expanding effect, making for a fairer curriculum treatment of other hitherto neglected groups, including women, Native Americans, Hispanic Americans, and Asian Americans.

Not a matter of concern on the elementary and secondary school levels, the enrollment and retention of black students in the colleges, universities, and professional schools was a problem that loomed large. During the early 1980s black enrollments were down at all types of higher-education institutions. Moreover, the black drop-out rate was high, even in the two-year community colleges, the group in which approximately one-half of the black post-secondary education students were to be found. One reason for the low black enrollment and the high black drop-out rate was the poor academic preparation of some students. But the major reason by far for black nonattendance and dropping out was economic. Many aspiring and prepared black students and their families simply could not cope with the steadily rising tuition fees and other college costs in general, a circumstance made all the worse by the reduction in financial aid from the colleges themselves and from the federal government, the state legislatures, and the local community governments.

During this period the predominantly black colleges found themselves in competition with white colleges that were increasingly seeking black matriculants. In ten of the southern states these white colleges were acting in part under a Supreme Court mandate (*Adams v Richardson,* 1973), ordering them to desegregate their dual systems of higher public education. In the more celebrated Bakke case (*Regents of the University of California v Bakke,* 1978) the high court upheld the use of race in the admissions programs of the colleges and professional schools, although the decision also struck down quota, set-aside special admission programs for blacks. In keeping with the spirit of the times, the admission of significant numbers of blacks to white colleges and universities was on the whole a step forward. Its full gain, however, could not be realized unless these racially mixed schools included black studies in their curricula, and in broader ways reflected the many-sided black presence in American life and culture.

The recruitment of blacks by white colleges, however, did bring about a decrease in the percent of black students enrolling in black institutions. Such sizeable declines in the number of black students attending black schools added to the chronic and pressing financial problems facing black colleges, private as well as public. Such difficulties raised questions in the academic community as to whether these predominantly black schools were worth saving. Who needed them, and why?

Their supporters had no doubts in the matter, making a persuasive case for their continued existence and strengthening. "Black colleges have always provided a sympathetic, socio-psychologically supportive environment for Black students, and educated economically disadvantaged students," reported the Institute For the Study of Education Policy, based at Howard University. The report went on to note that the function of the historically black institutions was "not to shield Black students from whites but to prepare them developmentally to deal with the heat of competition."

Supporters of black colleges also maintained that such institutions placed the necessary emphasis on the significant Afro-American heritage and its present-day manifestations. Blacks needed schools that "connect Black people [and the nation] to their roots and sense of history," wrote Luther Brown. Another concurring black educator, Steven Jones, said that "the custodianship of the Afro-American culture by black colleges" should rank as one of the more vital reasons for their existence. A white supporter of the continued existence of black colleges, Ernest Holsendolph, asserted that these colleges "have been important repositories of Afro-American literature, history, and culture." Certainly it would seem logical to expect that even as the black colleges and universities continued to operate ever more fully in the mainstream of higher education, they would retain their commitment to the task of identifying, preserving, and expanding the rich black component in American culture.

The increased interest in black history by Afro-Americans themselves went beyond the ranks of the black academicians, reaching the rank and file. As in the case of black culture in general in recent decades, this interest in black history had a mass base in the black community, cutting across class and occupational lines and levels of schooling and thus becoming broadly functional in black life. For those who were nonbookish and those with limited formal education there were black history card games, trivia games, puzzles, calendars, greeting cards, and illustrated history magazines that presented their stories in comic-book format. Black history by means of radio and television took a decided spurt as it did in other audiovisual forms and fashions.

Blacks of this period became more familiar with the field of oral history, a kind of history that recognizes that memories held by the living are sources and resources well worth tapping. Oral history had a strong appeal to blacks since its devotees made a special effort to place on record the recollections of the common people, the previously unrecorded, and thus lent itself to the newer trend of reconstructing history "from the bottom up."

Another aspect of history coming to the fore in recent years is the role of black women in this country's past. Prior to the 1970s those who studied or wrote in the field of Afro-American history tended to concentrate on the black forefathers, saying relatively little about the black foremothers. When these researchers touched upon black women, they generally cast them in subordinate roles, as bit players, whether in quest of black freedom and equal rights or in the movement for women's liberation and advancement. Today's black women are reviewing their past anew, redefining their roles, then and now. They are "looking at themselves as a distinct black voice, not just a black voice," observes the knowledgeable Paula Giddings. "A lot of the challenges we face today are not new," she continues. "It is an inspiration to see how the women who came before us dealt with them—how they transcended." One indication of this growing interest by Afro-American women in the activities of their female predecessors was the founding in 1977 of the Association of Black Women Historians, incorporated in Washington, D.C.

The interest of blacks in their past embraced the field of genealogy, their quest for racial group identity having stimulated them to probe into family history. "Looking up" one's ancestors provided the seeker with a more personalized pride, a deeper and more rounded sense of self, of belonging. To a mounting degree, blacks began to collect family papers and otherwise to engage in family heritage research. Indicative of this interest in black lineage was the founding of the Afro-American Historical and Genealogical Society, chartered in the District of Columbia in 1977. Interest in black genealogy was sparked by the appearance of guide books on how blacks could trace their ancestors. Typical of such "how-to-do-it" helpers was *Black Genealogy* (1977), by Charles Blockson with Ron Fry.

The single published work that riveted attention on the black family was *Roots: The Saga of an American Family,* by

Alex Haley, published in 1976. Its success phenomenal, it appeared on bestselling book lists week after week, was republished in some thirty languages, and was serialized on commercial television, the final of its eight on-the-air episodes attracting 80 million viewers and smashing all records. Haley's autobiographical novel focuses on his ancestor, African-born Kunta Kinte, and his descendants in the United States, describing the manner in which they proved themselves capable of coping with the harshest adversity, of making resourceful and self-respecting adjustments to racial discrimination. From one generation to another the family that emerges from Haley's pages was a stable, two-parent household, characterized by binding marriages, a respect for the elders, a tenacious family bond, and a sense of mission.

Haley's book bore the subtitle, *The Saga of an American Family,* and indeed it conveyed to its American readers a sense of shared identity despite the lines of race and color. The broad theme and inclusive outlook of *Roots* explains in part its wide appeal to Americans of a non-African background. The work struck a national chord, addressing itself to the central theme in U.S. history—the expanding concept of liberty. Haley dedicated the book "as a birthday offering to my country." Its publication during the year of the Bicentennial, 1976, was appropriate and timely. For *Roots* was a summons back to first principles, to the high goals set forth at the birth of the nation two centuries earlier.

The strong American note struck by *Roots* was accompanied by equally strong African overtones. Haley's family had originated in a land of which they were proud; indeed, they always spoke of their founding father as "the African." With its opening scenes set in Africa, *Roots* conveys this sense of an Africa rediscovered, of a heritage that embraced two continents. Haley thus reflected this newer awareness of their ancestral heritage by black Americans and the pride they took in it. In black circles the feeling grew that the African past was to be esteemed rather than rejected and that they had good reason to be proud of their pre-American origins. They were looking at Africa anew, viewing her as a creator of culture, and a land looming larger and larger in any rational evaluation of man's past. They would concur with native son K. O. Dike in his observation: "The actions of Africans have not only shaped the patterns of conduct on this continent but have also played their part in the development of the civilizations of the New World, Europe, and Asia." The pervasive influence of Africa's creative spirit was felt in the world of modern art, whether in painting or sculpture, and in music and dance. To demonstrate outwardly their identification with such a richly endowed motherland some wore African dress styles and braided their hair. With encouragement from such organizations as the African Studies Association and the African-American Institute, black students at colleges called for the installation of courses on Africa.

A cultural and racial identity with Africa by black Americans led to a growing interest and concern as to current affairs, political and economic, in that continent, an interest and concern shared by many Americans of non-African lineage. "Africa is important to us in cultural and historical terms," said Chester Crocker, U.S. Assistant Secretary for African Affairs, on March 18, 1986. "About 11 percent of the American people trace their ancestry back to Africa," he explained. "Afro-Americans are today a more cohesive and activist constituency than at any time in the past, not only on the emotionally charged issue of South Africa but also on the range of America's African interests and policies."

In the sphere of politics the supporters of the independent movements south of the Saharas hailed the establishment on April 16, 1980, of the Republic of Zimbabwe, formerly Rhodesia, marking the end of ninety years of colonial rule. The emergence of Zimbabwe stimulated the movement to bring freedom to the blacks in the adjacent Republic of South Africa, a nation with white minority rule (22 million blacks, 4.5 million whites), with a rigid system of segregating blacks from whites (apartheid), and with a system of passing laws requiring all blacks over the age of sixteen to carry passbooks that stipulated where they could live, work, and travel. In the United States the "free South Africa" movement drew strong support from black churches and from such organizations as the National Urban League, the N.A.A.C.P., the Congressional Black Caucus, and Trans-Africa, a Washington-based lobby founded in 1977 for the advancement of independence and home rule in Africa's white-ruled regions. Afro-Americans were conspicuous in the numerous protest demonstrations held outside the South African embassy in Washington and at other sites, the participants inviting and welcoming arrest and detention. Led by Jesse Jackson and organized by Britain's Anti-Apartheid Movement, an estimated one hundred thousand people took part in a demonstration march in London in November 1985, in which 140 of them were taken into custody by the police. The mounting anti-apartheid protests in the United States led many business firms to pull out of South Africa and led colleges, states, and municipalities to adopt a similar policy of disinvestment, withdrawing their South African investments, entirely or in part. Bestirring itself, the South African government in April 1986 announced that it would abolish the pass laws, but by then such a reformist measure was viewed by many black inhabitants and their supporters abroad as being too little and too late.

Africa's economic objectives and concerns were also of interest to black Americans. The continent's independent black nations faced a chronic indebtedness, estimated at $120 million in 1985. During the preceding decade these countries experienced their worst droughts in a century and a series of famines equally unprecedented. Their plight was duly noted by black Americans. "I am especially pleased that in recent months, black Americans have rallied to the cause of the starving millions in Africa," wrote P. Bertrand Phillips, an official of the United States Committee for UNICEF, an agency of the United Nations, in January 1985. "As an Afro-American," continued Dr. Phillips, "I am extremely proud to be a part of this effort of so many black Americans to reach out to over 150 million endangered people in the twenty-four African countries severely affected by the results of this prolonged drought." In December 1984 the N.A.A.C.P. called a meeting of some twenty-five black fraternal, religious, and civic groups for the purpose of "discussing ways in which we could provide emergency assistance for the victims of famine and develop a strategy for making sure that Africa's needs would not be forgotten when the immediate crisis is over." Not to be left out, show people, white and black, gave rock concerts and dance presentations to raise funds for the cause. On the African front itself the black-led organization, *Africare,* founded in 1971 in Washington, D.C., was a leading force in supporting grassroots developments. By 1976 *Africare* had offices in ten African countries in which it sponsored projects in a variety of fields, among them drought relief, agriculture, and forestry, its program expenses for the year ending June 30, 1985, running to over $6.5 million.

The interest of black Americans in Africa, its present and past, and their awareness of their African heritage retentions in music, the arts, and literature, were factors in the Afro-American cultural heritage that took hold in the 1970s and 1980s. It was a development, a consciousness, that historian Robert Weisbord described in 1973 as "Afro-America's African Renaissance." In turn this mounting interest in the creative arts made for an ever-increasing company of productive blacks whose works received greater attention. This growing audience cut across the color line, many whites becoming aware that black culture was an enduring flame in American aesthetic expression, having a revitalizing effect.

The Afro-American arts drew a broad-ranging constituency. Among blacks there was a variety of tastes in music and the arts, a circumstance resulting from the differing socio-economic and age levels within the group. But in Afro-American life much of its art was socially conscious, its function to bring about a change in group relationships and the status quo. To Afro-Americans in general, the appeal of the arts was not solely aesthetic—they were not advocates of art for art's sake. In black life the arts were designed to convey a message, and this message, if in varying forms of artistic expression, had to be conveyed to the low as well as to the high, to the unschooled as well as to the intelligentsia. Designed to inspire, advance, and uplift the people, the arts must be designed so as to reach the people, speaking to them in accents they could understand and to which they in turn might make their own creative responses. In addition to helping blacks retain their cultural heritage, the arts provided them with a psychological escape from oppressive conditions, affording them with needed intervals in which they could put away the troubles of the world and march to the beat of their own drums and drummers.

In the visual arts, the performing arts, and in literature, Afro-American creativity had increasingly come to the fore, reaching an ever-widening audience. Blacks themselves had come to share Larry Neal's belief that "Afro-American life and history are full of creative responsibilities." This encouraging attitude was shared by leaders of black improvement organizations, the N.A.A.C.P.'s Benjamin Hooks gratefully acknowledging in 1986 that "We recognize that the arts are a vital part of the fabric of our society and our legacy as a people."

In the visual arts the black renaissance brought new and well-deserved attention to the works of such well-established living painters as Romare Bearden, Jacob Lawrence, and Lois Mailou Jones, and the sculptor Elizabeth Catlett-Mora. Such artists had an international reputation, their works having been exhibited in and owned by galleries and museums in Latin America, Europe, and Africa.

The role of the dance lost none of its influence in the social structure of black life in the late twentieth century, and the field attracted a growing retinue of nonblack performers and viewers. "Contemporary Afro-American dances are frequently a recycled version of dances performed in previous generations," some of them dating back to slavery and others traceable to Africa, wrote authority Katrina Hazzard-Gordon in 1985. In the 1970s and 1980s tap dancing experienced a notable revival, rejuvenating itself while changing its forms. Branching out, the Alvin Ailey American Dance Theater and Arthur Mitchell's Dance Theatre of Harlem presented both traditional ballet and Afro-American choreography, sometimes in combination. Mitchell indeed described the offerings of his multiracial company as "classical ballet with soul."

Afro-American singers likewise made their influence felt in spheres hitherto assumed to be off-limits to them. This breed included such diverse performers as operatic soprano Leontyne Price on the one hand, and country singer superstar Charley Pride on the other. Among Afro-Americans, however, such venturesome developments tended to intensify their ongoing appreciation of black vocal music's own rich repertoire of spirituals, gospel songs, secular folksongs, and blues. In the mid-eighties black music's most celebrated entertainer, singer-dancer Michael Jackson (who inspired the kind of fan adulation aptly characterized as "Michaelmania") described his goal as seeking "to try to integrate all races into one through the love of music."

Afro-American writers of this period similarly experienced a receptive response to their outpourings. Amiri Baraka (LeRoi Jones) had an explanation for this ongoing influence of literary expression in black life. "People want to know," he wrote, "why Jesse Jackson speaks in rhymes. Black people have to be poets, otherwise the people would not listen!" For many of their themes black writers drew upon the vast storehouse of bygone times and places. Seeking to discern the thrust and meaning of current Afro-American fiction, Michael Cooke, a qualified appraiser of twentieth-century black literature, concluded that "more and more we find brought into a decidedly modern setting the forms and values of the historical past."

Recent black literature has been characterized by a greater sense of realism than formerly. While continuing to point with pride to the creative and wholesome aspects of the Afro-American experience, current black writers have not flinched from portraying its seamy side, its unsavory and self-destructive manifestations. In a similar vein of constructively meant self-criticism, recent black literature has come to grips with the differing outlooks of black men and black women. In the 1970s and 1980s black women writers were more determined than ever to be heard, their voices taking on a more urgent and confrontational tone. Theirs was a dual battle against both racism and sexism.

"We fight the central oppression of all people of color as well as the oppression of women by men," asserted prolific freelance writer Alexis Deveaux. The voluminous writings of these latter-day black female liberators ranged widely, embracing Alice Walker's enormously popular 1983 Pulitzer Prize–winning novel, *The Color Purple*, to the periodical *Sage: A Scholarly Journal on Black Women*, founded in early 1984 in Atlanta, Georgia.

Reflecting the influences of the Afro-American art, music, and literature of this period, as they related to its mission, the black church remained a dominant force in black life. Broadly based, as in the past, its members were drawn from the widest ranges of educational and occupational groups. The Afro-American church had an inclusive theological outlook, its elements a cooperative spirit on the local level, a reverential respect for the black past, an impassioned cry for social justice, and a tradition of reconciliation, of cutting across the lines of race, class, and color in pursuit of "the beloved community."

The local black church continued to teach its congregation how to work together, to be mutually supportive in organizing and promoting programs and activities. Black churches of the 1970s and 1980s have shown a greater appreciation of the history and culture of their racial group, including the African heritage, and they have urged their congregations to search out their theological roots. Today's black church reaffirms the value of its antecedents, its spiritual forebears. More strongly than ever before, the current black church has addressed itself to social concerns, identifying the Christian gospel with the struggle against injustice, oppression, and racial discrimination. This liberation theology holds that God sides with the dispossessed and the downtrodden, and hence that the church must address itself to the resolution of deep-seated inequities in the social order, that the church should be a resource base for needed change. A black church that was truly Christian, expounded theologian James Cone, "was Christian precisely because it had identified the gospel with the struggle for freedom and justice in society." Without question the dramatic civil rights battles of the 1960s had their effect on the black church, impelling some black sects with an otherworldly orientation to take a new look at conditions in the here and now rather than to devote all their attention to the afterlife "in bright mansions above." Moreover, blacks who were members of white churches increasingly raised their voice in protest against racial discrimination, some of it in their own congregations.

Somewhat less nationalistic than its counterpart of the 1960s, the recent black church has been more in line with the integrationalist approach, of coalition building with nonblack groups, secular and religious. On the part of the black church there has been a wider reaching-out effort, a more ecumenical spirit. More than any other black leader the embodiment of this ideal of "the beloved community" was Martin Luther King, Jr., and since his death in 1968 his image and his message had taken on new lustre with every passing year. His host of admirers would not forget his broad outlook and sympathies, his concern for the unfortunate, wherever they might be, his example as a citizen of the world. They remembered his admonitions pointing out that "We are caught in an inescapable network of mutuality, tied to a single garment of destiny." His continuing influence became dramatically apparent on January 20, 1986, when the United States celebrated his birthday, now designated as a national holiday by a bill passed by the Congress and signed by President Reagan. This high and lasting honor was graciously acknowledged by his widow, Coretta Scott

King. "His memory is engraved in the hearts and minds of his fellow Americans, and it is appropriate . . . to remember and honor the principles for which he stood," she noted. "Each year, Martin's national birthday celebration will rekindle in the hearts of all our people a new pride in America, a determination to make it an even greater nation."

It is the centrality of the Afro-American experience that makes its past so significant, a past that has a sobering but redemptive quality for our nation, not as an escapist journey to some gossamer glory of bygone days but possibly as a vehicle for present enlightenment, guidance, and enrichment.

Selected Bibliography

Designed for those who may wish to examine some topic more fully than is done in these pages, this bibliography is confined to one-volume works that are more or less readily procurable. The titles are arranged to conform with the chapter sequences, with eight titles for each chapter. Works that cover broad periods are listed in a final group under the heading "General Readings." The titles are arranged alphabetically by author within groups.

Chapter 1
From Africa to the New World (to 1619)

Paul Bohannan, *Africa and Africans.* New York, 1964.
Philip D. Curtin, *The Atlantic Slave Trade.* Madison, Wis., 1969.
Basil Davidson, *A History of West Africa: To the Nineteenth Century.* New York, 1966.
Melville J. Herskovits, *The Myth of the Negro Past.* New York, 1941.
Robert July, *A History of the African People.* New York, 1970.
Roland Oliver and J. D. Fage, *A Short History of Africa.* Baltimore, 1962.
Robert I. Rotberg, *A History of the African People.* New York, 1970.
Ivan Van Sertima, *They Came Before Columbus.* New York, 1976.

Chapter 2
The Colonial and Revolutionary War Negro (1619–1800)

Ira Berlin and Ronald Hoffman, *Slavery and Freedom in the Age of the American Revolution.* Charlottesville, Va., 1983.
David Brion Davis, *The Problem of Slavery in the Age of Revolution, 1770–1823.* Ithaca, N.Y., 1975.

Lorenzo J. Greene, *The Negro in Colonial New England, 1620–1776*. New York, 1968.

A. Leon Higginbotham, Jr., *In the Matter of Color: Race and the American Legal Process: The Colonial Period*. New York, 1978.

Winthrop D. Jordan *White Over Black: American Attitudes Toward the Negro 1500–1812*. Chapel Hill, N.C., 1968.

Duncan J. MacLeod, *Slavery, Race and the American Revolution*. Cambridge, England, 1974.

Benjamin Quarles, *The Negro in the American Revolution*. Chapel Hill, N.C., 1961.

Arthur Zilversmit, *The First Emancipation: The Abolition of Slavery in the North*. Chicago, 1967.

Chapter 3
The House of Bondage (1800–1860)

John W. Blassingame, *The Slave Community: Plantation Life in the Antebellum South*. New York, 1979.

John W. Blassingame, ed., *Slave Testimony: Two Centuries of Letters, Speeches, Interviews, and Autobiographies*. Baton Rouge, La., 1977.

Mark Miles Fisher, *Negro Slave Songs in the United States*. Ithaca, N.Y., 1953.

Larry Gara, *The Liberty Line*. Lexington, Ky., 1961.

Eugene D. Genovese, *Roll, Jordan, Roll: The World the Slaves Made*. New York, 1974.

Nathan Irvin Higgins, *Black Odyssey: The Afro-American Ordeal in Slavery*. New York, 1977.

Kenneth M. Stampp, *The Peculiar Institution*. New York, 1956.

Richard C. Wade, *Slavery in the Cities: The South, 1820–1869*. New York, 1964.

Chapter 4
The Nonslave Negro (1800–1860)

William L. Andrews, *To Tell a Free Story: The First Century of Afro-American Autobiography, 1760–1865*. Champaign, Ill., 1986.

Howard Holman Bell, ed., *Minutes of the Proceedings of the National Negro Conventions, 1830–1964*. New York, 1969.

Ira Berlin, *Slaves Without Masters: The Free Negro in the Antebellum South*. New York, 1974.

John H. Bracey, Jr., August Meier, and Elliott Rudwick, eds., *Free Blacks in America*. Belmont, Calif., 1970.

Luther P. Jackson, *Free Negro Labor and Property Holding in Virginia, 1830–1860*. New York, 1942.

Rudolph M. Lapp, *Blacks in Gold Rush California*. New Haven, Conn., 1977.

Leon F. Litwack, *North of Slavery: The Negro in the Free States, 1790–1860*. Chicago, 1961.

Benjamin Quarles, *Black Abolitionists*. New York, 1969.

Chapter 5
New Birth of Freedom (1860–1865)

Ira Berlin, ed., *Freedom: A Documentary History of Emancipation, 1861–1867. Series II: The Black Military Experience*. Cambridge, U.K., 1982.

James H. Brewer, *The Confederate Negro: Virginia's Craftsmen and Military Laborers, 1861–1865*. Durham, N.C., 1969.

Dudley T. Cornish, *The Sable Arm: Negro Troops in the Union Army, 1861–1865*. New York, 1956.

Louis R. Gerteis, *From Contraband to Freedman: Federal Policy Toward Southern Blacks, 1861–1865*. Westport, Conn., 1973.

Thomas W. Higginson, *Army Life in a Black Regiment*. Introduction by Howard N. Meyer. New York, 1962.

James M. McPherson, *The Negro's Civil War*. New York, 1965.

Benjamin Quarles, *The Negro in the Civil War*. Boston, 1953.

Willie Lee Rose, *Rehearsal for Reconstruction: The Port Royal Experiment*. Indianapolis, Ind., 1964.

Chapter 6
The Decades of Disappointment (1865–1900)

Lerone Bennett, Jr., *Black Power, U.S.A.: The Human Side of Reconstruction, 1867–1877*. Chicago, 1967.

Robert Cruden, *The Negro in Reconstruction*. Englewood Cliffs, N.J., 1969.

Philip Durham and Everett L. Jones, *The Negro Cowboys*. New York, 1965.

John Hope Franklin, *Reconstruction After the Civil War.* Chicago, 1962.

Leon F. Litwack, *Been in the Storm So Long: The Aftermath of Slavery.* New York, 1979.

Rayford W. Logan, *The Betrayal of the Negro: From Rutherford B. Hayes to Woodrow Wilson.* New York, 1968.

Nell Irvin Painter, *Exodusters: Black Migration to Kansas After Reconstruction.* New York, 1977.

Howard N. Rabinowitz, ed., *Southern Black Leaders of the Reconstruction Era.* Urbana, Ill., 1982.

Chapter 7
Turn-of-the-Century Upswing (1900–1920)

Herbert Aptheker, ed., *The Autobiography of W. E. B. DuBois.* New York, 1968.

Alfreda M. Duster, ed., *The Autobiography of Ida B. Wells.* Chicago, 1970.

Louis R. Harlan, *Booker T. Washington: The Wizard of Tuskegee, 1901–1915.* New York, 1983.

Charles Flint Kellogg, *NAACP: A History of Colored People,* Vol. I: 1909–1920. Baltimore, 1968.

August Meier, *Negro Thought in America: 1880–1915.* Ann Arbor, Mich., 1963.

Alfred A. Moss, Jr., *The American Negro Academy: Voice of the Talented Tenth.* Baton Rouge, La., 1981.

Emmett J. Scott, *Official History of the American Negro in the World War.* Chicago, 1919; reprinted New York, 1969.

Mary Church Terrell, *A Colored Woman in the White World.* Washington, D.C., 1940.

Chapter 8
From "Normalcy" To New Deal (1920–1940)

Jervis B. Anderson, *A. Philip Randolph: A Biographical Portrait.* New York, 1973.

Dan T. Carter, *Scottsboro: A Tragedy of the American South.* Baton Rouge, La., 1969.

Edmund Cronon, *Black Moses: Marcus Garvey and the Universal Negro Improvement Association.* Madison, Wis., 1960.

David Levering Lewis, *When Harlem Was in Vogue*. New York, 1981.

Alain Locke, ed., *The New Negro: An Interpretation*. New York, 1925.

Roi Ottley, *'New World A-Coming': Inside Black America*. Boston, 1943.

Wilson Record, *The Negro and the Communist Party*. Chapel Hill, N.C., 1951.

Nancy J. Weiss, *Farewell to the Party of Lincoln: Black Politics in the Age of F.D.R.* Princeton, N.J., 1983.

Chapter 9
War and Peace: Issues and Outcome (1940–1954)

Ulysses Lee, *United States Army in World War II: The Employment of Negro Troops*. Washington, D.C., 1966.

Philip McGuire, *Taps for a Jim Crow Army: Letters from Black Soldiers in World War II*. Santa Barbara, Calif., 1983.

Lee Nichols, *Breakthrough on the Color Front*. New York, 1954.

Louis Ruchames, *Race, Jobs, and Politics*. New York, 1953.

Seymour J. Schoenfeld, *The Negro in the Armed Forces*. Washington, D.C., 1945.

Mabel Keaton Staupers, *No Time for Prejudice: A Story of the Integration of Negroes in Nursing in the United States*. New York, 1961.

Robert C. Weaver, *Negro Labor: A National Problem*. New York, 1946.

Walter White, *A Rising Wind*. New York, 1945.

Chapter 10
Democracy's Deepening Challenge (1954–1963)

James Baldwin, *The Fire Next Time*. New York, 1963.

James Farmer, *Lay Bare the Heart: An Autobiography of the Civil Rights Movement*. New York, 1985.

Martin Luther King, *Stride Toward Freedom*. New York, 1958.

Richard Kluger, *Simple Justice: The History of Brown versus Board of Education and Black America's Struggle for Equality*. New York, 1976.

C. Eric Lincoln, *The Black Muslims in America*. Boston, 1961.

Louis E. Lomax, *The Negro Revolt.* New York, 1962.

Aldon D. Morris, *The Origins of the Civil Rights Movement: Black Communities Organizing for Change.* New York, 1984.

Whitney M. Young, Jr., *To Be Equal.* New York, 1964.

Chapter 11
A Fluid Front (1963–1970)

Floyd Barbour, ed., *The Black Power Revolt.* Boston, 1968.

Stokely Carmichael and Charles V. Hamilton, *Black Power: The Politics of Liberation in America.* New York, 1967.

Clayborne Carson, *In Struggle: SNCC and the Black Awakening of the 1960s.* Cambridge, Mass., 1981.

William H. Grier and Price M. Cobbs, *Black Rage.* New York, 1968.

The Autobiography of Malcolm X (with the assistance of Alex Haley). New York, 1965.

Howell Haines, *My Soul Is Rested: Movement Days in the Deep South Remembered.* New York, 1977.

Benjamin Muse, *The American Negro Revolution: From Nonviolence to Black Power, 1963–1967.* Bloomington, Ind., 1968.

Report of the National Advisory Commission on Civil Disorders. New York, 1968. Also see *One Year Later: An Assessment of the Nation's Response to the Crisis Described by the National Advisory Commission on Civil Disorders.* Washington, D.C., 1969.

Chapter 12
Widening Horizons (1970–1986)

Theodore Cross, *The Black Power Imperative: Racial Equality and the Politics of Nonviolence.* New York, 1984.

S. Wilmore Gayraud and James H. Cone, *Black Theology: A Documentary History, 1966–1979.* Maryknoll, N.Y., 1979.

Faustine Childress Jones, *The Changing Mood in America: Eroding Commitment?* Washington, D.C., 1977.

Steven E. Lawson, *Southern Blacks and the Electoral Process, 1865–1982.* New York, 1985.

C. Eric Lincoln, *Race, Religion, and the Coming American Dilemma.* New York, 1984.

Harvard Sitkoff, *The Struggle for Black Equality, 1954–1980.* New York, 1981.

SELECTED BIBLIOGRAPHY

Claudia Tate, ed., *Black Women Writers at Work*. New York, 1983.
Wallace Tery, *Bloods: An Oral History of the Vietnam War by Black Veterans*. New York, 1984.

General Readings

John Hope Franklin, *From Slavery to Freedom: A History of Negro Americans*. New York, 1980.
John Hope Franklin and August Meier, eds., *Black Leaders of the Twentieth Century*. Urbana, Ill., 1982.
Herbert G. Gutman, *The Black Family in Slavery and Freedom, 1750–1925*. New York, 1976.
Vincent Harding, *There Is a River: The Black Struggle for Freedom in America*. New York, 1981.
William H. Harris, *The Harder We Run: Black Workers Since the Civil War*. New York, 1982.
Lawrence W. Levine, *Black Culture and Black Consciousness: Afro-American Folk Thought From Slavery to Freedom*. New York, 1977.
Dorothy Sterling, ed., *We Are Your Sisters: Black Women in the Twentieth Century*. New York, 1984.
Edgar A. Toppin, *A Biographical History of Blacks in America Since 1528*. New York, 1971.

Index